THE COMMONWEALTH AND INTERNATIONAL LIBRARY
Joint Chairmen of the Honorary Editorial Advisory Board
SIR ROBERT ROBINSON, O.M., F.R.S., LONDON
DEAN ATHELSTAN SPILHAUS, MINNESOTA
Publisher: ROBERT MAXWELL, M.C., M.P.

EDUCATION AND EDUCATIONAL RESEARCH DIVISION
General Editor: DR. EDMUND KING

SOCIETY, SCHOOLS AND PROGRESS IN INDIA

The author after experience as a teacher and inspector of schools became Deputy Education Officer at Birmingham (1920–27), then Chief Education Officer at Southend-on-Sea County Borough (1927–31) and then Chief Education Officer in the County of Essex (1931–38). He was President of the Association of Directors and Secretaries for Education (now the Association of Chief Education Officers) in 1935–36 and President of the Education and Psychology Section of the British Association for the Advancement of Science, 1937–38.

In 1938 he went out to India as Education Commissioner—the title was subsequently altered to Adviser—with the Central Government. When his contract with the Government of India expired in 1948, he returned to India from 1948–51 to supervise the establishment of British Council centres in that country and Pakistan.

SOCIETY, SCHOOLS, AND PROGRESS IN INDIA

BY

SIR JOHN SARGENT, M.A., D.Lit.

PERGAMON PRESS

OXFORD · LONDON · EDINBURGH · NEW YORK
TORONTO · SYDNEY · PARIS · BRAUNSCHWEIG

PERGAMON PRESS LTD.,
Headington Hill Hall, Oxford
4 & 5 Fitzroy Square, London W.1
PERGAMON PRESS (Scotland) LTD.,
2 & 3 Teviot Place, Edinburgh 1
PERGAMON PRESS INC.,
44–01 21st Street, Long Island City, New York 11101
PERGAMON OF CANADA LTD.,
207 Queen's Quay West, Toronto 1
PERGAMON PRESS (AUST.) PTY. LTD.,
19a Boundary Street, Rushcutters Bay, N.S.W. 2011, Australia
PERGAMON PRESS S.A.R.L.,
24 rue des Écoles, Paris 5^e
VIEWEG & SOHN GmbH,
Burgplatz 1, Braunschweig

Copyright © 1968 Pergamon Press Ltd.
First edition 1968
Library of Congress Catalog Card No. 68-21106

Printed in Great Britain by A. Wheaton & Co., Exeter

08 103808 9 (flexicover)
08 203808 2 (hard cover)

Contents

Comparative Studies

An Introduction to the Series "Society, Schools and Progress"

by EDMUND KING

THIS volume is one of a mutually supporting series of books on SOCIETY, SCHOOLS AND PROGRESS in a number of important countries or regions. The series is intended to serve students of sociology, government and politics, as well as education. Investment in education, or satisfaction of the consumer demand for it, is now the biggest single item of non-military public expenditure in many countries and an increasing proportion in all the rest. The systematic use of education to achieve security, prosperity and social well-being makes it imperative to have up-to-date surveys realistically related to all these objectives; for it is impossible to study one effectively without reference to the others or to assess the objectives without reference to education as the chosen instrument.

Comparative studies of all kinds are in vogue. We find university departments of comparative government, law, religion, anthropology, literature and the like. Some comparison is taken for granted in a contracting world of closer relationships. But not all comparative studies are forward-looking or constructive. Comparisons based solely or mainly on backward-looking interests can have their own kind of respectability without necessarily drawing lessons for the present. However, some contemporary comparisons show utility as well as interest or respectability, particularly when observers are enabled to analyse social organization, formative customs, value systems and so forth.

More important still are area studies based upon a comprehensive survey of a whole culture, showing the interpenetration of its technology, government, social relationships, religion and arts; for here we see our neighbours making man—and making him in an idiom which challenges our own assumptions and practices. This concerted and conscious making of posterity by a multiplicity of interlocking influences is perhaps mankind's most astonishing feature—at least on a par with rationality and speech, and inseparable from them. As the last third of the twentieth century begins, however, we are witnessing the struggle of competing educational prescriptions for the whole future of mankind.

THE MAKING OF THE FUTURE

The most important studies of all in the world today are those undertaken with a view to modifying deliberately the formative conditions in which our children and their descendants will live— that is to say, their education. In the pre-industrial past there was plenty of time for the slow evolution of civilization and technology. Even in this century people used to think of societies and educations as growing empirically and evolving. Today's world cannot wait upon the spontaneity that sufficed yesterday. It is often said that the Industrial Revolution is entering on its second and more important phase—the systematic application to *social* relationships of mechanized and urban-style abundance, with a corresponding transformation of all learning opportunities.

Certainly that is the dream of the hitherto underprivileged majority of mankind. All countries are involved in this social stocktaking and reckoning for the future, no matter whether they are called socialistic or capitalistic. In any case, the pace of change is so fast everywhere that some co-ordination or phasing of development is accepted as a critical responsibility of statecraft in all countries.

THE TRANSFORMATION OF EDUCATION

In relation to education, this sequence of events has already been attended by remarkable changes. Education used to be undertaken largely at home, by society at large, by working relationships or by voluntary organizations. Now it is a publicly regulated, publicly financed activity for the most part. It is provided as a necessary service by an expanding range of public employees. Of course, unofficial people and social groups continue to take a keen interest, especially in their own children; but increasingly it is the State which co-ordinates and directs the process for all children. In some countries the State claims a monopoly of education; in most others that claim is hotly resisted, though inevitably the State is conceded a growing share in the partnership.

In any case, the State or its professional subsidiaries will assume a mounting responsibility for the allocation of funds, for increasingly expensive instruments and premises, for ensuring fair distribution of opportunity, for preventing the waste of talent, for safeguarding economic and social well-being and for setting the national priorities into proper order. Therefore, no matter what education has been in the past, the logic of the Industrial Revolution has turned it into publicly regulated and publicly provided activities, directed towards the deliberate construction of a more satisfactory future.

That commitment is now implicitly indivisible within any one country. It is also accepted that internationally, too, everyone's education is likely to be to the advantage of everyone else in the long run. For this reason alone, international comparisons and assessments are of the utmost importance.

Whole countries are finding that their external context is changing in unprecedented ways. The emancipation of formerly subject peoples is a conspicuous example. Another instance is seen in the large regional developments whereby food production, commerce and mutual protection are ensured in "developing countries"—usually with some notable reliance on educational improvements. Even quite powerful and well-established countries (like several in Western Europe) co-operate increasingly with their neighbours for commercial and political reasons; and all these changes necessitate some adjustment of school orientation and programmes, if only for the interchange of personnel. Apart from such specific instances, it is increasingly obvious that no education anywhere is worth the name unless it is viable in world terms.

Great though these adjustments are between sovereign nations, the changes that transcend all national boundaries and apply to all school systems alike are even more radically influential. In all countries, the area of education monopolized by the schools and other formally instructive institutions is diminishing in relation to educative forces outside. For example, the first public television programmes in the world began in 1936; yet within twenty-five years television and radio absorbed almost as much of children's time and interest (taking the year all round) as the formal school hours in a number of countries. The appeal of such external influences may be greater than the schools'. The universal teacher problem accentuates the change.

In any case, all instruction offered in school is largely conditional for its success on subsequent reinforcement. This it does not always get in a world of expanding opportunities and experiences for young people, which challenge schools' previous prerogatives and sometimes their precepts. A whole new range of "service occupations" provides alternative perspectives. Furthermore, technological and social change necessitate much professional retraining and personal reorientation in all advanced countries. There is far less idea of a once-for-all preparation for life. Learning the unknown is taking the place of teaching the certainties.

In all countries we share this uncertainty. Deeply rooted though we all are in our own ways of life, our scrutiny of the future becomes increasingly a comparison of our hypotheses and experiments. No really adequate answers to any educational or social problem can be determined within one country's confines any longer. Comparative Education is above all the discipline which systematizes our observations and conclusions in relation to the shaping of the future.

COMPARATIVE EDUCATION IN GENERAL

Comparative studies of education are necessarily based upon existing practices, institutions and background influences which have shaped the present variety of educational idioms throughout the world. It is essential to acquaint ourselves with the most important systems, not as alien phenomena but as variations upon the preoccupations of every family and every school in our own country. To be both civilized and scientific we must try to "feel inside" the common human concerns of our neighbours. By this transference of sympathy we achieve some sort of detachment which will enable us to appreciate our own involvement in circumstances—quite as much as theirs.

What adds up to education in our own country is as confused a tangle as any to be found in those other countries where we more easily assume the role of critical advisers. Much of it is habituation, and much is emotionally bound rather than rational. Advice and rational planning that do not take account of these actual influences on education at any one place and time are unscientific as well as failing in humanity. From a practical point of view, too, they will fail, because they lack a sense of the local and topical dynamic. We must know the living present. It is this that gives momentum to the future and conditions it. Thus, even at this first or informative stage of Comparative Education, we are made analytically aware (not only descriptively) of today's climax of forces. We inevitably envisage some possibilities for the future—if only with reference to our own reactions and purposes.

Therefore, though Comparative Education must go on to study particular problems (such as control or university expansion), it must begin with area studies or dynamic analyses of concurrent influences such as this series provides. Without awareness of what "education" seems now to be to its participants, no student or planner can effectively share in the shaping of the future. He may have falsely identified his "problems". He will probably misjudge their topical significance. On the basis of unrealistic generalizations he will certainly fail to communicate acceptable advice. The climax of local culture which amounts to education in any one place is emotionally more sensitive even than language issues or religion, because it includes within itself these very influences and many others.

THE PURPOSE OF THIS SERIES

SOCIETY, SCHOOLS AND PROGRESS are here surveyed in the world's most significant countries—significant not simply for reasons of technological or political strength, but because of the widely relevant decisions in education now being taken. Since the end of the Second World War a ferment of reform has been going on. No reform takes place in the sterile conditions of a laboratory. In the social field not even research can be isolated and sterilized. Experiment in education involves all the untidiness and unpredictability of human responses, which are the source of all creative ingenuity. Every planner or theorist, every student of "problems" that seem abstract and general enough, needs an opportunity of studying again and again the forensic application of his theories.

Nevertheless, so that some general study may be made of frequently recurring tendencies and problems, the books in the SOCIETY, SCHOOLS AND PROGRESS series are arranged in a fairly uniform pattern. They all begin with the historical and institutional background. They then go on to describe administration, the school system, family influences and background social forces in much the same order of progression. Thus it is easy to make cross-references from one volume to another. Cross-cultural analysis of particular problems or interests is facilitated, but always in relation to the living context which so often reveals unexpected pitfalls or opportunities.

After this second or "problem" level of cross-cultural analysis in detail, the serious student can go on to a third stage. He can assess as a dynamic whole the collective preparation for the future of each of the countries featured. This third level of assessing orientation, or of planning, is not always marked by logic alone within any one of the countries concerned; but an international survey of discernible trends can be of great practical importance. The evolving form of the future can at least be surmised, and continuing research can guide it.

Public investment in education (and consumer demand still more) has often been a precarious venture from the half-known into the unsuspected. Yet buildings, teachers and the children's lives may be committed for generations. For this third level of comparative analysis it is therefore necessary to work closely with specialists in other disciplines, such as economists and sociologists. But the specialist in Comparative Education gives insight and information to them, just as he receives from them. Making the future is no project for any one man, any one discipline, any one interpretation.

This brings us to a last general point. It is more important than ever to have soundly based comparative studies of education, because the relevance of even the best of systems has limits imposed by time. Reorientation and retraining successively throughout life will be the experience of most people in advanced countries for generations to come. That trend is already evident at the most educated levels in the United States, Sweden, Britain and some other countries. All human roles are being transformed, too, not just subjects and occupations. Therefore it is useless to rely on what has been done, or is being done, in schools. We must try instead to think of what will be required, and to observe experiments now being undertaken on the very frontiers of education, where new matrices, new media, new elements and methods of learning are being revealed.

The less settled educational patterns of "developing countries" (where most of mankind live) make it easier for them to be radical. They can by-pass the institutions, methods and curricula of older-established school systems in their eager pursuit of unprecedented but valid objectives. This is all immediately important to us, because the whole world's educative relationships are being transformed, our own along with all the others. For that reason, one or more of the books in each batch of volumes published in the SOCIETY, SCHOOLS AND PROGRESS series will deal with a developing country, whose experience is particularly relevant in assessing education's contribution to the future.

THE PARTICULAR CASE OF INDIA

Of India it has been said that she displays all the problems of mankind in accentuated form : over-population, malnutrition, ignorance on a scale which remarkable increases in school provision have been unable to overcome—and, in addition, the difficulties of multilingualism, religious or communal diversity, discrepancies of wealth and technical development, and a clutter of unreconciled legacies from the past. Therefore, the study of Indian progress towards educational advance is full of lessons for any observer. It excites admiration and sympathy for much that has been achieved, but leaves an overwhelming sense of the need for further endeavours in which the whole of mankind is somehow involved. For it is not only a matter of human concern or technical assistance; the solution of many Indian problems may represent a turning point for much educational and social decision likely to influence the future of the majority of mankind. That majority already lives in southern or eastern Asia; and the fantastic explosion of population in low-income countries may aggravate problems already severe yet representative of most human beings. In Singapore, for example, and in Mexico and Algeria, about half the population are under 21; and in Singapore one-third are under 10 years of age. These are therefore beginning to be representative (not isolated) human problems.

No better author could be found for this volume than Sir John Sargent, a friend of Gandhi and many distinguished Indians. Sir John's masterly survey of Indian educational problems in the "Sargent Plan" earned world recognition before independence (and some Indian criticism for its measured analysis of the time-scale necessary); since that time its statesmanship has been acknowledged on all sides, and Indian educational progress might have been smoother if its recommendations could have been fully implemented. Now, twenty years after independence, Sir John has been able to draw on Indian experimentation, on his own insights as adviser and friend of India, and on the more recent planning by Indian experts.

At a time of radical decision for mankind, *Society, Schools and Progress in India* tells the story of many educational turning points. They include crises of quantity, quality, resources and orientation. The institutions of a vast and complex civilization are challenged by the need to catch up with the material achievements of the outside world, as well as the tasks of independence and of a newer concept of human dignity. Two alternatives to parliamentary democracy and to the "Western way of life" are found on India's borders. In the past, India has been the battleground of conflicting cultures, yet has produced her own amalgam; the present study reveals how that process may be repeating itself now.

Preface

IN VIEW of the size and complexity of the subject with which this book attempts to deal it may be helpful to readers if I explain briefly how it is arranged.

The first three chapters will aim at giving a concise account of the historical events and the political, social, religious and other influences, which have combined to create the India of today. The following chapters will describe what has been thought about educational problems during the last thirty years, what has actually been done about them during the last twenty and what it is hoped to do during the next twenty.

It may make for clarity, if the same line of approach is followed throughout in surveying the educational system. It is proposed to deal in the first place with its main branches, viz. pre-primary, primary, secondary, university, technical and adult (or social, as it is now called) and then with its essential services, viz. the supply and training of teachers, the school health service, provision for the mentally or physically handicapped, vocational guidance, administration and finance. The final chapters will examine the more important issues with which Indian educationists today are concerned, and in particular those which still await agreed solutions.

The publication of this book has been delayed because two reports, which may have a vital bearing on education and social welfare, are due in 1966. The first is the Fourth Five-year Plan for 1966–71 and the second is that of the Education Commission (EC) which was set up by the Government in 1964 to make a comprehensive survey of the whole educational system and to submit its recommendations for future developments by the end of March 1966. It will obviously add to the value of this book, if it is able to take into account these latest official pronouncements. Their main conclusions and recommendations will be reviewed in the final chapter.

Some people who read this book may well feel surprised at the prominence given to the Report of the Central Advisory Board of Education (CABE) on Post-war Educational Development, which was published in 1944. I feel that I owe them both an explanation and an apology about this, especially since many Indians used to, and still do, attach my name to this report. I am both glad and sorry about this; glad because I am proud to have had a part in preparing what may fairly claim to have been the first constructive attempt to plan a national system of education for India, and sorry for more reasons than one. The attachment of an English name to this report may suggest to those unaware of its genesis that it was yet another attempt to foist alien ideas on a long-suffering society—it has in fact been recently described by an Indian writer as "the product of an alien Government"—or that it was a mere gesture, destined, like so many previous reports, to lead nowhere; or, at the best, that it was a kind of death-bed repentance on the part of the British Raj for not having done more to provide India with better social services.

It must be admitted that there is a certain validity in the last of these criticisms, for when, in 1937, the then Viceroy, Lord Linlithgow, offered me the post of Educational Commissioner, he told me that as we should be giving the Indians the control of their own affairs in the near future, he would like the education system to be handed over—to use his own words—"in running order". Apart from that, however, the truth is, as anyone who looks at the first two pages of the report may see, that the plan it contains was devised for India (then, it must be remembered, unpartitioned) by a body mainly Indian in composition. Of the thirty-six people who signed the report, only nine were British. I do not think that anybody who knew the Indian members would regard them as the sort of people who would have allowed themselves to be coerced, or even persuaded against their better judgement, by their British colleagues.

There is another and still stronger reason for regarding the report as, both in intention and substance, a genuinely Indian production. It is true that, during the period of its gestation, political tension was high, that the Congress Ministries had resigned and that there was little or no co-operation, at any rate on the official plane, between the servants of the Government and the adherents of the Nationalist Movement. Fervent Congressites might, therefore, have had some reason to think that any Indian who would assist in the work of an official body like the CABE was either a British sympathizer or at best a luke-warm patriot. They would, however, be quite wrong, and for a reason which I believe is not generally known even now.

Shortly after I arrived in India, I was flattered to receive an invitation to spend a weekend with Mahatma Gandhi at his ashram at Sevagram, a few miles from Wardha, which gave its name to his famous education scheme. The Viceroy raised no objection to my accepting it but warned me that I would prob-ably find living conditions pretty austere. He turned out to be wrong, for the Mahatma, with typical consideration for a new boy like myself, had arranged for me to be lodged with a local raja. In the course of our talks over the weekend I found myself more and more in agreement with him as to the educational (as distinct from the economic) aspects of his scheme, and I came away with his promise that so long as my views were not repudi-ated by those in authority, he would regard education as outside the field of current controversy. This meant that Congress educationists would be free, provided they were not in gaol, to serve on the CABE or its committees or to help it in any other way.

During the years 1937–47, among the people who served on the Board or its committees were Dr. S. Radhakrishnan, the present President of India, Dr. Zakir Husain, the Vice-President and formerly chairman of the Wardha Committee, and the late Mr. B. G. Kher, Chief Minister and Education Minister of Bombay. On the women's side there were the late Rajkumari Amrit Kaur, the first Minister of Health in the new India, a former President of the World Health Organization (WHO) and for many years Mahatma Gandhi's personal secretary, Mrs. Renuka Ray, who has held ministerial office in West Bengal, and Mrs. Hansa Mehta, the wife of the present Indian High Commissioner in London and a former Vice-Chancellor of Baroda University. These few names should be enough to show that the Board spoke for India as a whole and was not merely the mouthpiece of British authority.

In case, however, some people who were not in India at the time may think that I have exaggerated the importance of the CABE Report, especially since they will find only three direct references to it in the Report of the EC of 1966, may I quote what was written about it in the *Year Book of Education, 1949*, by one of the most distinguished of Indian educationists, Dr. K. G. Saiyidain, himself a member of the EC. He wrote :

> It is the first comprehensive scheme of national education; it does not start with the assumption, implicit in all previous government schemes, that India was destined to occupy a position of educational inferiority in the comity of nations; it is based on the conviction that what other countries have achieved on the field of education is well within the competence of this country. . . . Secondly, it is inspired by the desire to provide equality of opportunity at different stages of education. Thirdly, it stresses in clear terms the importance of the teaching profession and makes proposals for inceasing its miserable standard of salaries and poor conditions of service.

If I owe to the members of the CABE an apology for having unintentionally appropriated more than my fair share of the credit to which their labours entitle them, I should also like to take this opportunity of paying a most deserved tribute to my colleagues in the Department, later the Ministry, of Education. Lord Linlithgow, as a consequence of his desire to put education on its feet, accepted the necessity for the Central Government to take a much greater share, financial and otherwise, in the responsibility for development than it had done hitherto. This meant among other things the creation of a separate Department of Education at New Delhi. Education was then, even more than it is now, a provincial subject and such educational matters as concerned the Central Government were dealt with in the Department of Education, Health and Lands. The education staff, apart from the Education Commissioner, consisted of a superintendent and a few clerks. I was told that one of my first duties was to recruit through the Public Services Commission Indians with good qualifications and experience, who would in due course become the senior officers in the new Department or Ministry when it was set up. My first recruit was Dr. D. M. Sen, who previously had held the interesting post of secretary and general ADC to Dr. Rabindranath Tagore at Santiniketan. He remained my deputy until after Independence, when he chose to leave the Central Ministry and become Secretary of the Ministry of Education in his home state of West Bengal. Two years ago he was appointed Vice-Chancellor of the new University of Burdwan. I cannot speak too highly of the loyal help which I received from him at all times, or of the service which he has rendered to the cause of Indian education over many years.

I only wish that space would allow me to thank individually all those to whose help and advice I owed so much in building up the Department but I must at least express my indebtedness to Dr. S. R. Sen Gupta. In my time he was head of the technical branch of the Department and the first secretary of the AICTE. Subsequently he rendered most valuable service to the cause of higher technical education as Director of the IIT at Kharagpur, a post from which he has recently retired.

I was extremely fortunate in my early colleagues and so I was in the later ones, but the Department expanded so rapidly between 1944 and 1947 that I was not able to get to know many of them as well as I should like to have done. Since 1947, some of them have gone to Pakistan and others have retired, but most of those still at work occupy key posts in the education service with great credit both to themselves and to India.

It is only fair to my first colleagues to put on record their share in the preparation of the CABE report. We were up in Simla in the summer of 1942 when it occurred to me that it might be a good exercise for all of us if we worked out how long it would take and how much it would cost to provide India with the same range of facilities in the way of public education as were available in Great Britain in 1937. We split up the various branches among us and then met from time to time to discuss difficulties and register progress. As the whole picture began to take shape, I realized more clearly than I had done before what a vast place India was, and how complex were its problems. When we had got all our financial and other statistics checked by experts, and gazed at the result, we felt rather like "stout Cortez and his men", only our peak was in Simla and we had a woman in our company. So it happened that when, in 1943, with victory in sight, the Government began to think about post-war reconstruction and invited departments to submit their plans, the raw materials so far as education was concerned, were ready.

The CABE can at least claim credit for one feature of its report which is by no means common among official reports, especially in India. Its length was deliberately kept within one hundred pages, so that to read it would not be too much to expect of the busy men who would ultimately be called upon to decide its fate. As a result of this it had the rare experience of becoming something like a best-seller. Nearly 20,000 copies were disposed of, many being sold on station bookstalls, and only the paper shortage stopped further editions being printed. For the sake of the pedagogically minded, the reports of the various committees set up by the Board since its reconstitution in 1935 were issued at the same time in a separate volume.

May I, before ending this preface, offer a word of congratulation and encouragement to all those who, since 1947, have been "facing fearful odds"—perhaps Macaulay is not the happiest source from which to quote to Indians—in the cause of Indian Education? Even if progress on the whole front may not have kept pace with all their desires, there have been notable achievements, particularly in the technical sphere. But even if, as all lovers of India must hope, the present political and economic difficulties are overcome and the path of peaceful progress is again open, the need to make haste slowly will still remain. Democracies, and especially the new ones, have to learn by their own as well as other people's trials and errors. After all, it is nearly a hundred years since Britain, a small country and then much richer than India, set out to provide itself with a national system of education—and it has still a good way to go. I do not think that many Americans or Frenchmen or Germans, or members of any other of the so-called advanced countries, would claim that the millennium is yet at hand so far as education and the social services are concerned. Even the Russians, with all the machinery of autocracy at their command, admit that after nearly half a century of communism they still have problems to solve.

If it was tactless to quote Macaulay a little earlier, it may be far more so in present circumstances to go to China for inspiration. There is, however, a Chinese saying, no doubt older than the present régime, that has sustained me when I have felt depressed at the slow grinding of the educational mills. Here it is :

> If you are planning for one year, plant grain,
> If you are planning for ten years, plant trees,
> If you are planning for a hundred years, plant men.

In any case, *fas est et ab hoste doceri* or, in other words, there is nothing wrong in taking lessons from the opposition.

For facts so far as the historical background up to 1947 is concerned, I have relied on a number of authorities, both ancient and modern, Indian and foreign, to whom I can only make a general acknowledgement of my indebtedness. Although I have read a good many books and articles dealing with education and the social services since Independence, I have thought it best to confine myself for facts and figures solely to official publications. I accept full responsibility for all the opinions expressed in this book, except where they are clearly indicated as quotations.

Finally, I should like to thank very warmly all those friends, both in India and this country, who have helped me with information and advice, and above all, Mr. G. S. Bozman, C.S.I., formerly of the Indian Civil Service (ICS), whose wide knowledge of and affection for India and its people have been of inestimable value to me in the preparation of this book.

Introduction

PEOPLE who have never visited India or have only crossed it by road, rail or air on their way to other places, may be excused for failing to realize that it is a country of infinite variety and violent contrasts. Even those whose stay there has been restricted to a short time or a limited area may not appreciate what a vast and exciting assortment of people and scenery it contains. A cynic, familiar with certain parts of India at certain seasons, might perhaps feel that the Supreme Being had planned them as a kind of steeplechase with fences like heat, drought, flood, famine, disease and wild animals to test the faith and endurance of the men and women whom He had created and put there. The difficulties and dangers by which the life of the Indian peasant has been beset through the ages may help to explain why the principal incentive to the good life offered by the Hindu religion is the prospect of never being born again.

Nevertheless, those who know and love India will agree with a distinguished traveller who declared that it was one of the loveliest parts of the world, provided that one was able to live in the right places at the right time of the year. For a long while prior to the outbreak of the Second World War, the members and employees of the central and most of the provincial governments, as well as a few private individuals, enjoyed this advantage. The war stopped it, however, and since 1947 the many problems confronting the new India have ruled out any prospect of resuming this idyllic existence, at least as a normal routine.

Before turning to the main subject of this book, it may be well to take an early opportunity of saying something about the more striking contrasts to be encountered in India, because through the centuries, they have done so much to determine the conditions under which most of the population have lived, and, whatever the changes that may result from national planning, are likely to go on doing so for a long time to come.

First of all, there are what may be loosely termed the geophysical contrasts. Some parts of the country are very flat; others, particularly on the northern frontiers, are extremely hilly; some areas have too much rain but most have far too little—which makes the control of river water supply a crucial issue with Pakistan. In some districts, notably those with modern irrigation, the soil is very fertile, while elsewhere it is exhausted, eroded or in other ways unproductive. In a recent speech, the late Prime Minister laid stress on the disturbing effect which climatic conditions were having on plans for accelerating agricultural development. He took justifiable pride in the fact that in spite of the widespread floods and droughts in 1964 no one was reported to have died of starvation, whereas, in the old days, such calamities caused the death of millions. At the same time he admitted that it would be a long time before planned development in the agricultural field would relieve India of the necessity to import foodstuffs from abroad.

The climate on the coast is very humid for most of the year, but inland, and especially in the northern plains, there is another contrast, for the weather is usually magnificent from October to March but unpleasantly hot from April until relief comes with the arrival of the monsoon.

It is in the human sphere, however, that the contrasts are most striking. It is not difficult to understand why they present what is probably the most intricate problem which the new Republic has to solve, that is, how to weld a number of races, each with its own language, culture and traditions, into a community conscious of its essential oneness as Indians; how to secure what is currently termed "emotional integration" before fissiparous tendencies may become active, is a matter about which patriotic Indians are much concerned.

Genetically, the main contrast is between the Aryans of the north and the Dravidians of the south. Their looks, cultures, languages, scripts and other characteristics make it clear that they come from entirely different stocks. The people who live in the central and northern regions, and claim descent from the Aryan invaders, are more closely related to one another but it is doubtful whether their affinities are any closer than those which unite— and not infrequently divide—the inhabitants of Europe.

There are, however, other important human contrasts in India which have little to do with racial differences. The first of these is inherent in the traditional structure of Hindu society. Most people will be familiar with the caste system and the effect that it has had in stopping or slowing up social changes of the kind that have been taking place in most Western nations over the last 200 years. More will be said about its ethos in a later chapter. It will be interesting to see how far and how long it will be able to maintain itself—on the one hand against a democratic constitution which has specifically abolished "untouchability", one of its main features, and on the other against the new caste system which is already being produced by the industrial revolution. This new development overlaps to a considerable extent what is perhaps the most significant contrast in relation to the social problems in India today; that between the educated and the uneducated classes. India is often included among the backward or underdeveloped countries, but the educated Indian is anything but backward and is quick to resent being treated as such by tactless, if well-intentioned, foreigners.

For the mathematician and his kin, statistics are no doubt lovely and revealing things, but for the ordinary person, trying to give or to get a conspectus of a vast place like India, they tend, if incomplete, to be misleading, and if complete, to be overwhelming. However, there is no escaping from some figures, if the racial and religious make-up of the Indian population and its social implications are to be made at all clear.

At the time of Partition the population of the old India was about 450 million, of whom 90 million went to Pakistan. The 1961 census gave the population of the new India as 438 million, which represented an increase of 77 million over the 1951 figure.

It is estimated that by the end of the Fifth Five-year Plan in 1976 it will have risen to over 600 million.

An analysis by religions of the 1961 figures shows that there were, to the nearest thousand, 366,503,000 Hindus, 46,939,000 Muslims, 10,726,000 Christians, 7,845,000 Sikhs, 3,250,000 Buddhists and 2,027,000 Jains. Although, by religion, Hindus make up roughly 80 per cent of the population, Hindi, the language, is spoken by less than half. With the possible exception of the Sikhs and the Buddhists—there is some political significance in the growth in the number of Buddhists from 181,000 in 1951—these religious groups are neither racially nor linguistically homogeneous. Diversity in language is shown by the fact that the eighth schedule to the Constitution names fourteen main Indian languages, while the 1951 census lists no less than 845 languages and dialects.

From the political angle, another striking contrast in the pre-1947 era was that between British India proper and the princely states. The latter had their own autocratic rulers and some of the larger ones had their own treaties with the British Crown. There were over 300 of them, and they varied in size from a small estate to a dominion like Hyderabad with some 17 million inhabitants. Some of the bigger ones were progressive in their outlook, in some cases more so than British India, but in the great majority living conditions remained distinctly feudal. At the time of Partition many people thought that one of the major problems facing the new India would be to come to terms with the princes. The way in which this was solved was one of the outstanding achievements of the new Republic.

There are many other contrasts in the Indian scene but enough has perhaps been said to show that few rulers of an emergent democracy have had more difficulties to cope with than Mr. Nehru and his colleagues from 1947 onwards.

Explanatory Notes

ABBREVIATIONS

After the first mention of the bodies listed below they will subsequently, in order to save space, be referred to by their initials:

AICTE   = All-India Council for Technical Education.
APTI   = Association of Principals of Technical Institutions.
CABE   = Central Advisory Board of Education.
EC   = Education Commission, 1964–6.
IAS   = Indian Administrative Service.
ICAR   = Indian Council for Agricultural Research.
ICS   = Indian Civil Service.
IES   = Indian Education Service.
IIT   = Indian Institute of Technology.
ITI   = Industrial Training Institute.
IUB   = Inter-University Board.
NCERT   = National Council for Educational Research and Training.
NPC   = National Planning Commission.
UGC   = University Grants Commission.
UNESCO   = United Nations Educational and Scientific Organization.
UNO   = United Nations Organization.
WHO   = World Health Organization.

PLACE NAMES

Normally the spellings in common use before 1947 will be followed but note will be taken of the more important changes that have taken place since Independence, e.g. United Provinces is now Uttar Pradesh, Central Provinces is now Madhya Pradesh, Benares is now Banaras, etc.

MONEY

Financial estimates and figures generally will be given in Indian terms, except where they are definitely quoted in sterling or some other currency. The rupee was devalued in June 1966. Equivalents in sterling are given below:
1 rupee = pre-1966 1s. 6d.: post-1966 1s. approx.
Rs. 1 lakh (100,000) = pre-1966 £7500: post-1966 £5000 approx.
Rs. 1 crore (10,000,000) = pre-1966 £750,000: post-1966 £500,000 approx.

Approved by the High Commission of India, London

CHAPTER 1

The Historical Background. I

THE aim of this and the following chapter will be to summarize the main events in the history of the sub-continent which used to be called India or Hindustan, but which, since 1947, has been divided between the new India and Pakistan. Comment will be avoided as far as possible, because the ways in which the impact of races and religions, both within and from without, have moulded the political and social structure as well as the character of the inhabitants of the India of today, will form the subject of succeeding chapters.

The first section will record briefly the principal events from the Indus civilizations of the third millennium B.C. to the middle of the eighteenth century A.D., when the British began to arrive in force. The second will cover the period of the British Raj and will deal in somewhat greater detail with the growth of the Nationalist Movement which finally brought it to an end in 1947. The third will chronicle the events, expected and unexpected, and the pressures, internal and external, which have presented so many problems to the rulers of the new India and have created or accentuated many urgent issues. The final section will concentrate on the main happenings in the educational sphere from the time of Warren Hastings up to 1937, when Mahatma Gandhi's Wardha Scheme at last made a national issue of educational planning. Developments since 1937 will be reserved for the chapter in which the assumptions underlying the present social set-up will be examined.

FROM THE INDUS CIVILIZATIONS TO THE BEGINNING
OF BRITISH RULE

So far as is known at present, the so-called Indus civilizations
date back at least as far as 2500 B.C. and appear to have endured
for about 1000 years before they were destroyed by invaders from
the north-west, generally known as the Aryans. The main centres,
unearthed to date by archaeologists, were at Mohenjo-daro about
200 miles from the mouth of the Indus and Harappa some 300
miles further up. Whether they formed part of a single political
unit is uncertain, but their cultures were closely akin. Their
political structure seems to have had a theocratic basis with rank
gradations suggestive of a conservative and static society. The
absence of fortifications implies immunity from external threats,
at any rate until the Aryans fell upon them. Living conditions
were at a high level, with domestic bathrooms, water supply and
sanitation. Their religious system has certain affinities with
Hinduism, which no doubt it influenced.

The Aryans were tribes who originally lived round the Caspian
Sea, but about 2000 B.C. they began to confederate and move
south-east. They were a rough and warlike people who grew
grain and kept animals, about the slaughter of which, unlike
their Hindu descendants, they had no inhibitions. Their religion
was a crude form of anthropomorphism and their chief god,
Indra, was little more than the deification of the ideal Aryan
warrior. A raja with a council of elders ruled each tribe. Although
their early incursions were mostly in search of booty, somewhere
about 1500 B.C. their minds turned to conquest, and the Indus
cities were overwhelmed and obliterated. From then on they
spread steadily over the north of India and penetrated as far
south as the River Narbudda.

The Indo–Aryans' earliest extant literature is the four Vedas
(*Veda* = knowledge), of which the oldest and most important is
the Rigveda. This was composed probably between 1500 and
1000 B.C. and reflects a society divided into ranks or orders but
not yet into castes. These orders were the warriors, the priests and

the workers. In the early days, as is not surprising among primitive, warlike folk, the warriors appear to have had the precedence over the priests. Gradually, however, the invaders began to be influenced by the superior civilization of the people whom they had subdued, particularly in religion. The old anthropomorphism and fire-worship began to be superseded by something much more subtle and sophisticated, and this change marked the growing ascendancy of the priests and a transition from the idea of social ranks to that of caste divisions with a religious sanction. No more will be said here about the origin and nature of Vedic Hinduism, its subsequent ramifications and the impact on it of rival faiths like Buddhism and Jainism, which made their appearance towards the end of the sixth century B.C. The bearing of these and other later religions like Islam and Christianity on the Indian social and economic complex will be examined in the next chapter.

The first really world-famous event in Indian history is the invasion by Alexander the Great in 326 B.C. Oddly enough, there is no extant Indian record of this, though it was well reported on the Greek side. Until a few years before Alexander arrived on the scene, northern India seems to have been split up into a number of independent states without any cohesion or acknowledged suzerain, but shortly after Alexander's brief but dramatic appearance, Chandragupta Maurya established himself in Bihar and founded the Mauryan Dynasty. Before he died in 298 B.C. he had extended his sway over all India north of the Narbudda and some parts of Afghanistan as well. Seleukos, who was Alexander's successor in Asia, sent an envoy, named Megasthenes, to Chandragupta's court, and he has left a vivid account of contemporary Indian life and institutions. The Emperor lived in great state and maintained a large regular army and a highly organized civil service. The most distinguished of his successors was the Emperor Asoka, who came to the throne in 269 B.C. His inscribed pillars and rock edicts, which have been discovered as far south as Maski, not far north of Madras, indicate not merely the extent of his dominion but also an enlightened conception of a ruler's responsibilities, which was far in advance of his time. His sculptured lions have been adopted as the emblem of independent India. He was a Buddhist but after his death Buddhism made little headway in the land of its origin as compared with its progress in other parts of Asia.

The Mauryan Empire slowly collapsed and for several centuries anarchy reigned in northern India. It was the fourth century A.D. before a new power, the Gupta Dynasty, made its appearance. Their rule seems to have been much on the same line as that of the Mauryans, if slightly more lenient. We are again dependent for an account of life under the Guptas on a foreign visitor, this time Fa-hien, a Chinese pilgrim who spent the first decade of the fifth century A.D. in India. He was greatly impressed by what he saw, and particularly by the piety of the people. Although he may have been over-polite to his hosts, his account makes it clear that the power of the Brahmin caste had grown considerably since Mauryan days. It is also clear that during the Gupta period civilization reached a high level. Mathematics, architecture and sculpture flourished, and the University of Nalanda attracted students from many parts of Asia.

At the end of the fifth century the power of the Guptas was shattered by an invasion of nomadic tribes from central Asia, to whom the Indians gave the name of "Huns". A last competent ruler, Harsha, reasserted his authority over much of the Gupta Empire during the first half of the seventh century but on his death northern India again disintegrated and disorder reigned until the arrival of the Muslims at the end of the twelfth century.

Between A.D. 800 and 1200 parts of northern India, including the modern State of Rajasthan, were ruled by the Rajputs, the heroes of many chivalric legends.

In central and southern India during the medieval period there were a number of dynasties whose power, impressive while it lasted, was generally short-lived. Of these the most important were the Chalukyas in the Deccan and Maharashta, and the Pallavas, Pandyas, Cholas and Cheras in the Dravidian south. These kings almost without exception were Brahminical Hindus.

Although today their names and deeds are of no great interest to anyone but scholars, they did, in fact, leave a legacy in the way of distinctive languages and cultures. From these derive the linguistic loyalties which have caused some embarrassment to the present rulers of India.

The Muslims, after a period of sporadic raiding like the original Aryans, began to invade India in earnest towards the end of the twelfth century A.D., and by the middle of the fourteenth century the Sultanate of Delhi controlled most of the north. By A.D. 1400, however, decline set in : provincial governors, in some cases, succeeded in asserting their independence and, to complete the collapse, the Emir of Samarkand, the famous Tamerlaine, burst into India and sacked Delhi. For the next 200 years, although Muslim rulers survived in some areas, there was no central authority until Akbar arrived.

The anarchy which followed the downfall of the Delhi Sultanate paved the way for a revival of Hindu power in the centre and south. Vijayanagar was founded in A.D. 1336 and its kings seem to have recreated much of the splendour of the Mauryans and Guptas. Like their predecessors in this area they were orthodox, if not particularly ascetic, Hindus, and were much in the hands of their Brahmin ministers. They were notable patrons of the arts, and under them, Telegu culture was much enriched. Their dominion lasted nearly 200 years but then, after the usual preliminary internal upheavals, a confederation of Deccan princes defeated their army and destroyed their capital.

Seventy years before the fall of Vijayanagar, Babur, King of Kabul, started the Mogul assault on India, but it was not until his grandson, Akbar, came to the throne that the Moguls made themselves masters of all of northern and much of central India. Akbar was a man of great parts. He remodelled the administrative system and reformed the traditional methods of revenue collection. Unlike his predecessors and most of his successors he was not a fanatical Muslim. He married Hindu princesses and gave important posts in his government to Hindus. Men of all faiths were welcome at his court, and at a later stage in his reign he invented a new religion with a supreme deity, whose earthly mouthpiece he naturally was. This, however, made little appeal either to Muslims or Hindus.

Akbar was succeeded in 1605 by his son, Jehangir, who continued his tolerant policy. He was also a liberal patron of the arts, and the famous Mogul school of painting dates from his time. There is not much that can be said for the next king, Shahjahan (1627–58), except that posterity is indebted to him for the Taj Mahal. He was a ruthless tyrant and a persecutor of all non-Muslims. His successor, Aurungzeb (1658–1707), was no better. The semblance of Muslim power was maintained during his long reign but cracks were beginning to appear in the fabric, and by the middle of the eighteenth century the time was ripe for the British to step in.

THE BRITISH RAJ

The British were not, of course, by any means the first foreigners to interest themselves in India and its commercial attractions. The trading links of the Malabar Coast not only with other parts of Asia but also with East Africa, Egypt and perhaps even with Greece and Rome can be traced back almost to the dawn of history. Nor were the British the first Europeans in the market, for they had been preceded by the Dutch and the Portuguese. By the end of the sixteenth century, however, the former had moved their main interests further east, and the latter had spoiled their prospects and alienated the local population by a religious intolerance rivalling that of the Muslims.

The East India Company was founded by Royal Charter in 1600, its primary objective being the spice trade. In 1611 it secured from Shahjahan the grant of its first trading station at Masulipatam. This was followed by Surat in 1612, and Madras, which became its first presidency, in 1641. Before long it was also operating from the two other future presidencies of Bombay and Calcutta. Before the seventeenth century ended, the rival French company had also established successful trading posts in the south, east and north. The war between the two countries, which broke out in 1742, naturally involved their foreign outposts and proved to be the first step towards British supremacy. Whether it wanted to or not, self-preservation forced the Company to shoulder political and military, as well as commercial, responsibilities. Clive's ability as a soldier and the presence of the British Navy ensured victory, and, by 1760, France's hold on India was finished.

Once the French were gone, the Company, in the guise of agents for the still surviving but moribund Mogul Empire, had little difficulty in dealing with local opposition, apart from the Maratha confederacy in the north-west.

The story of the Company's early years as a political power does not make very pleasant reading. Its main object was still trade and many of its servants were out to amass fortunes regardless of the interests of the inhabitants. It was the age of the "Nabobs". It can, however, be put to their credit that whatever the morality of their business dealings, their social contacts with Indians, if one may judge from the memoirs of William Hickey and others, were on an equal and friendly footing.

In 1772, a man of ability and vision, by name Warren Hastings, became Governor of Bengal, and not long afterwards the Company appointed him to the new post of Governor-General, which gave him control over the other two presidencies of Madras and Bombay. During his fourteen years in office he did much to improve administration and check the more flagrant forms of corruption, though this did not save him from being impeached on his return to England.

It was about this time that the British Parliament began to realize that one of its chartered companies was becoming an imperial power. In 1784, at the instigation of William Pitt, it passed an India Act, which made the Crown and the Company jointly responsible for Indian affairs. In 1813 the Company suffered a further blow when Parliament abolished its trading monopoly. Twenty years later it ceased altogether to have commercial interests and became the political agent of the Crown.

Although the India Act of 1784 had deprecated any idea of extending British dominion by conquest or other means as "repugnant to the wish, honour and policy of this nation", the confusion and lawlessness caused by rival claimants to thrones or by princes with expansive ambitions often forced the British to intervene for their own protection. Lord Cornwallis, who succeeded Warren Hastings as Governor-General, had taken steps to restrict incursions by the Marathas, and the Marquess of Wellesley with the aid of his brother, afterwards the great Duke of Wellington, not only defeated them but also extended British authority over practically the whole of the south. When the Muslim Sultan of Mysore was overthrown, the former Hindu rulers were restored subject to a treaty which gave the Governor-General the right to intervene if maladministration or any other sufficient cause gave him reason to do so. This is noteworthy because it laid down the line to be subsequently followed in settling the relations between the British Crown and the princely states.

Under Lord Hastings, who became Governor-General in 1813, conquest was coming to an end and consolidation began. There was trouble with Nepal in 1816 but after an initial success which impressed British soldiers with the military virtues of the Gurkhas, Nepal gave in. The only remaining independent power of any importance was the Sikh kingdom in the Punjab but, at the time, its rulers were friendly. Hastings repaired the canals, which had become derelict since the Moguls, and started to improve communications by road. He also gave some encouragement to education and, unlike his predecessors, appointed some Indians to senior posts in the judiciary and civil service.

Lord William Bentinck, who was Governor-General from 1828 to 1835, continued the work of consolidation and initiated reforms in many directions. For the first time since the British Raj began, serious attention was given to developing local industry and improving agriculture by irrigation and other means. Persian was replaced by the vernacular or English as the judicial language and English became the prescribed medium of instruction at the higher stages of education. How far this was done on the advice of Macaulay, who was the education member of his council, will be discussed in the last section of this chapter. Bentinck also departed from the previous policy of not interfering with local customs by making illegal the practice of burning widows on the funeral pyres of their husbands, known as *sati*. His work on communications was carried further by Lord Dalhousie (1848–56), who not only extended the road system but also started railways. Apart from this he should go on record as the first person in authority to give official endorsement to the idea of trusteeship rather than conquest.

The Indian Mutiny, which broke out at the end of Dalhousie's time, is important neither for its extent, for the mutineers received little support from the mass of the population, nor for its duration, as it was suppressed within a year, but for its causes, effects and implications. There is little doubt that the British were primarily responsible for it. Their efforts to modernize the country had antagonized many whose prosperity had suffered or whose orthodoxy had been offended, particularly since the former policy of discouraging missionaries had been reversed. Then the Company had created a modern army, the pay and prestige of which had attracted into its ranks many high-caste Hindus. Such people, already disturbed by British innovations, were easily inflamed by rumours that the new Enfield cartridges were greased with the fat of cows, sacred to Hindus, or pigs, an abomination to Muslims. No serious attempt seems to have been made to contradict the rumours or withdraw any suspect cartridges. The Mutiny began at Meerut in May 1857, when some soldiers were punished for refusing to use the cartridges and were rescued by their comrades. In the course of the fighting that ensued, some savage acts were done by both sides and these left bitter memories.

In some ways, however, the immediate results of the Mutiny were not unbeneficial to India. The India Act of 1858 saw the disappearance of the East India Company as a political factor, and a Secretary of State in London became directly responsible to the British Cabinet for Indian Affairs. The Governor-General acquired the additional title of Viceroy as the personal representative of the Crown, and three years later his Executive Council was enlarged and each member put in charge of a department of government. At the same time, steps were taken to improve the lot of the peasants by protecting them from extortionate landlords and tax-collectors and giving them greater security in respect of their holdings. On the economic side a good deal was done to increase the output of coal and iron as well as the manufacture of cotton and jute. Other new industries made their appearance, and the growth in the demand for tea was remarkable. Further road and railway expansion expedited progress on the economic side. For reasons similar in some ways to those which have operated in India since 1947, such educational development as took place was concentrated on the higher stages and no serious effort was made to cope with the problem of mass education at the primary level.

Although quite a lot was done during the last half of the last century to develop India's natural resources, the steps taken to implement Dalhousie's conception of trusteeship and to associate Indians in the management of their own affairs were at best half-hearted and sporadic. From the seventies onwards the ratepayers in the big cities like Calcutta and Bombay began to have some say in the election of municipal committees, and in the eighties Lord Ripon, the then Viceroy, in order to provide, as he said, "a measure of political and popular education", set up district boards in rural areas, at least half of whose members were popularly elected. The subjects entrusted to them included education, health, sanitation and public works, and they were given limited powers to levy taxes. The fact that elementary education was remitted to these inexperienced bodies is yet another indication of how little those in authority were concerned with this problem.

It is hardly surprising that government measures to stimulate industry or arouse interest in local self-government made little appeal to the Indian intelligentsia, except to those engaged in government service or in the new industries. Some sought escape from frustration in various forms of religious revival like the Brahmo Samaj, founded by Raja Ram Mohan Roy as early as 1828, and the Arya Samaj, which won many adherents from 1870 onwards. Perhaps the most significant of these movements in view of its impact on society today was the Ramakrishnan Mission, which propagated an all-embracing faith derived from the essential tolerance of pure Hinduism, and insisted that religion divorced from good words became sterile.

But while some Indians found solace in a return to the purity of Vedic Hinduism, there were many others who did not. These, in the main, belonged to a new class of educated and, in some ways, Westernized Indians, whose aspirations were not to be satisfied by religious revivals. This new society, unlike the old aristocracy, which was prepared to accept British rule, albeit without any great enthusiasm, felt that the time had come for a new India to abandon its age-old acceptance of foreign domination and assert its right to manage its own affairs. This feeling, fortified by the liberal ideas current in many parts of the world since the second half of the eighteenth century, found expression in the first meeting of the Indian National Congress, which was held at Bombay at the end of 1885. The seventy members who attended were nearly all professional men, and the views expressed were both moderate and along Western lines. Liberal British opinion approved the new body—between 1885 and 1900 it had three British presidents—and even the administration showed no hostility to it.

Through the normal machinery of local branches and conferences, Congress soon made its influence felt over a wide area, but differences began to develop as to the best way of pursuing its object. The "moderates", led by Mr. G. K. Gokhale, found themselves at odds with the "extremists", whose leading spokesman was a Bombay newspaper editor, Mr. B. G. Tilak. The cause was not helped by the arrival, in 1899, of Lord Curzon as Viceroy. He soon came to regard Congress as an obstacle in the way of his plans for Indian betterment and made no secret of his desire to see it disappear.

Curzon was a man of ideas, and he was unquestionably desirous of doing his best in his own way for the country of which he was the temporary ruler. As is not uncommon in the case of would-be benefactors, his gifts were so designed and distributed as to excite anything but gratitude from the intended beneficiaries. Nevertheless, he did do a number of things from which India is today still deriving benefit. With the possible exception of Warren Hastings, very few of his predecessors had taken any practical interest in Indian arts and antiquities. He established a department of archaeology, which was just in time to avert the threatened decay of some of India's most famous monuments. He created the Imperial Library and his personal interest did much to revive the Bengal Asiatic Society, which Hastings had founded. In other branches of the administration he again revised the land revenue system in order to provide increased protection for the cultivator from avaricious landlords. He brought science to the aid of agriculture by setting up a special department with laboratories, experimental farms and a research institute. On the industrial side he also created a new department and put a member of his Council in charge of it. His incursions into the educational field, or rather the ways in which they were made, were ill-conceived and will be examined later in this chapter. The outstanding instance of his inability to combine sound theory with tactful practice was his partition of Bengal. His object was more efficient administration and there is no reason to think that he was in any way influenced by the religious issues that led to it being again partitioned in 1947, but Congress suspected him of trying to introduce a communal rift into their movement.

The partition of Bengal was revoked in 1911 but in the meantime two things had happened which acted as powerful stimulants on the Congress leaders. The first was the triumph of the Japanese over the Russians in the war of 1904–6, which implied that Easterners were as good as Westerners when they met on level terms, and the second was the sweeping victory of the Liberals at the 1906 General Election in Britain, which raised hopes that the new Government would be more sympathetic towards Indian aspirations than its predecessor.

These events encouraged Congress to step up its programme and in 1908 its political aim was defined as a form of colonial self-government on similar lines to that of Canada. The reaction of the British Government took the form in 1909 of what are known as the Morley–Minto reforms, Morley being the Secretary of State for India and Minto the Viceroy at the time. The object of these reforms was to give Indians a bigger part in the administration. The enlarged Legislative Council of sixty members contained thirty-three nominated members, twenty-eight of them officials, with twenty-seven members, not officials, to be elected by the provincial legislatures. The provincial legislatures, on the other hand, were given non-official majorities; these non-officials were not popularly elected but were the nominees of local interests. For the first time seats were reserved for Muslims both in the Legislative Council and in the provincial legislatures. When Lord Hardinge succeeded Lord Minto, further conciliatory gestures were made. Apart from revoking the unpopular partition of Bengal, he had the seat of government moved from Calcutta to Delhi, which became the new capital.

On their first publication, the Morley–Minto reforms received a mild welcome from Indians both in and outside Congress, where Gokhale and the moderates were in control, but on closer examination it became clear that they fell far short of what Congress wanted. The Central Council was still controlled by officials and even in the provinces where non-officials were in the majority, the governors retained the power to veto measures of which they did not approve. No provision was made for popular representation, and the reservation of seats for Muslims stirred communal feelings.

However, before Congress had decided what form future agitation should take, the outbreak of the First World War in August 1914 rallied most educated Hindus to the British side, though the fact that Turkey, the home of the Khalifa, was in the

other camp alienated many Muslims. Large sums were con-
tributed to the war funds and over three-quarters of a million
Indians joined the armed forces. When, however, the early
victory that most people expected did not arrive and the cost of
living rose steeply, disillusionment set in. Victory, when it did
come, coincided with the world influenza epidemic, which hit
India with special violence. The war did have one effect that was
to prove of some benefit thirty years later. A desire to help the
war effort and/or the attractive wages offered drew many high-
caste Hindus into munition and other factories, and made a
breach in the accepted convention that such people did not
engage in manual labour.

During the war, Congress lost, by death, two of its early
leaders and, though it received an unexpected reinforcement in
the shape of the theosophist, Mrs. Besant, it badly needed someone who would give it the leadership that would appeal to the
masses as well as the intelligentsia. The man was at hand in the
person of Mr. M. K. Gandhi, soon to be known and revered
throughout India as the Mahatma or Great Soul. He was a
Gujarati who had studied law in London and other places before
going to live in South Africa, where he became the leader of the
local Indians in their struggle against racial discrimination. There,
he developed his strategy of non-violence or passive resistance,
which he was to employ with success against the British Raj.
"Satyagraha", as it was called, was not merely a political weapon,
it was also a form of self-discipline which embodied the ancient
Hindu concept of "Ahimsa" or the sanctity of all living things.
Gandhi himself practised certain austerities in regard to food,
dress and other matters, which did much to enhance his reputation as a holy man among the peasantry. He has sometimes been
criticized on the grounds that the saint and the politician in his
make-up tended to get confused at moments of crisis but whether
this was so or not, the verdict of history will certainly place him
among the greatest men of his time. Apart from getting rid of
the British, his main object was to improve the condition of the
Indian villagers. The fact that he once said that he considered

William Morris to be one of the finest Englishmen will suggest his attitude towards modern industrialization, and it may be that the assassin's bullet that ended his life in 1948 saved him from seeing the new India embark on an economic policy of which he could never have whole-heartedly approved.

Gandhi's task as Congress leader, which he became soon after his return to India, was made easier by the fact that one of Tilak's last acts was to come to terms with the Muslims, so that with the exception of a few Liberals who continued in the role of "honest brokers", there was now something like a united front in the fight for self-government.

Not long after the end of the war, the nationalist cause got some quite unexpected assistance from the British Government. In 1917, Mr. Montagu, then Secretary of State for India in the Coalition Government, had given a specific assurance that steps would be taken to ensure the progressive realization of responsible government in India at the earliest possible date, but victory and Lloyd George's enormous majority at the Coupon Election encouraged the die-hards to assert that the force which had at last broken the Germans might be used with effect to overcome opposition in India. To make matters worse, in 1919, the Indian Government, no doubt with the consent of the authorities at home, passed two unnecessary and highly provocative laws. One allowed judges to try certain political offences without juries and the other gave provincial governments power to imprison trouble-makers at their discretion. Protests against these were followed by "hartals" or hold-up of all business, and then by riots, one of which ended in a massacre at Amritsar.

The consequent widespread resentment did nothing to smooth the way for the next serious attempt at political evolution. In fact, the Montagu–Chelmsford reforms, which came at the end of Lord Chelmsford's time as Viceroy in 1921, represented a considerable advance on previous schemes. The Viceroy's Executive Council was enlarged and for the first time Indians were made members of it. A Council of State and a Legislative Assembly, both with non-official majorities, took the place of the

Imperial Legislative Council. Another important innovation was the introduction of what was called "dyarchy" into the provincial administration. By this, certain subjects, termed "transferred subjects", which included education, agriculture, public works and local government, were entrusted to ministers responsible to the provincial councils, while others termed "reserved subjects", such as justice, revenue, irrigation and labour, were left in the hands of counsellors responsible only to the Governor. There was also to be a new electoral system, with a limited franchise based on a property qualification, for the election of members of the Council of State, the Legislative Assembly and the provincial councils. The reservation of constituency seats, already operative for Muslims, was extended to other communities like the Sikhs and Anglo–Indians in those provinces where they formed a substantial element in the population.

In some respects, the Montagu–Chelmsford reforms marked a definite step forward on the part of the British Government, but they still left the ultimate control in the hands of the Viceroy and the provincial governors. For this reason, Congress, on Gandhi's advice, rejected them and started a campaign of non-co-operation, which included taking no part in the new elections. This meant that those who went to the polls were mostly moderates, and the ministers who then took office were nearly all Liberals and must have been conscious that they did not have the support of the mass of the people. The doubling of the salt tax to meet a deficit in the budget did nothing to diminish public disaffection.

During the next few years the manœuvres of the two sides bear some resemblance to a country dance, the parties engaged advancing towards each other, then retreating and occasionally turning their backs on their own partners. Advances on the government side were the securing for India of membership of the League of Nations and an increased proportion of officers in the army. On the other side, an advance by Gandhi—or perhaps it was more in the nature of a strategic move—was the calling-off of the civil disobedience movement on the ground that it was leading to disturbances, which conflicted with the principle of non-violence. This did not please some leading Congressites, among them Motilal Nehru and his son, Jawaharlal, who favoured using the elections to attack the Government. The Swaraj (Home Rule) Party, as they called themselves, secured enough seats to cause some embarrassment but it achieved little else and when Gandhi, who had been arrested, was released, Congress turned to him again.

The next significant moves took place in 1927. The British Government sent out a commission under Sir John Simon to survey the constitutional situation but again made the mistake of not associating any Indians with it. Congress, on their side, declared independence, and not dominion status as previously, to be their ultimate aim. This was followed by a scheme for self-government drawn up by Motilal Nehru. This may or may not have laid the egg, from which Pakistan subsequently emerged, for it turned down the idea of separate constituencies for Muslims, and the 1916 entente between the parties, which had never been exactly "cordiale", became progressively less so from then on.

In 1929 there was a new Labour Government in Britain and it announced that it accepted dominion status for India and was prepared to call a round-table conference to work out ways and means. Since, however, there was no promise of dominion status at once, Gandhi, once again in full command of Congress, rejected the offer outright and launched a fresh campaign of civil disobedience. With a few companions he staged a spectacular defiance of the law by going to the sea and making salt on the shore. This gesture against a highly unpopular tax appealed to the imagination of the people and before the year was out thousands had got themselves into gaol through following his example.

The Simon Report, when it appeared, did little to appease the opposition, for although it advocated self-government for the provinces, the centre would have to wait for this until the princes were prepared to join in a federation. Congress not unnaturally interpreted this as putting it off indefinitely. Lord Irwin—better known later as Lord Halifax—who was Viceroy from 1926 to

1931, convened a round-table conference at the end of 1930 but, as most of the Congress leaders were in prison, those who attended were mainly Liberals. It reached no definite conclusions but it led to a pronouncement by the British Prime Minister, Ramsay Macdonald, that "with the legislature constituted on a federal basis" his government would be prepared "to recognize the principle of the responsibility of the executive to the legislature". This, at least, offered some prospect of a settlement; the Congress leaders were released and civil disobedience stopped. After talks between Gandhi and Irwin, which seem to have convinced the former that the latter was in earnest, it was agreed that there should be a second conference, in which Congress would take part.

At this point, however, external events once more interfered. Before the conference could be held, the international financial slump hit Britain and led to the supersession of the Labour Government by a "National" Government, which was conservative in outlook and consequently less inclined to come to terms with the Indians. The result was that when the second conference did meet, the Indian members soon felt, as Jawaharlal Nehru notes in his autobiography, that the British were again employing delaying tactics and were not prepared to face up to the main issue. They had some excuse for this in view of the fact that a new obstacle to a settlement had made its appearance. The rift between Hindus and Muslims had been widening, and the communal issue had become a live one, even if it did not, as Nehru says, dominate the conference.

As the Indian members were unable to reach agreement among themselves, the British Government had to reach a decision, which, as usual, proved unacceptable. There followed, also as usual, civil disobedience, riots, terrorism and numerous arrests, including those of the Congress leaders. The fact that Gandhi's presence at the conference table had failed to produce the desired result added greatly to the general disillusionment. Under its influence, civil disobedience petered out and the political prisoners were soon at liberty again.

At this stage another actor, who was to play a prominent part in future negotiations, began to make his presence felt. This was Mr. M. A. Jinnah, who, for some years as leader of the Independent Party in the Legislative Assembly, had had sufficient votes at his command to make him a force to be reckoned with, both by Congress and the British. At first, he usually gave his support to Congress but during the twenties Muslims began to wonder whether, in the long run, they might not get more from the British than from the Hindus. There were several reasons for this but the chief one was the approval by Congress of the Nehru Report, which rejected the idea of separate Muslim electorates. The reappearance of Gandhi as Congress leader was another factor in dividing the two parties, for, in spite of his fervent belief in and public advocacy of Indian unity, he had never been able to convince the Muslims that he was other than a typical Hindu at heart.

In the middle thirties, Jinnah, after a temporary withdrawal into private life, returned to the political arena as head of a much strengthened Muslim League, and from that time the Hindu–Muslim struggle intensified. It is a moot point whether, if the British had acted more promptly in granting self-government, Hindus and Muslims might have got down together to make it work. The opportunity was not taken, the policy of drift went on and led to what impartial observers, in the light of what has happened since, can only regard as a catastrophe. In the words of Lucretius, "Tantum religio potuit suadere malorum" ("So many ills could religion prompt"). In 1933 the name "Pakistan" was first heard, and thereafter its establishment became the overall objective of the Muslim League.

In 1935 the British Government, endeavouring to make the most of such slight signs of accord as had emerged from the second round-table conference, passed the Government of India Act. The constitution which it embodied was a federal one, and legislative powers were classified under three heads : federal, provincial and concurrent. The provinces were given popularly elected assemblies, to which ministers, though appointed by the

governors, were responsible. A lowering of the property qualification multiplied the electorate by six, and women got the vote.
There was a reservation of seats for Muslims in all provinces and
for other communities, like the Sikhs in the Punjab and Europeans in Bengal. Dyarchy disappeared and governors were
required, subject to their reserved powers, to act on the advice
of their cabinets. At the centre, all the main branches of administration except defence and foreign affairs were to be under
ministers responsible to the Assembly but the paramount authority
of the Viceroy remained much as before. He appointed the
counsellors in charge of the reserved departments and could issue
ordinances which had the force of law for limited periods. It was
further enacted that the new central executive was not to become
operative until a specified number of the princely states had
acceded. Even if and when this happened, which in fact it never
did, federal legislation could still be refused assent by the
Viceroy, as Governor-General, acting under instructions from the
Secretary of State in Britain.

There were enough loopholes in the Act to justify the criticism
that it was just another delaying action, but both Congress and
the Muslim League decided to give it a trial. The first election
under the new franchise was held in 1937 and gave Congress clear
majorities in five provinces, in two others it got control with the
help of allies and only Bengal with a Muslim ministry and the
Punjab with a Unionist bloc stood out. On the whole, the new
provincial ministries were soon in satisfactory working order and
had few causes to complain of lack of co-operation on the part
of their governors or members of the ICS and other imperial
services.

The outlook would have been more promising if the leading
members of Congress had not abstained from taking office instead
of deciding to pull the provincial strings from off-stage, while
devoting their energies to attacking the central executive. This
direction from the wings led to one unfortunate result, which
it is difficult to believe that such shrewd minds as Gandhi and
Vallabhai Patel did not foresee. In the Congress provinces, even

where Muslims were numerous, no member of that community was given or offered a ministerial post. It seems strange that such an obvious chance of closing the communal breach should have been missed. The explanation may be that Gandhi, with an independent and unified India in the forefront of his mind, felt that Congress must adhere to its role of representing all Indians who wanted to be free, whatever their caste or creed, and that, therefore, any recognition of Muslims as such was both unnecessary and undesirable.

This was almost the last straw so far as Jinnah was concerned. During the recent election, he had made several public offers to support Congress in the struggle for self-government but these had evoked no response from the Working Committee, who probably regarded them as merely tactical moves. From then on, the League took up with increased energy the work of rousing Muslims throughout the country, and when, on the outbreak of the Second World War, the Congress ministries resigned, Jinnah hailed it as a day of deliverance.

The coming of war at this particular time put Congress in a dilemma. The ideals of nazism and fascism were naturally anathema to Gandhi and all believers in "ahimsa" and non-violence. On the other hand, it was clear that so long as the war lasted, the British would not relax their control of anything in India which might affect the war effort, and might even take occasion to go back on some of the concessions recently made. When, in 1940, it looked as if Germany might win, some of the Congress leaders like Nehru would have been ready to join in the fight against totalitarianism, subject to satisfactory guarantees as to what would happen when the war was won. Gandhi, however, adhered to his pacifist principles. There were some tentative negotiations about a post-war constitution but these came to nothing, largely because the third party now in the field, the Muslim League, were insistent not only that they should be consulted in regard to any possible settlement but also that they should be given a share in any national government that might be set up as a result of it.

When Japan came in on Germany's side, the threat to India emphasized the urgent need for some definite decision. Sir Stafford Cripps, a cabinet minister of notably progressive views, was sent to India with a new offer. This was that India should have dominion status as soon as possible after the war ended with the option of leaving the Commonwealth, if and when it so desired. It was further proposed that the new constitution should be worked out by a constituent assembly, elected by the provincial legislatures and then embodied in a formal treaty with the British Government. Provinces which disliked the new constitution could remain out but would have the right to come in later, if they so wished.

Nehru was prepared to consider this offer, but Gandhi and most of the other leaders were not, in default of some tangible proof that the British were in earnest this time. As this was not forthcoming, the offer was rejected. Congress then approved the "Quit India" campaign, which caused some loss of life and much damage to property before it was suppressed. It also led to the arrest of Gandhi and the Working Committee, an event of which the Muslim League took full advantage.

Lord Linlithgow, an able administrator whose intentions had been rather unfairly mistrusted by the Indians, was succeeded as Viceroy in 1943 by Lord Wavell, a brilliant soldier and a man of unquestioned integrity. In spite of the respect in which he was held by all sections of the community, his efforts to find an acceptable solution were no more successful than those of his predecessors. He was unable to get Congress and the League to agree as to their allocation of seats in the Executive Council and, to make things still more difficult, Gandhi persisted in his refusal to recognize the League as the only mouthpiece of Muslim opinion. The League's claim to be this was much enhanced by the results of the election held at the end of 1945.

Meanwhile, the general election in Britain had been won by Labour, and Mr. Attlee was Prime Minister in place of Mr. Churchill. Attlee had got to know and like India when he was a member of the Simon Commission. He sent out a new mission, which was led by Lord Pethick-Lawrence with Sir Stafford Cripps and Mr. A. V. Alexander as his colleagues. The mission promptly endorsed the proposal for a federation of the provinces, for admission to which the princely states would be at liberty to apply. This union would control foreign affairs, defence and communications. A novel suggestion was that individual provinces might join in some form of regional organization, for the more effective exercise of some of their powers. To bring the new system into operation, a national government should be set up. The mission was opposed to partition on the ground that any geographical division of the country would be bound to leave too many Muslims in India and too many Hindus in Pakistan.

At first, both parties appeared ready to accept the mission's plan, but owing to some ambiguous statements by leaders and some malicious reporting by sections of the press the League began to suspect that the plan was regarded by Congress as a basis for subsequent negotiations rather than a blueprint for a permanent settlement. Nehru did his best to remove this impression, and when he was invited by the Viceroy to form the transitional government, he offered Jinnah a choice of places on the Executive Council. Jinnah refused the offer and prepared to take direct action in support of the demand for Pakistan. Once more there were riots and bloodshed in the north-east, and this might well have spread but for Gandhi's personal intervention. A month or two later the League changed their minds and agreed to join the Executive Council, but it soon became clear that their object was not to co-operate but, by obstructing business, to convince all concerned, and Congress in particular, that the only escape from the impasse was Pakistan.

After further fruitless discussions, this time in London, Attlee took the bull by the horns and announced that Britain would leave India not later than June 1948. Lord Mountbatten, a member of the British Royal Family who had been Supreme Commander in south-east Asia during the last phase of the war, was sent out to succeed Wavell and organize the transfer of power.

He found, on his arrival, that the tension was so high that there was no chance whatever of Britain handing over to a united India. He soon established friendly relations with both Gandhi and Nehru, and managed to persuade the latter, if not the former, that the sooner Pakistan came into existence, the better the chance of avoiding civil war.

The task that remained was to fix the dividing line in the case of the provinces of Bengal and the Punjab. A boundary commission did its best, but in the prevailing atmosphere the resentment of those who found themselves left on the wrong side of the line led to lamentable disturbances. Some decided to make the best of it and stay put but many others, especially in the districts where murder and looting were rampant, fled in terror. Those who saw the columns of refugees many miles long going in either direction will never forget the appalling spectacle.

On 15 August 1947 India and Pakistan became independent states within the British Commonwealth. About a quarter of the previous population of India, just over 90 million, became Pakistanis, but over 40 million Muslims remained in the new India, either by their own choice or because they had nowhere else to go.

The army, the civil services, finances, assets and liabilities were divided proportionately between the two new states.

Deplorable atrocities followed close on Partition, but most impartial observers on the spot at the time were agreed that some sort of decision had to be taken swiftly if far worse things were to be avoided.

CHAPTER 2

The Historical Background. II

INDIA SINCE INDEPENDENCE

IT IS not proposed to deal with the history of India during the two decades which have elapsed since Independence in anything like the same detail as has been done in the case of the British period. There are several reasons or excuses for this. In the first place, the intricate political manœuvres that led in the end to Independence and Partition are not generally known to people outside India, including the British public at large. In the second place, Indo–British contacts over the last two centuries have done much to influence the institutions, both political and social, of the new India. In the third place, many Britons, deeply concerned for India and its future prosperity, like to think that the struggle for independence, in spite of some regrettable incidents, inevitable when strong emotions are aroused, was conducted with commendable restraint on both sides. It has been explained in the preface how and why, at the height of the struggle, both sides felt able to co-operate in the social sphere. On one of the occasions when Gandhi fell foul of the law, a British judge, in sentencing him to a term of imprisonment, gave him what reads like a testimonial. Personal friendships between Indians of all parties and Britons, which were formed before 1947, are still maintained and treasured.

Apart, however, from purely Indo–British relations, so many things have happened in India and in the world outside since 1947 and so many of the resulting problems still await solution, that it would be premature to do more than record them, except in so far as they have a direct bearing on the subject of this book.

25

The rejoicings that greeted the coming of Independence were hardly over before the clouds, which had been gathering for years past, banked up for a storm. As the last British Commission had foreseen, however earnestly the Boundary Commission might strive to demarcate equably the frontiers of the new India and Pakistan, too many people were going to resent being left on what they regarded as the wrong side of the line. This applied particularly to Bengal, and, above all, to the Punjab, where the Sikhs were bitterly aggrieved by the final decision which Mountbatten found himself forced to take. In the old days, it had never taken much to provoke a local flare-up between Hindus and Muslims, and now the ingredients for a large-scale explosion were ready to hand. As soon as migration from one side of the border to the other began in a big way, the criminal elements in the population seized the opportunity for pillage; rape and murder followed. It is impossible to say with any accuracy how many refugees were involved. Some Indian writers claim that as many as 8 million fled into India, while some Pakistanis maintain that their share of this burden was no less than India's. The point has already been raised as to whether this terrible business could have been avoided if the British had made quite clear their intention to hand over India before the Hindu–Muslim antagonism emerged as a major political issue, but the religious and emotional differences between the two parties make it unlikely that they would ever have got together to shoulder the responsibilities relinquished by the British.

Grim as the refugee problem was in terms of human suffering, the political and economic issues arising out of Partition were even more distracting to the new governments. Difficulties over the divorce of raw materials, like jute, from the processing plants, and the control of essential supplies of river and canal water were bad enough, but the quarrel over Kashmir has proved the worst of all. Whether India was too quick in accepting the accession of a Hindu maharajah whose subjects were mainly Muslims, and whether this justified subsequent aggression by Pakistan are questions which, in view of the recent Tashkent Agreement, one may hope will soon be handed over by the politicians to the historians for argument. The really serious aspect of this protracted dispute has not merely been the risk of total war, which has been near more than once, but the very grave handicap imposed by defence preparations in peaceful development. There is no space here to record in any detail the complicated series of negotiations which have taken place directly between the two countries or indirectly through intermediaries appointed by the United Nations. The Minority Treatment Pact of 1952, which provided for no discrimination against minorities on either side and no hostile propaganda, raised hopes that were soon dashed, and a more serious setback was the failure of the Rawalpindi Conference between Nehru and Ayoub Khan a year later.

That this effort by the two national leaders to reach a settlement proved abortive is generally ascribed to the fact that, not long before the meeting, Pakistan had signed an agreement with China which affected the Kashmir borders. But there was a lot more behind it than a mere demarcation of frontiers. It was an incident in the tangle of international relations created by Nehru's policy of non-alignment. Although India remained a member of the British Commonwealth, Nehru was probably right in believing that it was neither in India's interest nor in that of the world at large that it should attach itself either to the democratic or the Communist bloc. There was room in his opinion for an honest broker in the international market both in Asia and outside, and India would best serve itself and humanity by assuming this role. Unfortunately, the tension with Pakistan and trouble on the horizon with another powerful neighbour, China, soon converted non-alignment from a peaceful progress down the middle of the road into a tight-rope balancing act, that often failed to earn applause from either pavement. India badly needed money for internal development, and the obvious place to look for it was the U.S.A., but the U.S.A., though it provided a lot, would have been even more liberal if it had been assured of India's political support. Armaments also entered into the matter. India was offered arms by the U.S.A. but refused the offer as not in accord with the policy of non-alignment. Pakistan, on the other hand, accepted, and the agreement with China left no doubt in Indian minds that these weapons would be put to other uses than combating Communist aggression.

The origins of the dispute with China provide another headache for the political layman. The friendly feelings, based on agelong associations, which most Indians used to have for their great neighbour, were shaken when the new régime in Peking made no secret of its intention to "liberate" Asia from the imperialists and colonialists. This might have been discounted as no more than a typical Communist gesture if a more concrete issue had not soon arisen over Tibet. India had accepted China's claim to suzerainty over it, but drew a sharp distinction between suzerainty and sovereignty when Chinese forces began to occupy Tibet and the Dalai Lama fled to India for safety with a large number of his subjects. In 1962 Chinese armies appeared in strength on the Indian frontiers in Kashmir and Assam, and in the clashes that then took place the Indian forces suffered severely. It is difficult to forecast how long the present formal and informal truces on both fronts will remain operative. The chances of anything like a permanent, peaceful settlement between India on the one hand and Pakistan and China on the other are bedevilled by the fact that, at the moment, world tensions seem to be coming to a head in South-east Asia, and their involvements in Vietnam alone rule out several of the great powers who might otherwise have been called in as mediators.

It is all the more regrettable that India has been deflected from the path of peaceful coexistence, which, there can be little doubt, the Government genuinely wished to follow after 1947, because India's voice was being listened to with increasing respect in the international councils. The present president, Dr. Radhakrishnan, played a prominent part in starting UNESCO and since then several Indians have played a leading part in shaping the policy of that organization. Rajkumari Amrit Kaur, India's first Minister of Health, became president of WHO; Nehru's sister, Mrs. Pandit, was the first woman to be elected president of the United

Nations Assembly, and for all his modest presence, the late Prime Minister, Lal Bahadur Shastri, was making his moderating influence increasingly felt in the counsels of the Afro–Asian nations. Is it too much to hope that his last contribution to peace, the Tashkent Agreement, will become his permanent memorial?

Only a few months after the new India came into being, Mahatma Gandhi was assassinated. By an irony of fate, his assassin was a fanatical Hindu who thought that he was being too kind to the Muslims. In view of the state of public feeling at the time, it is fortunate that the killer was not a Muslim. That the new State, in the midst of all its early perplexities, should have been deprived of the guidance of the man who had done more than anyone else to create it, was a blow the impact of which, on Indians and on their sympathizers all over the world, it would be hard to exaggerate. It came, however, at a time when economic policies were beginning to take a shape which the Mahatma might not have found it easy to approve. There is no doubt that he and Nehru had a real affection and respect for one another. They had fought together for independence and both were dedicated to see that it brought their fellow countrymen not only freedom but also prosperity. But rapid industrialization on Western lines was not Gandhi's panacea, nor did his gospel of peaceful persuasion coincide with Nehru's readiness to use coercion, if necessary, to overcome factious opposition to the removal of social injustice.

A matter which called for prompt attention by the new Government was the future of the princely states, some of which might prove intractable in view of their own treaties with the British Crown. Many people in 1947 feared that this might be the cause of serious trouble. The Transfer Agreement prescribed that these states should have the option of deciding whether they would accede to India or Pakistan. It was not, however, laid down who should decide about accession, the ruler or his subjects. Among the larger states there was, as already mentioned, Kashmir, where a Hindu maharajah ruled over a Muslim majority. On the other hand, there was, in the middle of India, the State of Hyderabad, where a Muslim, the Nizam, ruled over an even larger Hindu majority. Its size, position and mineral resources made its accession a matter of vital importance to India. Fortunately, the man was at hand to tackle this thorny problem in the person of Vallabhai Patel, the Minister directly concerned. He lost no time in making it clear that he was prepared to be tough, should the necessity arise. Most of the leading princes were either patriotic enough to accept the new conditions or realized that it was useless to kick against the pricks. Apart from Kashmir, the only state to cause serious trouble was Hyderabad, and, although force had to be employed, there was very little bloodshed. The smaller states were either amalgamated with larger ones to form convenient administrative units or absorbed into adjacent provinces, now themselves called states. The princes were treated quite generously from the financial point of view, and some of them were made rajpramukhs or governors of the new units. The title of rajpramukh has since been abolished. As a result of this settlement the new India came to be divided into sixteen states and nine union territories.

After much labour and discussion, the Constitution was finally adopted by Parliament in January 1950. Its salient features and the legislative, judicial and administrative systems which emerged from it, will be described in a later chapter. All that need be said here is that it constituted India a Sovereign Democratic Republic. In the previous year the Conference of Commonwealth Prime Ministers had to decide how such a state could remain a member of the Commonwealth, which had a monarch at its head. It was agreed that India should remain a full member and accept the Queen as "the symbol of the free association of its independent nations and, as such, the head of the Commonwealth".

On the home front, the two major tasks facing the new Government, apart from the integration of the princely states and the rehabilitation of the refugees, were the reorganization of the local government areas and the preparation of plans for national prosperity. A States Reorganization Commission was set up to deal with the former, and, in most cases, its decisions were influenced by linguistic considerations. Since no less than fourteen major languages were listed in the eighth schedule of the Constitution and local patriotisms were aroused, the job was not an easy one. The effect of the linguistic problem in the sphere of education will be examined later. All that can be done here is to mention the principal results of this reorganization. To satisfy Telegu aspirations, a new State of Andra Pradesh was created in 1956; it took in part of Madras and part of the former Princely State of Hyderabad, the remainder of Hyderabad being absorbed in Bombay. The two princely states of Travancore and Cochin were merged and became the State of Kerala, which soon became a political trouble spot owing to Communist activities. Finally, after a long and bitter controversy, Bombay was divided into two new states, Maharashtra and Gujarat.

The new Government was quick to recognize the fact that if the ideals explicit in the Constitution were to be realized and the living conditions of the people as a whole were to be raised to a much higher level, this could only be done by mobilizing all available resources, both public and private. This, in turn, meant a survey of national needs with a view to determining the best and quickest way of satisfying them within the means likely to be accessible. A National Planning Commission was accordingly set up and it soon came to the conclusion that the economic and social problems, existing and prospective, could not be solved through annual budgets. The means to be adopted, therefore, should be Five-year Plans, which would allot priorities to the national services in the light of the resources, in money and manpower, likely to be forthcoming during the period in question. The new India was not, of course, the first country to go in for long-term planning; the CABE, in fact, realized in 1944 that even in the case of a single service like education, such a procedure was essential to any progressive and sustained development. But the new Government certainly deserves credit for a thorough exploration of the task before it and for the production of programmes designed to implement the policy upon which it had decided.

The First Five-year Plan covered the years of 1951–6. Not surprisingly, it gave top priority to agricultural development, including irrigation, and assigned to it 45 per cent of the estimated funds. Communications were allotted 26 per cent, and the social services 21 per cent. It is difficult to exaggerate the predominance of agriculture in the Indian economy or to see any likelihood of this being affected for a long time to come by industrial development, however rapid and widespread. On the one hand it absorbs 90 per cent of Indian labour, on the other the need to make it more efficient is urgent. The yield per acre is only about one-third of that in China or Japan and of the cultivated land only one-quarter is irrigated. It is worth noting the stress laid on electrification in the communications sector in view of its bearing on the spread of social education.

In the Second Five-year Plan the main emphasis shifted from agriculture to industry, mostly of the heavy type. This, with power, transport and communications, was allotted nearly half the budget, while agriculture and the social services got about 30 per cent and 20 per cent each. Roughly the same basis of allotment was followed in the Third Plan, though there was a slight drop to 16 per cent in the case of the social services.

The First Plan was very nearly successful in achieving its objectives. There was a substantial rise in both agricultural and industrial production, partly due in the one case to favourable weather and in the other to a special demand for commodities, stimulated by external events like the Korean War. As Nehru himself said, when urging the country to still greater effort, "We had rather an easy time in the First Five-year Plan". An interesting supplement to the First Plan was the establishment of the National Extension Service, which aimed at creating a permanent organization for rural development. Out of this emerged the Block System, of which more later. Contrary to pronouncements before 1947 by Congress leaders and Nehru in particular, the First Plan envisaged no drastic action in the way of nationalization. "The public and private sectors", it stated, "should function side by side as integral parts of a single organism."

The Second Plan was less successful than the First in promoting the prosperity of the country as a whole. The various areas of production were not sufficiently co-ordinated, with the result that too much progress and profit in one direction meant too little in another. This led, in turn, to inflation and a general rise in the cost of living, so that, although the full sum provided for the Plan, Rs. 4600 crores was spent, it was only sufficient to finance 80 per cent of the projects listed. Naturally, such a situation played into the hands of market manipulators, and, as an Indian economist notes, a serious diversion of resources took place for the benefit of the privileged upper classes. On the agricultural side, there was also reason to believe that the funds made available by the rural credit schemes, started during the First Plan, were not reaching the poorer cultivators whom they were intended to benefit, an undue portion going into the pockets of landlords and moneylenders. The hired labourers, who, in 1961, constituted about a quarter of the agricultural working population, fared even worse, as was revealed by two government inquiries between 1950 and 1956. Nevertheless, quite a lot was done to help agriculture through the irrigation and power schemes, and the experts attached to Block Development, although not always helped by their village panchayats, brought the knowledge of new techniques to a large number of agriculturists.

Towards the end of the Second Plan in 1959, Nehru gave a new impetus to land policy by what has come to be known as the Nagpur Resolution. This put a ceiling on individual land holdings, surplus land to be handed over to village panchayats for working on a co-operative basis. To check hoarding and profiteering there was to be state trading in food grains. It also advocated the establishment, in the course of three years, of a number of voluntary farming co-operatives, in the produce of which all concerned, including the hired labourers, would receive a share. This was a definite step in the direction of socialism—some critics called it communism—and its success or otherwise would clearly depend on the efficiency and integrity of the panchayats.

It may be well to reserve comment on the Third Plan until its final results have been assessed, as they probably will be when the Fourth Plan is published. The general emphasis, as in the previous Plans, is laid on industrial and agricultural development. The proposed outlay in the public sector is Rs. 7500 crores, which is Rs. 3000 crores more than in the Second Plan. The percentage of the total allocated to the social services is slightly less than before. The Third Plan has been described by a rather austere foreign critic of contemporary India as an "intricate exercise in wishful thinking". The way in which the planners have faced their task since 1951 hardly justifies this criticism, but certain features in the Plan itself, as well as the adverse effect of recent events, make it doubtful whether sufficient funds will be forthcoming to meet the proposed outlay, unless there is a substantial increase in the financial subventions from abroad. Since the threat from China has become more menacing from 1962 onwards, it involves a still greater diversion of resources to defence, and, to that extent, will reduce industrial growth, especially in the export field. On top of this came the bad harvest in 1964, which caused an alarming rise in prices. Moreover, the Plan expects an addition of 17 million persons to the labour force during the five years but can only see its way to providing 14 million new jobs. This means that with the backlog from previous Plans there may be nearly 12 million unemployed by 1966.

EDUCATION UNDER THE BRITISH RAJ

After the foregoing summary of the main events in the general history of India, this chapter will end by taking a closer look at what happened to education and the social services during the 200 years preceding Independence, which cover roughly the period of the British Raj.

The first steps, like many of the later ones, were not inspired by devotion on the part of the British rulers to any idea of social welfare for the population at large. The object was to meet the need of the Company, as its responsibilities grew, for an expanding administrative service. People destined to fill the senior posts could be imported from Britain, but if Indians could be trained to fill the lower grades, it would mean a considerable saving of time and money. There were in existence a number of Hindu schools (Tols) and Muslim schools (Madrassas), which provided education on traditional lines for the sons of the well-to-do. Since Persian continued to be the official language, Hindu boys often attended Madrassas. These schools were private institutions, unconnected with Government.

As the eighteenth century moved on into the nineteenth, two factors combined to create what has been described as an Indian Renaissance. One was the awakening of enlightened scholars like Raja Ram Mohan Roy and of devoted servants of India like David Hare to the need for bringing Western literature and science within reach of educated Indians, and the other was a new interest in the culture of the East among British scholars like Sir William Jones, who, with the help of Warren Hastings, founded the Bengal Asiatic Society, and James Prinsep, the Mint Master of Calcutta, who, some years later, found the key to the Brahmi script and enabled the inscriptions on Asoka's pillars and other Buddhist monuments to be at last deciphered. Between them they caused what can be termed a genuine revival of learning, and, at the same time, started, or at least stimulated, the controversy between the Anglicists and the Orientalists, which raged for many years.

Earlier than this, however, the first official incursion into the educational field had come in 1781, when Hastings founded the Calcutta Madrassa. Ten years later, Jonathan Duncan founded the Sanskrit College at Benares. Other foundations followed on similar lines and with similar objects. Missionaries were also at work, but their scholastic enterprises were frowned upon by the Company, and, in any case, were mainly directed towards making converts among the lower orders. At the turn of the century liberal principles were much in vogue in Britain. The ideals of the French Revolution, the religious revival inspired by Wesley and his followers and, the championship of the under-dog wherever he might be, by Wilberforce, had all combined to create a new atmosphere and it was not long before these ideas began to impinge upon India. The reaction of the Company to them has its amusing side. When, in 1792, Wilberforce proposed the insertion in the Charter Act of a clause to send teachers to India, it met with strong opposition from the Court of Directors. One of them said, "We have just lost America through our folly in having allowed the establishment of schools and colleges. It would do us no good to repeat the same folly in regard to India. If the natives require anything in the way of education, they must come to England for it." Another argued, "The Hindus have as good a system of faith and morals as most people and it would be madness to attempt their conversion or to give them any more learning or any other description of learning than that which they already possess". In spite of this, when the Charter came up for renewal twenty years later, the Act directed that out of the surplus revenues of British India "a sum of not less than one lakh (100,000) of rupees should be set apart and applied to the revival and improvement of literature and the encouragement of the learned natives of India and for the introduction or promotion of a knowledge of the sciences among the inhabitants of the British territories in India". When, in 1815, Lord Moira, the Governor-General, said that it was the moral duty of the Government to encourage education, the Directors completed their about-turn by informing him : "We wish you to be fully apprised of our zeal for the progress and improvement of education among the natives of India and of our willingness to make considerable sacrifices to that important end, if proper means for the attainment of it could be pointed out to us." The Act renewing the Charter in 1813 also directed the Company to lift the ban on British missionaries. At the next renewal in 1833 foreign missionaries were also allowed to operate in the Company's area and the grant for education was increased ten times.

Even a million rupees (£75,000) was a microscopic sum when compared with the existing need, and there was no agreed policy as to how it should be spent, for the Anglicist–Orientalist controversy was very much alive. This was no racial issue for prominent Indians and British were to be found on either side. In 1817 Ram Mohan Roy, with the aid of David Hare, had founded the Hindu College in Calcutta to teach Western literature and sciences to the children of the Indian upper and middle classes. On the other hand, the General Committee of Public Instruction, a product of the 1813 Act and largely British in membership, was definitely in favour of priority for Eastern learning in Indian schools.

It does not appear, however, that any of the educational reformers of the period were seriously interested in the problem of schools for the masses. They accepted the "filtration" theory, which meant that if education were provided in the first instance for the upper classes, it would gradually seep down to those below. There were several prominent Britishers in India at the time, who did not subscribe to this theory; among them were Elphinstone, Moira and Adam, whose *Reports on the State of Education in Bengal*, published in 1835, stressed the need to develop indigenous schools. They were not successful in winning official support, for Macaulay's famous minute in 1835 put the Anglicists in the ascendant for the next twenty years. The following extract from this minute will explain why his memory is not generally cherished by Indians, though Sardar K. M. Panikkar, in his *Survey of Indian History* (1947), is at pains to defend him.

> I am quite ready to take the Oriental learning at the valuation of the Orientalists themselves. I have not found one among them, who could deny that a single shelf of a good European library was worth the whole native literature of India and Arabia. . . . It is, I believe, no exaggeration to say that all the historical information, which has been collected from all the books written in Sanskrit, is less valuable than what may be found in the most paltry abridgements used in preparatory schools in England.

In spite of the rough treatment which Macaulay still receives from some Indian writers, he was, in fact, full of liberal ideas and good intentions, and it is a pity that his uncalled-for denigration of Eastern learning should be the thing for which he is best remembered in India. Like so many of his successors, he failed to realize that the best way to help India was to get Indians to help themselves by giving them an effective share in working out plans for their national development.

The next important move came in 1854. In connection with the renewal of the Company's charter in 1853 a parliamentary committee had been set up to survey the educational scene in India. Its conclusions and recommendations were embodied in a dispatch from Sir Charles Wood, who was then President of the Board of Control. Wood's dispatch has been hailed as the first serious attempt on the part of the British Raj to consider the educational needs of the Indian people as a whole. It exhorted the Government of India to take steps for improving and extending educational facilities at all levels. For this purpose, the vernacular should be used as the medium of instruction at the lower stages, and English at the higher. More specific proposals were for the creation of universities at the presidency towns of Calcutta, Bombay and Madras, for the establishment of institutions to train teachers for all grades of schools, for the development of new "middle" schools, for increased support to indigenous and other schools providing elementary education, for grants-in-aid where desired and deserved and finally, in order to promote the carrying out of these proposals, the setting up of a separate department of the administration to look after education. It is interesting to note, in the light of subsequent events, that the dispatch recognized that poor students would not be able to climb the educational ladder without reasonably generous assistance in the way of free places and maintenance, and that if girls were to be encouraged to climb it, much more must be done to help them.

There is some reason to believe that the proposal in the dispatch to extend education to the lower classes was influenced by the Benthamite principle of the greatest happiness of the greatest number. Utilitarianism had some ethical affinities with the evangelism of Wesley and Wilberforce. Bentham's books were among those in use at Haileybury College, which was founded by the East India Company in 1809 to train its cadets and continued to do so until the Crown took over the Company's powers in 1858.

The dispatch was a wise and liberal document but it accepted the reigning official policy that education was a matter for private enterprise and that the function of government was to stimulate it by advice and finance, where required. Government institutions should only be set up where private enterprise had either failed or was not forthcoming. Many good schools and even colleges were already in existence thanks to the munificence of public-spirited Indians, and still more were to come, but there were too many others, the managers of which lacked either the means, or the will or the capacity to run them properly. It was not difficult, in view of the accepted policy, for the Education Department to shut its eyes to such inefficiency, particularly in times of financial stringency, which were only too frequent.

It was particularly unfortunate that the outbreak of the Mutiny should have stopped or postponed the carrying out on any comprehensive scale of the proposals contained in the dispatch, because the Governor-General, to whom it was sent, was Lord Dalhousie, a man of progressive ideas, who, as already mentioned, had publicly proclaimed his belief in the principle of trusteeship. However, the three universities were founded in 1857 and departments of public instruction were set up in each province.

Although the Mutiny had little effect on the population as a whole, it left behind it an atmosphere in official circles that was anything but favourable to large-scale developments in the social services. Consequently, little or nothing was done to implement the recommendations in the dispatch for the expansion of elementary education, and the policy that Government should abstain from building and running schools and confine itself to stimulating private efforts became more strongly entrenched than ever. Apart from some growth in the higher branches, little happened in education during the next twenty years, and it was left to the missionary societies, who were about the only organized bodies in the social field, to produce the next move. Pressure on public opinion, for which they were primarily responsible, led to the appointment, in 1882, of an Indian Education Commission under the chairmanship of Sir William Hunter. An unusual feature about it was the inclusion of several Indians among its members. Its terms of reference required it to explore the ways in which effect had been given to the Wood dispatch and to pay special attention to the extension of elementary education.

The Commission, after much labour, produced a voluminous report, or rather, series of reports, an example to be copied by many future commissions. The only noteworthy result of so much effort was the handing over of elementary education to the new district and local boards instituted by Lord Ripon. Experience soon showed the unwisdom of doing this. Except for this new departure the Commission generally endorsed the grant-in-aid policy for higher education and made some tentative suggestions for including some vocational or technical subjects in the secondary curriculum. What might have proved a useful innovation was not taken up, because Government decided that the curriculum was already overcrowded and that Indian industry was not sufficiently developed to justify separate technical institutions.

Following the rather abortive outcome of the Hunter Commission there was another lull so far as the state system of education was concerned, until Lord Curzon arrived as Viceroy in 1899. In the non-official sphere, on the other hand, there was considerable movement. The birth of the National Congress in 1885 and the activities of revivalist societies like the Arya Samaj combined to give education a new importance as a means of enlisting youth in the dissemination of patriotic ideals. Of the institutions privately established at this time, perhaps the most interesting and influential was Rabindranath Tagore's ashram at Santiniketan in Bengal.

Curzon, as statesman and administrator, is a more impressive figure than Macaulay, but he owes his unpopularity with most Indians to the same innate qualities. He was genuinely anxious to do his best for India but he had no intention of making Indians his partners in so doing. He soon satisfied himself that the existing educational system, if it could be so called, was on the wrong lines and stood in urgent need of drastic reform. He began by summoning the provincial directors of public instruction, all British officials, to a secret conclave in Simla. No Indians were invited and it does not appear that he subsequently discussed with any leading Indians the decisions at which the meeting arrived. This was all the more regrettable, because the main conclusion, which involved a complete reversal of previous policy, was one which Indian opinion might well have approved. Henceforth, the State would take the lead and provide private enterprise not merely with advice and grants but with models at all levels, and is now a flourishing university.*

Curzon was also concerned, as indeed were many other people, about the Indian Universities, now five in number. In 1902 he set up a Universities Commission and omitted to put any Indians on it, though a Hindu and a Muslim were added later, when the harm had been done. The Commission made a number of practical recommendations, most of which were embodied in the Indian Universities Act of 1904. These provided not only for raising standards but also for improving administration by reducing the size of the bodies responsible for it.

In the same year, the Viceroy's views about education in general were promulgated in the form of a resolution. This was a penetrating analysis of prevailing defects. It pointed out that from the quantitative standpoint, four villages out of five were without a school, and that three boys out of four and thirty-nine girls out of forty had no schooling. From the qualitative aspect, particularly in regard to higher education, the concentration on preparing pupils for government jobs meant that those who failed to get one were ill-fitted for obtaining other employment. More general criticisms were that courses were too literary, that pupils were trained to memorize rather than to think, that too much importance was attached to examinations and, above all, that the undue prominence given to English was leading to the neglect of the vernaculars.

Probably, most thinking Indians agreed with this analysis, but Curzon was already suspect and it was felt that the proposed remedy of a stronger lead from Government simply meant more autocratic interference by the Viceroy. This suspicion was strengthened by the highly unpopular partition of Bengal. The particular significance for education of the Swadeshi Movement, which this partition provoked, was that it marked the first serious attempt to bring students into the political arena.

As the outcome of Curzon's reforming zeal or the growth of the Nationalist Movement, or both, the first decade of the present century witnessed a considerable stirring of the educational waters. It is likely that the English Education Act of 1902 and the controversies which it provoked did not escape Indian attention. In any case, the reaction against the Curzon régime and the boycott of things British by the Swadeshi Movement led to the foundation, under Congress auspices, of a National Council for Education, the aim of which was to provide education outside government influence or control. This, however, produced no permanent result except the Jadavpur Technical College in Calcutta, which, under wise direction, overcame many difficulties and is now a flourishing university.*

Another contemporary step, which deserved a better fate, was a motion by Mr. Gokhale in the Imperial Legislative Assembly to make elementary education free and compulsory. It was a modest measure, for it only proposed to apply compulsion to boys between 6 and 10, and then only in areas where the number of children already attending school indicated a local demand for education. Gokhale failed to carry his motion against official opposition, which argued that the country was not ripe for compulsion and that there was still plenty of scope for expansion on a voluntary basis. However, the interest which this proposal aroused, both inside and outside the council chamber, did have some tangible result, for when the King Emperor came to India for the Durbar in 1912, he announced that the Imperial Exchequer was making an additional grant of Rs. 50 lakhs to be spent mainly on the primary stage. This allocation was confirmed

* It is very good news that the creator of this institution, Dr. Triguna Sen, has recently been made Minister of Education at the Centre.

the following year in an official resolution, which also dealt with universities.

Hitherto, the recognition of secondary schools had been a matter for the universities, but now it was to be transferred to the provincial departments of education. The ostensible aim was to relieve universities of a task which distracted them from their proper functions, but it may well be that the increasing part being played in politics by their members had something to do with this decision. It was also proposed that future developments at this stage should take the form of small, residential and teaching universities with facilities for postgraduate and research work. Apart from the foundation of new universities at Dacca, Patna and Nagpur, Government announced its intention to aid the Hindu University of Benares and the Muslim University of Aligarh, thereby giving countenance in education to the communal issue, which had already been accorded official recognition in the Morley–Minto reforms.

It has often been remarked that it takes a war to awaken the public conscience to the obligation to repay the sufferings of one generation by doing something to improve the prospects of the next. This is certainly true of Britain, where the major Education Acts of this century were passed in 1902, 1917 and 1944. In India, 1917 saw the appointment of the Calcutta University Commission under the chairmanship of Sir Michael Sadler. Priority was once more given to the higher stages, but on this occasion, at any rate, there were some Indian members, among them Sir Asutosh Mukherji, a big figure in Bengal.

The primary object of the Commission, as shown by its title, was the reform of Calcutta University, which, by common consent, had become unwieldy and amorphous, but, either by official prompting or on its own initiative, it extended its survey not only to universities as a whole but also to their relations with the institutions from which they were fed. This enlargement of the scope of the inquiry was justified by the fact that, in addition to the universities covered by the resolution of 1913, two of the bigger princely states were starting their own universities, Mysore in 1917 and Hyderabad in 1918, the latter with Urdu and not English as the medium of instruction.

The Commission's report, an impressive document both in size and content, appeared in 1919. So far as Calcutta University itself was concerned, it proposed that in the interest of co-ordinated development, postgraduate teaching and research in all subjects should be done by the University and not by the colleges, the only exception being that Presidency College was allowed to keep its M.A. and M.Sc. classes. It then turned to the relation between university and secondary education, which had engaged the attention of former commissions. Unlike them, it found the general level of secondary education so low that the prospect of its ever being raised high enough to absorb the work then being done in intermediate classes was too remote to be worth serious considerations. Since it was imperative to leave universities free to devote themselves to making a success of the new three years' course for the first degree, the Commission recommended that a new type of intermediate college should be instituted and that both these and the secondary schools should be administered by boards of secondary and intermediate education. These boards, while under the provincial departments of education, were to be given as much freedom as possible. A further sign that the communal issue was becoming a live one in education as well as politics was a provision that in a board of sixteen members not less than three should be Hindus and not less than three Muslims. Many provinces set up boards as suggested by the Commission but a striking exception was Bengal, where Calcutta University was powerful enough to maintain its hold over secondary education.

The Commission made some useful recommendations in regard to the training and qualifications of teachers, the content of courses of study, women's education and various forms of techni-cal and vocational instruction, but probably its most important conclusion was that relating to the lines on which university education in India should be developed. It came down strongly on the side of the residential and teaching type but accepted the fact that, in some places, under Indian conditions, some form of affiliation was inevitable. This advice had some effect, for of the eight universities founded after the war, only Agra was of the old affiliating type.

Up to the end of the First World War, in spite of Gokhale's effort and pious exhortations from many quarters, elementary education had been left very much out in the cold, but when the Montagu–Chelmsford reforms transferred the education of Indian children to the care of Indian ministers, it seemed that at last the lower stages might come into their own. A good deal was in fact done and more was in contemplation, when the financial slump in 1929 held up further progress. Nearly every province passed a Primary Education Act. These exhorted municipal and district boards to prepare schemes for the development of primary education in their areas but left it to their discretion whether to introduce compulsion and to levy a special cess or rate to help finance their projects. It was, perhaps, too much to expect that such bodies would have the courage to embark on potentially unpopular measures, and, in the absence of any legal provision that would have enabled the central authorities to force them to take action, the Acts remained for the most part inoperative.

As a complement to their plans in the primary sphere, many of the popular ministries launched campaigns against adult illiteracy. In Bihar and other places these evoked much enthusiasm, but as no practical incentives or facilities were offered to induce the new literates to remain literate, the permanent results were incommensurate with the energy expended.

Two years before the Second World War started, compulsion applied to some 15,000 out of a total of 700,000 villages and in these, in the absence of any machinery, e.g. school attendance officers, for making it effective, it achieved little. The voluntary system, which had long enjoyed government blessing, if little else, had managed to enrol roughly one out of every five children in the age group of 6–14 in some kind of school, but even these not very impressive figures mean little in view of the prevailing wastage and stagnation. Out of every hundred admitted to class I only twenty-three reached class IV and only thirteen class V, the remainder either having been withdrawn by their parents or having failed to receive promotion.

This was the state of affairs when the first dynamic attack was made on the problem by the Wardha Scheme of Basic Education, sponsored by Mahatma Gandhi. What this meant at the time to those seeking a new approach to the whole field of educational and social planning, and what it still means to the new and independent India will be examined in detail later in this book. It may also be convenient to postpone, for the moment, reference to other significant events in education which took place in the latter part of the 1930's, like the Sapru Report on unemployment among the educated, the reconstitution of the CABE and the Abbott–Wood Report, which dealt mainly with technical instruction.

CHAPTER 3

Important Formative Institutions

IT WILL be apparent from the foregoing brief account of the origins, so far as they can be traced, of the modern India, that there is an extraordinary complex of influences contributing to the habits of thought in the Indian mind. Of the moral or religious influences the predominant one is Hinduism, the second is Islam and there are a number of others the force of whose impact varies from place to place. It is true that India today is a secular state and that equal citizenship is enjoyed by all irrespective of religion; but the facts cannot be ignored. Muslims constitute not more than 10 per cent of the population; the mass of the Indian population is Hindu and all governments, both federal and state, are predominantly Hindu. The authorities, political or administrative, whether they want to or not, cannot escape the Hindu tradition which shapes so much of their outlook, both upon themselves and upon the world outside.

It is true that the origins of many Western states and nations as they are today are also highly complex but this complexity has, in the main, been racial. Since the Dark Ages, at least, there has been, in the West, a uniform background of Christianity. Differing interpretations of the Christian ethic have led to bloody wars, brutal repression and violence and inhumanity of every kind. Comparable wars and massacres find their place in Indian history also, but the point is that these were internal to India. A recent writer makes this point clear when he states : "Hinduism is the flow of India's life, as Catholicism was the flow of life in medieval Europe, informing the marketplace no less than the cathedral, giving to power its shape, to labour its content and to society its meaning." This implies that any Western inquirer into comparisons of organization and administration between India and the West needs to make the comparison with Europe and not with any one European state or nation.

Two further points have to be kept in mind. India today is governed by Hindus, and the Hindu mind inevitably reflects Hindu tradition and ethics. But Islam, though comprising so small a percentage of the population, remains an unyielding influence of which due account must be taken. More will be said later on this point. There are also many aspects of life in the non-industrialized countries of South-east Asia and of Africa, which, just as in India, raise difficulties and dilemmas for the would-be Western organizer. These will need to be considered, even though their impact is by no means confined to India.

Hinduism is pantheistic, discursive, absorbent and non-proselytizing but ever ready to adopt and adapt from other systems of ethics and philosophy. So simple a statement, incomplete and unsatisfying as it is, still tells something of the attributes of Hinduism. This has its value in so far as it suggests the mood in which a Hindu would examine ideas about organizing a system of education but it tells one nothing of what Hinduism is, and, indeed, this is by no means an easy thing to do. There is no room in this book to dilate upon the many confusing and even contradictory elements in Hindu doctrine and the even more confusing mythology which accompanies it. For the present purpose it may be helpful to indicate briefly some of the basic beliefs, which, often unconsciously, influence the Hindu outlook.

There are two basic concepts, *Kharma* and *Dharma*, which give a useful clue to the essence of Hinduism. The individual's *Kharma* determines the rank or stage of society into which he is born and into which he will normally be reborn. His *Dharma* is the function which he has to perform in accordance with his *Kharma*. If, for instance, his *Kharma* makes him a soldier, then his *Dharma* is to fight and practise the art or craft of soldiering. If he does so conscientiously and successfully, his *Kharma* may upgrade him at his next birth; if not, it may downgrade him.

It is in accord with these two concepts that the general outlook of Hinduism has developed.

The world is evil and human nature fallible; there are as many evil spirits active in it as beneficent ones. It is the responsibility of the individual to be on guard against the evil ones, to mislead, avert or placate them. There are circumstances—wars, famines and the like—where concerted action by society as a whole is necessary, but fundamentally it is the individual who counts, and, since death is not the end but only one further stage in life, it behoves the individual, if necessary, to ignore society, his village and his family, if by so doing he can make sure that his next incarnation will be in a higher station. For there is only one ultimate object, so to conduct oneself as at last to obtain release from life altogether, to lose one's individuality and merge in the Supreme Being, the infinite and ultimate life-force, which is both the creator and the destroyer. It is in this sense that life is all illusion; heaven is the escape from life to the absolute. It is in this sense too that it is true to describe the Hindu outlook as essentially pessimistic.

For the purpose of this book, what is needed is an inquiry as to how far such an outlook hinders or facilitates the provision of a controlled system of social services, including education. It is therefore necessary to examine some of the practical effects which have, in fact, flowed from it. One of the most important and complicated is the development of the caste system. There is much argument as to how this originated, and it may well seem that the establishment of societies, especially ones as closely knit and guarded as castes, is in conflict with the placing of the responsibility for seeking good upon the individual. Hinduism, however, has never found any difficulty in reconciling apparent contradictions of this nature. Life is admittedly imperfect and compromises are constantly required to meet its many vicissitudes. Moreover, it is always open to the individual to withdraw from society altogether and to seek his own fulfilment in silent communion with the absolute—a thing which still happens even today.

Whatever the origins of the caste system—and it is tempting to perceive in it an attempt on the part of the learned priesthood to establish its authority over the kings and temporal rulers—it is a fact that the doctrine of reincarnation requires higher and lower categories to which individuals can be promoted or relegated according to performance and deserts. The system, therefore, is not out of line with one of the most fundamental tenets of Hindu beliefs. There are four main recognized castes, Sudras, Vaisyas, Kshatriyas and Brahmans. The Sudras are the lowest, servile, menial, without rights against organized society. Next are the Vaisyas, traders and agriculturists, concerned, it is true, with the mean and illusory business of producing, buying and selling— and, incidentally, making a profit—but, at the same time, rendering an essential social service, for which recognition is due. Then come the Kshatriyas, the kings and governors and warriors, who, for society's continued existence, must have the authority to command and the power of life and death. Finally, the Brahmans, the high priests, with the key—or at least a key—to the will of the Infinite and a knowledge of the mysteries of creation, some of the benefits of which they are prepared to communicate at a price.

It will be apparent that such a system, here presented in skeletal form, must encourage a built-in resistance to reform. It is to the advantage of each caste to resist any intrusion upon its privileges from below, to reinforce the rigidity of the structure and the discipline of its constituents. This applies even to the lowest caste, the Sudras, since below them again are the people of no caste at all, the "outcasts". These are the people, the "untouchables", whom Gandhi called the Harijans, and by so doing ran the considerable risk of constituting them a new caste. For no contradiction in terms is impossible in Hindu thought; it was Gandhi himself, so it is told, who, on being approached to subscribe to a European-organized war relief fund, begged to be excused with the perceptive comment that he might be enrolled in the scheme as a non-joining member.

In the course of time, the system of caste has proliferated far beyond its original scope. There are now in India numberless castes and sub-castes, many of them established on an occupational basis, which has clearly little or nothing to do with basic Hindu ideas. There is nothing in Hinduism which necessarily calls for a fenced-off distinction between, say, a silversmith and a cloth merchant. Yet such distinctions have arisen and their importance lies in the influence which caste exercises upon the normal life of the individual. That members of a caste may not marry outside that caste does not necessarily pose an organizational problem of any size, however unwise it may be genetically in the case of some of the smaller castes, but that a man or woman may not eat, drink or bathe with others than those of the same caste, or even, in extreme cases, that they may not live in the same village, gives rise to problems, in industry for instance, that may not be wholly insoluble but are hopelessly uneconomic. It is no doubt true that with increasing industrialization many of the restrictions imposed by caste are weakening; a factory canteen, like an army canteen, can exercise a powerful influence. But in the sphere of education plans must be made for those not yet of the age to go out to work or join the army, and it is possible to foresee caste restrictions surviving for generations in rural areas.

It would, however, be a mistake to regard the caste system as a serious impediment to the organization of an educational system for all India. It has already been pointed out that the Hindu mind is traditionally disposed to compromise, to the point, at times, of apparent contradiction, and there is no reason to doubt that, as indeed is already happening, a way will be found to reconcile the strict demands of tradition with those of innovations and departures from it, which the practical benefits of a sound organization may necessitate. That this conclusion is not merely wishful thinking will be apparent not only from the developments in higher education, which will be discussed later, but also from a consideration of the structure of the principal administrative services in India today, where, in general, promotion goes with ability.

Moreover, there is an even more basic reason for being hopeful. The habit of compromise is directly related to that aspect of the Hindu outlook which has been described as absorptive. It is natural for a Hindu, without conscious effort, to regard any ethic other than his own with what may be called an acquisitive curiosity and interest. It is unnatural for him to reject it outright; it is automatic for him to seek in the new idea thoughts and arguments which may, by adoption and adaptation, enrich his own. Put in hard, practical terms, this means that organizational schemes of education and courses of study based largely upon Western experience will not meet with any automatic hostility or rejection. They will be examined with lively interest; they may be modified, or even thrown somewhat out of balance, but the examination will be primarily in search of the good.

Much the same is true of the Hindu joint-family system as of caste. The system itself is ancient and far-reaching. Basically it provides that the head of any family shares his home and his income with his children, grandchildren and their children. They, in turn, contribute their share to the upkeep of the family home and render obedience to the head of the family. In theory, this system could have a seriously restrictive influence on the younger generation. Not only would they be subject to control by outmoded ideas, a thing which happens in other countries besides India, but it could also mean, for instance, that an intelligent boy winning a scholarship would be compelled to contribute from it towards the upkeep of a ne'er-do-well and, no doubt, cordially disliked cousin living under the same roof. In theory, too, this system should militate strongly against women's education. The joint family is strictly controlled by the senior male member of it. This is not to say that his wife is not also a very potent and frequently conservative influence. Here, indeed, is another example of the ease with which the Hindu mind reconciles apparent contradictions. Woman is essentially the servant of man. She prepares his food but does not share it with him. She cleans the house and then retires to the kitchen or women's quarters.

She takes no part in her husband's official or public life and is content to know nothing about it. Yet once she has become a mother, she acquires an almost sacred aura and image, even though, in seclusion, she can exert an influence hardly less than that of her husband. This influence has traditionally been exercised with special emphasis over daughters-in-law and, of course, all grandchildren, and it is clear that by the nature of things it has been a restrictive influence. But, as in the case of caste, circumstances have combined to modify this system also. Education itself has brought about great changes among the professional classes, in particular among those who have lived and studied outside India. The rapid increase in industrialization has had its effect outside the cities. The higher and more regular wages to be earned are drawing young men and, occasionally, young women to the industrial centres, and these, when they marry, set up homes of their own. They may—or may not—contribute to family funds or assist needy relatives; the sense of family responsibility remains strong and displays itself at times of famine or similar distress, but the patriarchal type of control is on the wane. A rather curious outcome of this close-woven family fabric is that nepotism is regarded, if not as a positive virtue, at least as a matter of obligation on the senior members of the family circle. It is their duty to use such influences as they may possess to secure jobs for their younger relations.

The Hindu custom of early marriage may cause difficulties. Under the Sarda Act of 1927, as amended after Independence, marriage below the age of 15 for girls and 18 for men is a criminal offence. It must be admitted that the Act is honoured as much in the breach as in the observance, and, in any case, the urge for a Hindu to have sons is still strong. It is by no means uncommon for a student at a university to be already burdened with the responsibility of a family. This problem is, of course, closely connected with that of family planning and birth control, which is a matter of grave concern to Government. Schemes for dealing with it have found a place in the first three Plans and there is reason to expect that it will be given a very high priority in the Fourth Plan. The social problem is aggravated at the time of writing by the fact that India is facing disastrous famine after successive years of inadequate rainfall. Climatic conditions in India are notoriously fickle, and while much has been done to improve water conservation and irrigation facilities, these measures, by reason of the cost alone, can do little more than provide a palliative. The ugly fact remains that the population is increasing at a pace with which improved agricultural techniques and facilities can hardly keep level. The sense of fatalism, inherent in much of the Hindu ethic, imposes a heartbreaking handicap upon those who plan and those who try to give effect to the plans. When food and life themselves are seen to dwindle and fade, education, whether in theory or practice, seems to have little to offer.

The population increase and the failure to step up food production at a satisfactory rate are, of course, matters which directly affect all non-Hindus in India as much as Hindus. This may, therefore, be an appropriate stage at which to give a short account of these people, among whom the Muslims form the largest group, numbering nearly 50 million, or just about the whole population of the British Isles. The differences between Hinduism and Islam are profound and it is not surprising that after centuries of coexistence the two communities have achieved no more than that. While the Hindu is pantheistic, the Muslim is devoutly monotheistic. Where the Hindu seeks to adopt and adapt from other ethics or religions, the Muslim seeks to proselytize. Where the Hindu looks for the merging of the individual in the ultimate life force, the Muslim looks for the individual attainment of heaven. Here indeed are divergencies which have all the appearance of being irreconcilable, and so, in fact, they have proved. Moreover, it should not be forgotten that for 700 years the Muslims were the rulers of much of India, during which time they could not and did not fail to exercise their authority in the service of proselytization. To the Muslim, therefore, there is the traditional fear of being swamped by a vast majority of infidels; to the Hindu there is the traditional fear of authority in the hands of those who, in the last resort, have not refrained from proselytization by force.

In this connection, it is worth recalling what has already been said about India being a secular state. All citizens, irrespective of religion, are now entitled equally to all government services. What, then, are the specific points about Islam which the planners must bear in mind? To the Muslim, the individual has only one life in this world. The character of his life, still as the same individual, in the next world, depends upon the use which he or she had made of the life in this world. Thus, life in this world is a gift from God to an individual soul and it is the one and only chance for that soul to forward God's design for the world. That design is that all the world should follow the precepts of Islam as revealed by Mohammed. But what precisely are these precepts? Mohammed spoke in the language of his time and his own account of what God revealed to him in visions and dreams was recorded with an apparent dedication to accuracy which is remarkable. The sources of a saying by the Prophet are often documented bearing an account of all those, by name, who have quoted the particular saying right back to the authority who heard it from the Prophet himself. Such historical precision is not only remarkable in itself, it is also clearly, over the generations, a potent source of sectarianism and dogmatism. It is just these two aspects of the historical development of Islam that have given rise, in India at least, to the backwardness of the rural Muslim population.

This is not the place to discuss the origins or the principles of the various sects which have influenced Islamic teaching, but it will be clear that two handicaps have been imposed upon educational development along Western lines. The original precepts announced by Mohammed were designed to guide a semi-nomadic, semi-commercial people, and, to some extent at least, must have been influenced by the constant strife between Medina and Mecca. What Mohammed meant and what he thought God's message was could no doubt be understood by the people of his own time and for a generation or two later. But the rapid spread of Islam, partly by official decree, in what we should now call the Arab world and in Africa, introduced considerations which were not and could not be in Mohammed's mind. Islamic scholars thus found interpretation of the original precepts in the light of later and different circumstances forced upon them. It is not surprising, then, that different scholars offered different interpretations or that, however worthy or unworthy their motives, they and their disciples fought strenuously and bitterly for the superiority of the view held by them.

It is from this internal conflict that the main difficulty for the Western-orientated administrator springs. Islam being a revealed religion founded upon the words of God uttered to his prophet Mohammed, must, in the last resort, claim to "know all the answers". But since, in fact, difference of opinion exists as to what these "answers" are, judgement upon new, non-Islamic ways of thought or ideas of social organization must come second to decisions upon what Islamic principles, if any, are involved, and how. The position is put clearly by an authority on Islam, who says : "Islam in thinking of itself as a community observing a divinely given law, tends to think ideologically. . . . Because of the ideological distortion of these ideas, Muslims have been impeded in their adjustment of themselves to the West." An outstanding example of how this impediment subsists is to be seen in the failure, so far, of Pakistan to produce an Islamic constitution. This is not said in any sense of disparagement; indeed, the fact that, in spite of the failure, Pakistan continues to exist and to prosper, may well be read as evidence that the idea of an Islamic constitution is something more than a dream. But it is also evidence that the Western social reformer or organizer, whether in education or anything else, must be content to hasten slowly. In so far as Muslims in India are concerned, it may be taken for granted that any pressure for official education plans to make special arrangements or allowances for them, will be measured against Pakistan's own success in adopting Western methods and ideas, and even more, perhaps, against Pakistan's willingness to make allowances for Hindus in that country. What would, in any case, prove a prickly and stubborn problem is thus accentuated by acute and very lively political considerations.

It is tempting to make an easy and seemingly rational transition from considering Islam to considering Christianity. Both religions are Judean in origin, both are monotheistic, both discern their origin in a prophet or direct human representative of God and both find much of their belief and teaching in the revealed commands and statements of God. The basic similarities are indeed strong, and it would be of great interest to study how and in what directions divergencies arose which, at their most acute stage, produced the bitterest forms of hostility. But historically in India the Christian faith has not left important traces on Indian society in general. There is a very small Christian community in the south-west corner of India, which is traditionally associated with a visit by St. Thomas the Apostle, though, in fact, it seems rather more likely that it originated towards the end of the eighth century A.D. Otherwise, Christians in India are descendants of converts dating at the earliest from the sixteenth and seventeenth centuries. To a very large extent they came from the "outcastes" or untouchables as a social revolt against the rigid impositions of Hindu caste. It is interesting that according to one account, the same social revolt is responsible for the Muslim population of East Bengal. However that may be, the point to note is that there is no original Christian ethic in India at all and such effect as Christianity has had on India's social development springs not from its built-in influence on the Indian mind but from outside circumstances and pressures of non-Indian origin. The impact has been missionary; the majority of Christians in India, who total some 11 million, are Roman Catholics, stemming from the work of the Portuguese and French missionaries. Thus, the earliest effect of Christianity cannot date from before the sixteenth or seventeenth centuries, and much of it is of shorter date than that. It is true that during the period of British rule the Protestant faith may have seemed, in some Indian eyes, to have official backing and so to be worthy of notice. But the effect of any such consideration has, in fact, been negligible, and it would be a mistake to think that among the Indians the Christians offer an easier or more receptive target for the social planner. The Indian who accepts the Christian discipline is no less an Indian than the Hindu Indian who does not, and the essentially Hindu tradition and history of the country continues to exercise a powerful influence. Superficially, it may be true that the removal of the most severe taboos of the caste system should facilitate social planning but not much can be accomplished by only $2\frac{1}{2}$ per cent of the population, and, as has already been shown, the Hindu system has a remarkable capacity for adjusting itself to inescapable facts.

It has just been posited that a Christian Indian is just as much an Indian as a Hindu Indian. The implication must be that an Indian can be distinguished from a non-Indian by his culture, his habits of thought and his natural reactions to events and people, as well as by his language. It is not easy to define any such distinction, but possibly, one way to approach it is by considering the outstanding cultural achievements of India as a whole.

At Ajanta, for instance, the unsurpassed frescoes represent Buddhist myth and story but they depict Indian people and places. The Taj Mahal is a Moghul monument—the finest in the world some would say—to a Muslim wife, but of Indian design and built by Indian hands. The superb lion-headed pillar which is now the symbol of the Indian Republic is a monument to Asoka, the Buddhist, but, at the same time, a work of purely Indian art. The exquisite Moghul miniature paintings are also Indian works of art, depicting the beauty to be found in Indian landscapes and interiors. The great rock-hewn temples of Ellora and the imposing remains of Vijayanagar are purely Hindu in conception but wholly Indian in execution. There can be no doubt that there is an Indian culture of as high a standard as anywhere in the world in sculpture, painting and architecture—and in music and dancing too, for those who understand the elaborate and almost mystical techniques which determine their expression —a culture which is specifically Indian, attuned to Indian climatic and geographical conditions. It transcends religious differences, though it may reflect them. It has produced master-pieces, which are part of India's heritage and of which every Indian, Hindu, Muslim, Christian, Sikh or Buddhist is proud.

This culture stands firmly upon its highest achievements in the past but it is encouraging, indeed, exciting, to note that there has been a powerful resurgence accompanying the drive for and the attainment of political independence. Though this movement originally based itself upon the traditional schools, for instance of painting, and aimed at developing them, art in India today is as questing and forward-looking as anywhere in Europe. It is not without significance that the man selected by the Government of India to design the new capital city of the Punjab at Chandigarh was Le Corbusier.

Indian culture, therefore, is not in any fundamental sense a hindrance to modern development in politics and administrative practice. Those who appreciate its splendour find it rather ridiculous that India should at times be classed among the backward countries. There are, however, unfortunately, certain features of Indian traditional life which are such a hindrance. The great bulk of the Indian population consists of peasants with a low standard of living. Peasants the world over tend to be reactionary, preserving the habits and customs of their predecessors without question and looking to the gods rather than themselves for help in time of trouble. It is a formidable task to attempt an explanation of new ways and new thoughts to over 400 million backward and, only too often, undernourished peasants. The present Government are making a gallant effort to face up to it with high ideals, if rather inadequate resources. The fact, already mentioned, that there are fourteen official languages and some eight hundred dialects, does not make the task any easier. While it may not prove a serious handicap to the individual social reformer working in a village or even in a region, it is a headache of considerable severity to the central organizer, who has not only to draw up overall central instructions and plans but also to study reports and returns from all parts of the country.

The lack of good communications, like the lack of electric

power, constitutes a major handicap for the social reformer. Most village roads are no more than rutted tracks, choking with dust in the hot weather, quagmires in the rains. Railways are still few and far between for such a vast area and can only cater for market centres at the lowest. The jeep and the Land-Rover can cope with most conditions, but to possess one is beyond the dreams of the ordinary peasant. Mobile cinemas, libraries and dispensaries can all contribute towards the amelioration of primitive living conditions but they cost money and the depreciation rate is very high; some of them depend for their efficiency on electric power, which can only be supplied by batteries or a self-contained generator. There has been no lack of research since 1947 into ways and means of improving the lot of the rural population and many plans have been prepared. What more can be done by education and the social services to help in this connection is one of the problems to be examined later in this book.

Stress has been laid upon the frustrations arising from the backward state of the peasantry in so much of the country, because it is for this teeming majority that social reform in general and education in particular are so urgently needed. If there is to be a social revolution in India, it must grow from below and cannot be imposed from above. This, indeed, is the political theory of the Congress Party, which has so far provided the governments since Independence. Sheer necessity, however, has compelled them to resort more and more to the imposition of change from above. This may be regretted but it is better than no change at all. Moreover, it makes it clear that the educated, middle-class minority is aware of the need for change. This is the background to the whole concept of the Panchayati Raj or Rural Devolution; guidance must come or at least be available from above but the actual administration of local affairs must be in local hands. If there is not a sufficient number of suitable people in any given locality, steps must promptly be taken to provide training courses in local government.

The division between "above" and "below", between the ruling party as government and the vast countryside population, closely represents the division between the educated and the uneducated, the educated rapidly including more and more skilled artisans as industry expands. This social cleavage occurs in most countries in some form or another, but in India it acquires particular importance on account of the sharpness and width of the gulf and the staggering imbalance of the numbers on either side. The width of the gulf is represented on the one side by a man who is at home and at ease in most capitals of the world, and on the other by a man who cannot read or write, a man most, if not all, of whose family and friends also cannot read or write and who has never switched on an electric light or drawn water from a tap. The numbers are some 20 million on the one side and some 450 million on the other. The problem thus posed is frightening in its size and calls for the highest determination and readiness for sacrifice if it is to be solved and the aims of social justice set out in the Constitution are to be realized. It can hardly be said that in the political field the ruling Congress Party has so far measured up to the effort required but here as elsewhere the Hindu capacity for reconciling irreconcilables reappears. The number of party members who recognize the need and are pre-pared to make at least some sacrifice is surprisingly large and the Government, that is to say the administration as distinct from the party, has shown an encouraging capacity for facing hard facts. India was fortunate in having at the time when independence was won a substantial core of highly trained civil servants to whom the principles of efficiency and impartiality had real meaning. Many of these men have now retired, but they have left their standards to their successors. Some of the problems which these men and their political masters have to face in stimulating and directing India's social revolution have been sketched in this chapter; so also have some of the Indian characteristics which, it may be hoped, will prove adequate to the task. It must be the earnest hope of all men of good will that this will prove to be so and that all available assistance to that end will be forthcoming from outside India. If India should fail in its task, the disastrous results would be felt far beyond its borders.

CHAPTER 4

The Political and Administrative Structure as it Affects Education

IT IS outside the scope of this book to examine in any detail the articles of the Constitution of 1950, except in so far as they concern education and the social services, but for the sake of those who are not familiar with the governmental organization of the new India, both in theory and practice, a brief summary of its contents may be useful. These may be classified under four headings, viz. (a) the constituent elements in the Union or Federation and their interrelation, (b) the machinery required to enable these to function, (c) directives to guide legislation, and (d) a statement of fundamental rights to protect and promote the well-being of the individual citizen.

On 26 January 1950 India became a Sovereign Democratic Republic comprising sixteen States and nine smaller units named Union Territories. In one sense it may be correctly described as a Union. The importance of maintaining and strengthening the feeling of unity among all sections of the people, which had been engendered by the struggle for independence, was very much in the minds of the first National Government. At the same time, it is also, in many respects, a Federation with a centre linking up and, within specified limits, controlling the constituent states.

It is interesting to note the change in the official attitude towards Centre–State relationship, which took place between the end of 1946, when the first Constituent Assembly began the task of framing the Constitution, and 1950, when it was finally adopted. When Pandit Nehru moved the "Objectives Resolution" in 1947, it was proposed that the Centre should only exercise such powers as were definitely vested in it. At that time, Partition had not yet been agreed upon and the Muslim League was unanimous in its opposition to a strong Centre. When this reason ceased to operate, there was a steady trend of opinion in favour of more power for the Centre. So in its final form, the Constitution prescribed that the Union should have the right to legislate in regard to any matters other than those included in federal, concurrent and state lists. Certain important subjects such as defence, international relations, currency, railways and ports belong to the Centre alone, but education and nearly all the other services which can be termed social are to be found in the concurrent list. This means that both the Centre and the States are empowered to deal with them.

A further reinforcement of the Centre's authority lies in its right in case of emergency or the failure of a State to govern in accordance with the Constitution, to intervene and, if necessary, take over any or all of its functions. Such action has to be approved by Parliament within a limited time. Finally, the Constitution provides a watchdog on both Centre and States in the form of an independent judiciary, which is empowered to pronounce invalid any legislation that, in the opinion of the Supreme Court, is not in accord with the letter or spirit of the Constitution.

With regard to the actual machinery of government, that at the Centre copies, in the main, the British pattern. At the top is the President, who, like the British monarch, enjoys, in theory, very wide powers but in practice acts and is expected to act in accordance with advice tendered to him by the Prime Minister on behalf of the Council of Ministers, with whom the real executive power rests. He is elected by a special college consisting of representatives of both the Central and State legislatures. His term of office is five years and he is eligible for re-election. He appoints the Prime Minister, but naturally chooses someone who commands the support of Parliament; he can also dismiss him or any of the ministers and even dissolve Parliament if he feels that Government is not being carried on as the people would wish. He must, however, abide by the result of the consequent election.

There is also a Vice-President, who is *ex-officio* chairman of the Council of States. If a digression may be permitted, it is very fortunate for education that the present President* and the Vice-President are two of the most distinguished educationists that India has so far produced.

The Prime Minister is, of course, the pivot or hinge on which the whole machinery of government turns. Gandhi's mantle and his own great personal prestige gave Nehru, so long as he lived and Congress remained in power, almost a divine right to the post. There were other men of acknowledged ability in the party, like Sardar Vallabhai Patel and Dr. B. C. Roy, but it is unlikely that any of them, even if they had wished to do so, could have challenged Nehru's claim to the premiership.

Tribute has already been paid to the outstanding service which Patel rendered to the Republic in its early years, above all, in connection with the "accession" to a unified India of the old princely states, many of which had their own treaties or guarantees with the British Raj. Dr. B. C. Roy, a prominent physician and a man of wide culture, was satisfied to become Chief Minister of his own State, West Bengal, and that rather difficult area was fortunate to have at its head during some critical phases a leader of his energy and integrity.

Another notable figure in 1947 was Mr. C. Rajagopalachari, known affectionately to many as Rajaji, but his age and occasional puckish reaction to current political issues put him out of the running for any but honorific offices.

The individual ministers who make up the Cabinet or Council of State are, as in Britain, in charge of the principal departments of government. They are appointed by the President on the advice of the Prime Minister.

Parliament, at the Centre, consists of two Houses, the Upper House, or Council of States (Rajya Sabha), and the Lower House, or House of the People (Lok Sabha). The Upper House has 250 members, twelve of them being nominated by the President in

* Dr. Radhakrishnan's term of office expired in 1966; he was succeeded by Dr. Zakir Husain, the Vice-President.

virtue of their special knowledge and experience of the arts, sciences and social service. The other 238 are elected by the legislative assemblies of the States, the number of seats allotted to each State being determined by its population. It is too early as yet to assess what effect the nominated members have had on education and social welfare. The members are elected for six years and one-third of them retire every second year, so that there is a certain continuity.

The Lower House has just over 500 members, who are elected by territorial constituencies, each having approximately the same number of voters. All citizens over the age of 21, except those disqualified owing to crime or insanity, are entitled to vote. This House, unless it is dissolved sooner, has a maximum duration of five years.

Apart from the raising and spending of money, control of which rests with the Lower House, Bills may be introduced in either House but require the consent of both Houses before becoming law. In case of disagreement, provision is made for a joint sitting and a final decision by the majority of those present. In the case of both Houses, procedures and privileges are much the same as in the British Parliament.

The pattern of government in the States generally follows that of the Centre. Each of them has a Governor, appointed by the President for a five-year term, with a Council of Ministers presided over by a Chief Minister. Their legislatures in nearly all cases consist of two Houses, the Upper, named the Legislative Council, and the Lower, the Legislative Assembly. Assemblies may not have more than 500 or less than sixty members and these are elected by single-member constituencies with roughly the same number of voters. Councils must not be more than one-third as large as the Assemblies and are made up of members, some of whom are elected by the assemblies, some by local authorities, university graduates and teachers, while others are nominated by the Governor for knowledge and experience of the arts, sciences and social service. The State legislatures carry on their business in much the same way as the Central Parliament.

There is also in each State an independent judiciary in the form of a High Court, the members of which are appointed by the President and have similar status to that of the members of the Supreme Court at the Centre. The existence of independent judiciaries both at the Centre and in the States is an important feature of the Constitution. Although in the discharge of their functions they may have caused some embarrassment to the powers that be, they have already established a reputation for integrity, which is particularly valuable in a society where so many pressures are at work and the need for a brake on ill-considered, if well-intentioned, legislation is urgent.

Although in the three years of its gestation the Constitution tended to vest more powers in the Centre at the expense of the States, recent political trends have been in the opposite direction and the States maintain substantial authority to manage their own affairs in the way that seems best to them. There are plenty of signs that the spirit of resistance to dictates from New Delhi, which used to inspire their predecessors, the provinces, is by no means extinct. Education, as it appears in the concurrent list, might be thought to offer an obvious arena for Centre–State conflicts, but fortunately there exist several co-ordinating bodies, which by their successful working are gaining increasing respect and authority. In addition to the CABE, there are the All-India Council for Technical Education (AICTE) and the University Grants Commission (UGC). Although these began as purely advisory bodies under the old régime, they have been acquiring executive and financial powers in recent years. A new body, which is likely to play an increasingly important part in stimulating and co-ordinating development, is the National Council for Educational Research and Training (NCERT). The Union Minister of Education is its President, and all the State Ministers of Education are members of it. Its precise relationship to the principal authorities in the field of education, such as the ministries and universities, has not yet been clearly defined and it may be wise to await the Education Commission's (EC) Report before doing so.

Valuable as these bodies are proving in formulating agreed solutions to national problems, the new factor, which has done most to bring Centre and States into line in regard to main issues, has been the greatly increased subvention from central funds in aid of State schemes. Whereas, in 1947, the Central Government's share of the total educational budget was less than 10 per cent of that borne by the provinces, it came to more than half in the Third Plan and may approach two-thirds in the Fourth. That this was inevitable if a national system was to be established was one of the major assumptions emphasized in the CABE Report.

So far as government below the State level is concerned, it is clearly the intention of the new India, as shown by the Constitution and the Five-year Plans, to encourage both enterprise and patriotism by giving the man in the street and in the village a say in the management of affairs. The size of most of the States and the fact that many areas are still without modern means of communication necessarily involve the delegation of authority in certain fields to smaller units of administration. This applies especially to the social services and to education most of all. Education, to be effective, must be able to establish satisfactory personal relations between the three parties directly concerned, namely children, parents and teachers. This cannot be achieved by circular, letter or telephone from a distant centre or even by the most devoted staff of visiting inspectors. For this reason great importance attaches to the new local authorities, the Panchayati Raj, as they are called, the Block Development system and the district boards for education.

It is not easy to give a clear picture of local government in India today. As the Third Five-year Plan pointed out, the carrying out of schemes for development has entailed the creation of new and the adaptation of a number of extension agencies, official, semi-official and private, from government level down to small communal units. So far as urban areas are concerned, the external features do not show any great change from British days, though much has been done through adult suffrage and other means to make the ordinary citizen conscious of his democratic rights and duties. In 1963 there were 22 municipal corporations, 1453 municipalities, 385 town area committees and 115 notified area committees. These bodies are responsible for the care of roads, water supply, drainage, sanitation, medical relief, vaccination and education at the primary and secondary stages. Their revenues are derived, in the main, from taxes on the annual value of land and buildings, octroi charges and vehicle licences. They make their own bye-laws and frame their own budgets, though the latter, except in the case of corporations, are usually subject to state approval.

In the rural areas the picture is much more complicated. During the last half-century of British rule it was the policy of Government to give encouragement of a somewhat tentative nature to local authorities, and, strange as it may seem today, education was chosen as a suitable subject on which they might try their prentice hands. As time went on, other matters were entrusted to them, but as there was no general policy, the nature and extent of their jurisdiction varied greatly from one province to another. It also depended largely on the extent to which they enjoyed the confidence of the government officer, usually called a Collector, who was in charge of the district of which they formed part. Under the new régime many of these local boards have been abolished, but the Collector remains, though with powers much circumscribed by the activities of the numerous new bodies now operating in the rural field. The first of these invaders were the extension agencies concerned primarily with the improvement of agriculture, to which, for obvious reasons, a very high priority was assigned in the early plans. It was realized that if a real boost was to be given to agriculture, the task of the experts would be simplified and lightened if the villagers' interest and support could be enlisted. To educate them and, at the same time, to co-ordinate the numerous co-operatives and other agencies already at work, a new system of local administration had been introduced, which is known as the Panchayati Raj or Democratic Decentralization. It operates at three levels, district, block and village. District and block panchayats deal with primary and secondary education, health and the construction and maintenance of roads other than highways. They have their specialist officers and can invoke the aid, when necessary, of experts employed by the State Government. Village panchayats are responsible for local amenities, sanitation, medical relief and the management of community assets. By 31 March 1964 the number of these bodies functioning was district 230, block 3155 and village 214,898, the last covering nearly the whole of rural India.

The success of this interesting experiment will largely depend on the tact shown by the expert advisers in their relations with the local bodies. In the old days there was a tendency for many local boards to treat the inspector of schools either as their servant or, if he refused that role, as their natural enemy. Jealousy of interference from above is a sentiment by no means confined to local authorities in India. It has even been known to show itself in totalitarian countries.

Whether in view of the many new responsibilities laid upon them these local authorities will have either the time or the ability to do justice to educational development, or whether as an interim measure, it might be wise to set up *ad hoc* bodies like the school boards under the English Education Act of 1870, is a matter that will be discussed in a later chapter.

Before turning to the executive arrangements designed to implement governmental decisions, whether at the Centre or State level, it may be opportune to have a brief look at one or two queries, raised by not unfriendly critics, as to whether, in actual operation, so far, the Constitution may not have hampered the policy of rapid development. In theory, the Constitution is a comprehensive and liberal document, embodying most of the more vital principles accepted by free and progressive nations as the basis of sound democracy. Its framers were plainly anxious to benefit by the experience of other countries with written constitutions like the U.S.A., Canada and Ireland, and to borrow from them anything likely to be of use to India. They were also fully familiar with the evolution of the British polity. The result of their labours on paper is certainly impressive but the first doubt that arises is whether, in fact, a new nation trying to find its feet and above all one like the new India beset by so many troubles, foreseen and unforeseen, is not handicapped in seeking a solution of its problems by having a large and inevitably rather rigid instrument tied round its neck. From the beginning some of the framers were doubtful as to the wisdom of including in it both directives and fundamental rights.

As it happened, these doubts were soon justified. About a year after the Constitution had been adopted, the Madras Government, satisfied that they were acting in accordance with its spirit, reserved places in their schools for children of the backward or depressed classes. They soon found themselves in trouble with the Supreme Court, which ruled that their action amounted to discrimination in favour of a particular section of the community, which is forbidden by the Constitution. Clearly what amounted almost to a contradiction in terms had to be sorted out and this led to the First Amendment. Other amendments have followed. The courts have also been kept busy dealing with cases where the litigant has claimed that his fundamental rights were being restricted by governmental action or even by the law of the land.

As a rule, where there has been a conflict between a directive and a fundamental right, the former has prevailed. Nehru himself defined the issue in his speech on the First Amendment. Directives, he pointed out, were meant to guide state policy towards desirable ends and so were dynamic. Fundamental rights, on the other hand, were designed to safeguard existing rights and to that extent were static. On the whole, the directives may be accepted as forming the basis on which the policy of any modern, progressive government would be founded. It is, however, interesting to note that the one referring specifically to education prescribed the provision of free, compulsory schooling for all children up to the age of 14 years within ten years. The period was subsequently increased to sixteen years and the age-range reduced to 6–11, but the framers could hardly have been unaware that the CABE Report had given chapter and verse for showing that this could not be done properly in less than forty.

There is, however, another reason for doubting the wisdom of laying undue emphasis on fundamental rights and high-minded directives in the Constitution of a new nation face to face with a horde of practical problems. Idealism has, of course, its rightful place in any Constitution, but there is a distinct danger that some of the ideals set forth in the Indian one may encourage the woolly-minded type of enthusiast to assume that the millennium is just round the corner. India has its fair share of people who go about with their heads in the air and need to be forcibly reminded, like the sages of Laputa, of the obstacles in their path. One has only to look at the history of some of the more successful Western democracies to realize how much time, patience and money it took to put them firmly on their feet. It is nearly a century since Britain set out to build a national system of education and no one would claim that the goal has yet been reached.

Nevertheless, it is no bad thing for individuals and nations, especially new ones, to have in their minds hopes as well as fears, together with the determination and enthusiasm to ensue the former and banish the latter. It was well said "Where there is no vision, the people perish". Few people who have visited India recently will fail to have been impressed by a new energy and urgency, both in public and private life. The only danger is that this sense of urgency may tempt some of those in posts of responsibility to try to find short cuts to Utopia.

After this brief account of the political aspect of the governmental structure, it is time to turn to the arrangements for implementing policies. It is perhaps open to question whether Pope's dictum "Whate'er is best administered is best" can be accepted without reservations in a democratic age and society, where the individual must be prepared to expect and endure a certain amount of inefficiency as the price of freedom. It is, however, beyond question that a newly emancipated country, which aspires to be a democracy, stands in special need of an honest and reasonably competent administrative service. Those who have taken a leading part in the fight for independence have some right to expect their services to be recognized when the fight has been won, but, unfortunately, the qualities that make a successful agitator are not merely different from but are often antithetic to those required in an efficient administrator. This may explain why so many of the new nations which have emerged since the Second World War are finding it so hard to put their houses in order.

India was unusually lucky to find in Vallabhai Patel not only a stout fighter for independence but also a man with practical ideas about what to make of independence, once it was won. But the experienced help available for him and his colleagues was strictly limited. At the end of the British period the Indian Civil Service (ICS) contained just under 2000 members, of whom roughly half were Indians, and this remnant was further depleted by the loss of those who opted for Pakistan. Although, in the years preceding 1947, a good many of the senior posts in the secretariats at New Delhi and the provincial capitals had been filled by Indians, the number of trained administrators at the disposal of the new Government was pitifully small when viewed in relation to the problems demanding immediate attention. A further call on existing resources was the need to staff the embassies and consulates, which the Republic had to establish in foreign countries. For prestige and other reasons their personnel had to be impressive. Prompt steps were taken to create an Indian Administrative Service (IAS) to replace the ICS; the standard of the recruits whom it has attracted has been higher than might have been expected in view of the openings offered to well-qualified young people by a rapidly expanding industry. It takes time, however, to give even first-class graduates the training and experience necessary to fit them to fill responsible posts, and, in the meantime, there was no administrative reservoir outside government service upon which to draw.

The manpower shortage was by no means confined to the higher ranks in the administrative hierachy : the subordinate grades were also affected both by outside competition and by the enormous increase in the amount of busines to be dealt with. The withdrawal of the British depleted not only the ICS but also the other former imperial services and, of course, the defence forces.

Education was particularly hard hit. The Indian Education Service (IES), which, in its heyday, had produced some notable figures, both British and Indian, ceased recruitment between the two wars and by 1947 had shrunk to a very small cadre. To replace it a good deal had been done to raise the standard of the provincial education services and a small but useful contribution was forthcoming in the shape of the new education department at the Centre, the genesis of which has already been described.

The IES, for all the distinguished service which its members rendered in its time, had two weaknesses which should be avoided in the course of building up machinery to carry out future developments. The first of these was that there was no demarcation at any stage between the teaching and the administrative side. A member who had spent all his time teaching might suddenly find that by virtue of seniority he had become next on the list for a top administrative post like that of Deputy Director or even Director of Public Instruction. Not long before the end of the British Raj, the post of DPI fell vacant in one of the larger provinces. The next senior man was a distinguished professor at a local university, who had never been outside his own department. He did not want the job, the Provincial Government did not want him and the Central Government agreed with the Provincial Government. It was then discovered that he could not be passed over without the consent of the Secretary of State in London and this was refused on the ground that there was nothing in the professor's record that would justify his supersession. Such a thing is not likely to happen in the new India but it does illustrate the importance of those selected for the higher administrative posts having had adequate experience of both teaching and administration.

There is, however, a much greater risk that the second weakness of the IES, which arose out of the first, may continue to exist under the new dispensation. The fact that some members, though excellent teachers, were not very efficient when called upon to administer, enabled the ICS to insert one of its own people as Secretary of the Education Department between the DPI and his Minister or Member of Council. So far from promoting the smooth transaction of business, this was liable to prove a frustrating situation for one or all of the parties concerned. "Administrators on top, experts on tap", which used to be a favourite apothegm with some members of the ICS in the old days, can hardly be accepted as an infallible guide to efficiency in this scientific age.

While on the subject of educational administration, there is another matter to which serious attention should be given when the time comes to deal comprehensively with the lower stories of the education structure. It is unlikely that any of those in administrative control will ever have taught in a primary school, except possibly in a model one attached to a training college. This, of course, is almost entirely due to the great difference in status, pay and other conditions of service which used to exist, and, in spite of improvements, still exists between the primary and the higher grades. Something will be said later on about possible ways of reducing disparities.

What has just been said about the importance of getting people with the right outlook and background, whether amateurs or professionals, to look after education does not apply only to India, but a country so large and diverse in its constituent elements needs something more than efficient central and state ministries and local authorities, if development projects are to be co-ordinated and, where necessary, integrated. The constitutional distribution of responsibilities between so many bodies makes the need for co-ordinating machinery more essential in India than in countries where the main responsibility rests either with the central or the local authority. This makes expert advice at all levels of special value to those in charge.

Democratic governments, whether seeking solutions of current problems or advice as to the lines which future development should follow, normally have recourse to standing advisory bodies or to *ad hoc* commissions. India started planning on a national scale in 1951, and, since then, the final recommendations as to what projects should find a place in the Five-year Plans have necessarily come from the National Planning and Development Commissions. Central and State ministries have submitted their proposals and these have been carefully examined and discussed before a decision has been reached as to which of them could be included in the final programme. Determining factors have naturally been the financial and personnel resources likely to be available and the contribution which departmental schemes would be likely to make towards implementing the approved national economic policy.

In education since the end of the British period there have been three important standing committees, which, though directly responsible to the Central Ministry, also represent State and other interests. It is a tribute to the value attached by Government to their advice that apart from special investigations set on foot by the Planning Commission, only two important *ad hoc* commissions were appointed between 1947 and 1964, one on university education in 1948 and the other on secondary education in 1953. In 1964, however, Government appointed an Education Planning Commission to survey the whole education field. In addition to its Indian members the commission has had the help of a number of experts from abroad. It is hoped that its report will be published in time for it to be reviewed in the final chapter.

The three standing committees are the Central Advisory Board of Education (CABE), the University Grants Commission (UGC) and the All-India Council for Technical Education (AICTE). Since they have been mainly responsible, so far at any rate, for framing the assumptions on which a national system of education should be based, a brief description of their constitutions and functions may usefully precede a more detailed exposition of the basic ideas now informing educational policy.

The CABE was originally established in the 1920s, but after a very short life was axed for economic reasons. It was reconstituted in 1935. In 1944, its membership, which has not altered materially since then, was as follows :

A. Chairman—The member of the Viceroy's Executive Coun-
    cil in charge of the Department of Education, Health and
    Lands, later the Minister of Education of the Central
    Government.
B. Ten persons, of whom not less than two must be women,
    nominated by the Government of India.
C. One member elected by the Council of State, now the
    Rajya Sabha.
D. Two members elected by the Legislative Assembly, now
    the Lok Sabha.
E. Three members nominated by the Inter-University Board.
F. The Provincial Ministers of Education or their representa-
    tives and the Directors of Public Instruction.

The Educational Adviser to the Government of India was an
ex officio member of the Board and the Deputy Educational
Adviser was its secretary.

Its main functions were to act as a power house for ideas and
a co-ordinating agency for development throughout the country.
Its importance in the latter connection has been much increased
since 1947 by the greatly enlarged financial commitments undertaken by the Central Government.

It meets annually at different places and, in its earlier days,
used to appoint one or more committees to survey special branches
or aspects of education and report to the next meeting. The
reports of these committees, which were available in 1944, when
the Board was called upon to submit its proposals for post-war
reconstruction, dealt with basic education (two reports); adult
education; physical welfare of school children; social service;
technical (including commercial and art) education; school buildings; recruitment, training and conditions of service of teachers
in primary, middle and high schools; recruitment of education
officers. Between 1944 and 1948 further committees covered
agricultural education; religious education; selection of pupils
for higher education; recruitment, training and conditions of
service of teachers in universities; examinations; textbooks;

education administration. Although there have been no material changes in the constitution or functions of the CABE since Independence, it has modernized its machinery by setting up five standing committees for basic, primary and pre-primary education; secondary education; higher (post-secondary) education, social education; general purposes.

The All-India Council for Technical Education (AICTE) was established in 1945 to advise about the co-ordination and development of technical education beyond the secondary stage. Like the CABE its membership represents the interested departments of the Central and State Governments as well as industry, commerce and professional associations. Among the latter is the Association of Principals of Technical Institutions (APTI), which has done much to correlate courses and unify standards in polytechnics and the higher institutes.

The University Grants Commission (UGC) is a much smaller body than either the CABE or the AICTE and the members are appointed by the Central Ministry of Education. Some indication of the way in which both its influence and its work have grown since 1947 is given by the fact that in 1962–3 the government grants to universities made at its instance amounted to nearly Rs. 11 crores. Among other useful bodies ancillary to the Ministry of Education which have come into existence since 1947 are the National Council for Women's Education and the NCERT, already mentioned, which has now absorbed the smaller units, which were previously concerned with particular subjects or branches. A new and interesting experiment is the National Discipline Scheme, the aim of which is to provide physical training and recreational activities for youth in ways designed to inspire patriotism.

CHAPTER 5

Prevalent Assumptions
Affecting the Development
of a Formal Education System

THE aim of this chapter and the following one will be to set out in some detail the principles upon which the present system of education is being built. Perhaps the simplest way to give some coherence to this inquiry will be to take the plan for post-war educational development, prepared by the CABE and published in 1944 and see how far its main recommendations have been accepted, modified or rejected by subsequent surveys or official decisions. This does not, of course, imply that the CABE plan was the first or even the most important attempt to explore defects or suggest improvements in Indian education. It was preceded, for instance, not only by the Commissions mentioned in Chapter 2 but also by Gandhi's Wardha Scheme, which put forward a new and dynamic conception of the kind of instruction to be provided for rural children at the primary and middle stages. Moreover, the last section of Chapter 2 will have made it clear that long before either of these plans appeared, both Indian thinkers and British rulers had been disturbed from time to time about the rate of educational progress and the direction in which it was going, but the CABE Report differed from earlier investigations in two important respects. It was the first attempt to survey the whole field from the nursery school to the university and beyond, and, what is more important, it tried to envisage the needs of an India verging on independence and anxious and determined to take its rightful place in the society of civilized nations.

The chapters in the CABE Report deal first of all with the six main branches of the education system, viz. pre-primary, primary (including basic education), secondary, university, technical and adult education, and then with the essential services, viz. the supply and training of teachers, the school medical service, the education of the mentally and physically handicapped, recreative and social activities, vocational guidance, and administration and finance. It may be convenient to follow these headings in the CABE Report and take up under each one what subsequent surveys have to recommend.

THE MAIN BRANCHES
PRE-PRIMARY EDUCATION

In its Report the CABE recommended that an adequate provision of pre-primary instruction should be regarded as an essential adjunct of any national system of education, though the main object of teaching at this stage should be to give young children social experience rather than formal instruction. In urban areas, where sufficient children are available within a reasonable radius, separate nursery schools or classes should be provided, but elsewhere, nursery classes should be attached to junior basic (primary) schools. Pre-primary education should in all cases be free. It may not be feasible to make attendance compulsory but no efforts should be spared to persuade parents to send their children to school voluntarily, particularly in areas where housing conditions are unsatisfactory and/or mothers are accustomed to go out to work. Nursery schools and classes should invariably be staffed with women teachers specially trained for this work.

On the basis of an age-range of 3–6 years it was suggested that one million places should be provided as a start. Owing to more urgent claims on the money available for education since 1947, little progress has so far been made in this branch, but such opinions as have been expressed recently by Indian educationists generally endorse the recommendations of the CABE.

It is perhaps worth mentioning that in the U.S.S.R. nearly 5 million children are now in kindergartens.

BASIC (PRIMARY AND MIDDLE) EDUCATION

One of the most important events in the history of Indian education—some people may still consider it the most important —was the appearance in 1937 of the Wardha Scheme of Basic Education. This was produced by a committee set up by Mahatma Gandhi under the chairmanship of Dr. Zakir Husain, the present President of India. Of the things that gave it both its educational value and its appeal to the public, two stand out; the first was Gandhi's sponsorship and the second the adaptation to the needs of the Indian masses of modern techniques already in operation in other countries, such as craft-centred curricula, activity methods and subject correlation. The CABE set up two committees to examine the Wardha Scheme, and these had the help of several persons prominently associated with the formulation of that plan. With one important exception both committees found themselves in substantial agreement with the Wardha Committee. Their reports were submitted to and approved by the CABE in 1938 and 1940.

The exception mentioned above was concerned with economics rather than pedagogy. The Wardha Committee, no doubt influenced by Gandhi's desire not to be under any financial obligation to the Government, expressed the hope that the cost of the scheme would be met from the sale of the articles made by the children. How many members really believed that this was possible is not known; the CABE did not, and although basic education is the official policy of India today, it is unlikely that the Education Minister or any of his colleagues expect it to pay for itself. Another point not covered in the Wardha Scheme but of interest to the CABE was how to fit basic education into the fabric of a national system. Gandhi himself once said that his main object was to do something for village children, who would very rarely get beyond the village school, and that he was content to leave it to the experts to link up his scheme with the higher branches.

Since, as has already been pointed out, there is, apart from the economic issue, no difference of opinion between the Wardha Scheme and what the CABE thought should be done about the primary and middle stages, it may be possible, without any disrespect to the former, to save time and space by concentrating on what was recommended by the latter and summarizing its main conclusions.

Basic education on the lines advocated by the Wardha Scheme should be first introduced in rural areas and the age-range for compulsion should be from 6–14 years. It should be free. The medium of instruction should be the vernacular of the pupils and English should not be introduced as an optional subject. Activity methods should be of as many kinds as possible in the lower classes but should lead up later to a basic craft, the produce of which should be saleable and the proceeds devoted to the upkeep of the school. This was as far as the Board would go to meet Gandhi's expectation that the scheme might become self-supporting. Turning to the all-important question of teachers, the Board was emphatic that to make a success of basic education the training courses would have to be completely remodelled. Also, to secure the numbers required, salaries and status would have to be raised and special efforts made to recruit more women. In view of what has happened since, the Board's advice that basic schools should only be started when suitably trained teachers are available is worth noting. It is also significant, in view of Indian addiction to external examinations, to find the Board laying it down that none of these are needed in basic schools but at the end of the course a leaving certificate, based on some form of internal assessment, should be given.

The Board's second committee, while generally endorsing the findings of the first one, devoted some time to considering how best to link up basic with the secondary stage for the sake of those children with the ability to go further. With this end in view it proposed that the basic course of eight years, while preserving its essential unity, should consist of two stages, the junior of five years and the senior of three. The first committee had already approved the diversion of able children from the basic to other types of school after the fifth class, but the second committee went beyond this by suggesting that the post-primary schools, to which basic pupils might transfer at the end of the junior stage, should make special arrangements for assimilating late-developers. It also paid attention to the needs of girls in senior basic schools and laid it down that their courses should include cookery, laundry, needlework, homecrafts, the care of children and first aid.

In concluding its report the second committee made two revolutionary proposals. The first was that subject to agreed conditions, the Central Government should contribute not less than half of the approved net recurring expenditure on basic education in each province, while the second was that capital expenditure on buildings and equipment should be met out of loans.

The CABE, while approving generally the findings of both its committees, made the reservation that provincial governments, if they so desired, might introduce English as an optional subject at the senior basic stage. It is perhaps not surprising to find that the official members of the Board were unable to commit themselves to the financial recommendations which have just been mentioned.

It will, therefore, be apparent that when the CABE was called upon to submit to Government a scheme for post-war educational development, they had ready to hand a considerable amount of relevant material, so far as the lower stages of a national system were concerned. Moreover, the Wardha Scheme and the reports of the two committees, which it was decided to publish in a supplementary volume to the main report, covered the pedagogical aspects of basic education and so relieved the Board of the necessity of dealing with that in any detail.

The main task was to work out how long it would take and

how much it would cost to provide basic education for all children between 6 and 14, other than those between 11 and 14, who would be in secondary or high schools. The cost would be largely determined by the number of teachers required and the salaries necessary to secure them. On the basis of one teacher to every thirty children in junior basic and one to every twenty-five in senior basic schools—this does not mean, of course, that classes would be limited to these numbers—it was found that about 1,800,000 teachers would be needed for an estimated school population at that time of 52 million, excluding the 20 per cent between 11 and 14, who might be expected to be in other than basic schools. It must be remembered that these figures relate to an unpartitioned India.

The salaries prescribed by the CABE for basic teachers, which will be found in Appendix B, may seem anything but generous today, but they were considerably in advance of those then being paid. The Wardha Scheme, in spite of its aim to make basic education self-supporting, had proposed a minimum salary of Rs. 25 per month, which was also well above the average at the time. It was agreed by all concerned that the essential academic qualifications for a basic teacher should be matriculation or its equivalent, followed by two years' professional training. It was optimistically assumed that with better salaries and conditions of service 30 per cent of future matriculates might be attracted into the teaching profession. This led the Board to the conclusion that a system of universal, free and compulsory education for all boys and girls between the ages of 6 and 14 should be introduced as quickly as possible, but that in view of the practical difficulty of recruiting the requisite supply of trained teachers, it could hardly be done in less than forty years. While the Government of the new India accepted the basic system as the pattern to be followed, the Constitution laid it down that free and compulsory education for all children up to the age of 14 should be brought into operation in ten years. This was subsequently extended to sixteen years. This decision has been largely responsible for one of the current problems, which will be examined later.

SECONDARY OR HIGH SCHOOL EDUCATION

In regard to the content and organization of the secondary or high school stage of education, the CABE had no recent or comprehensive survey from which to draw material or inspiration, as it had in the case of basic education. In one sense, the secondary school can be regarded as the backbone of a national system, since to it the country must look for the preparatory training of its future leaders and experts in all walks of life. For obvious reasons, the Board did not consider secondary education for all as a practical proposition in the near future.

The Board recommended that the secondary or high school course, as distinct from the senior basic course, should cover not less than six years and the normal age of admission should be about 11. Places should be provided as soon as possible for at least one child in every five of the appropriate age-group. Entry to secondary schools should be on a selective basis and the methods of selection to be employed should receive the most careful consideration. Only those children should be admitted who showed promise of being able to take full advantage of the education provided. In order that no poor child of ability should be excluded, liberal assistance in the form of free places, scholarships and stipends should be available throughout the course.

Secondary or high schools should be of two main types, viz. (a) academic and (b) technical. The aim of both should be to provide a good all-round education with some preparation, in the later stages, for the careers which pupils would be likely to enter on leaving school. The curriculum in all cases should be as varied as circumstances permit and should not be unduly restricted by the requirements of universities or examining bodies. The medium of instruction should be the mother-tongue of the pupils; English should be a compulsory second language. As in the case of basic schools, the Board based the cost of its proposals on the new scales of salaries for teachers, which had been worked out by one of its committees in the previous year. What these were and how they were arrived at will be explained in the section which deals with the supply and training of teachers generally.

In 1952, the Government of India appointed a special commission to survey the whole field of secondary education. This was presided over by a distinguished educationist, Dr. A. L. Mudaliar, for many years Vice-Chancellor of Madras University. In addition to the Indian members, it contained two foreign experts, one from Britain and the other from the U.S.A. It did its work with great thoroughness and expedition and its report of over three hundred pages was published in the middle of 1953. Of its many recommendations, those which deal with the supply and training of teachers, school health, vocational guidance, administration and finance will be reserved for examination in connection with those sections of the CABE Report which relate to these essential services over the whole educational field.

The Commission's first recommendations are concerned with the secondary course as a preparation for a university career. Here, the Commission agrees with both the Sadler Commission and the CABE that the two-year intermediate stage should be abolished and its place be taken by the addition of one year to the secondary course and one to the course for a first degree. This means seven years of secondary education, divided into three years of junior secondary education, covering the same age-range as the middle or senior basic school, to be followed by a higher secondary stage of four years. The CABE, however, went further than the Commission by expressing the hope that, ultimately, the whole of the existing intermediate course could be covered in the secondary or high school. Although it is not specifically stated in the report, it may be assumed that the CABE contemplated lengthening the secondary course by a year and the provision in the earlier years, as the Mudaliar Report suggests, of a special one-year pre-university course for pupils from secondary schools which had not yet been given the extra year, or in other ways failed to reach the requisite grade.

The Commission's next recommendations are for the creation of Multi-purpose Schools, wherever possible, to provide varied courses likely to be of use and interest to pupils with diverse aims, aptitudes and abilities, and for the starting of a large number of technical courses, either in separate institutions or as part of multi-purpose schools. Although emphasis is laid in the CABE Report on the need to provide a variety of courses, including technical, at the secondary stage, it does not mention schools of the Multi-purpose type. How serious this omission was will be discussed later on.

The Commission naturally gave particular attention to the ways in which secondary education could contribute towards the solution of the country's urgent problems, as set out in the First Five-year Plan, published in the previous year. Of these, priority was assigned to the improvement of agriculture and the expansion of industry. To assist the former the Commission recommends that courses with an agricultural bias should be provided in rural secondary schools. In the case of the latter care should be taken to locate technical schools in close proximity to the industries which they are designed to serve, and representatives of these industries should be associated with their management. The advice of the AICTE should be taken in the framing of technical courses for schools. A further proposal, novel for India but reminiscent of the French Loi Astier, is that a small cess, to be called the "Industrial Education Cess", should be levied on industries and the proceeds used for the furtherance of technical education.

Under the heading of "Other Types of Schools" the Commission gives a provisional blessing to "Public Schools", presumably of the British pattern. This calls for some comment, if only because it suggests that ideas as to the value of such institutions have changed considerably since pre-1947 days. An Association of Indian Public Schools was founded in 1940 but the only member comparable with a British Public School was the Doon School at Dehra Dun. This interesting experiment was opened in the 1930's under a headmaster who had previously been on the staff of Eton College. The other original members of the Association were the five Princes Colleges. These were established earlier in the present century with the object of giving the future rulers of the princely states the sort of training that would help them to discharge the responsibilities that would be theirs later on. In the beginning, the young rulers-to-be lived in considerable state with their own houses, tutors and servants but gradually, thanks to some enlightened rajas on their governing bodies and some far-seeing principals, the palace atmosphere was replaced by the normal discipline and domestic arrangements of a good British boarding school. In most cases their gates had been opened before 1947 to boys not of the blood royal.

The Commission advised that these schools, now seventeen in number, should continue with central or state assistance where necessary, until it is possible to absorb them without loss into the pattern of national education, and that to open their doors still wider to really able boys, free studentships should be awarded on merit. In addition to schools of this type, it advocated the need for more residential schools to serve rural areas and to cater for those children whose parents' work might take them away from home. In pursuance of the same idea it also suggested the establishment of residential day schools to facilitate pupil-teacher contacts as well as recreational and extra-curricular activities. There is no reference to public schools in the CABE Report, possibly owing to the prevailing atmosphere, but it clearly recognizes the duty of higher education to produce an élite, not for its own sake but for that of the community. It is worth noting that papers submitted to the Education Commission of 1964–6 stress the need in existing circumstances of "merit" or "quality" schools for the ablest children.

The next issue with which the Commission dealt is what to do for girls at the secondary stage. While it advises State Governments to open separate schools for girls wherever there is a demand for them, it raises no objection to mixed or co-educational schools, provided that home science can be studied in all of them and that definite conditions are laid down to satisfy the special needs of girl pupils and women members of the teaching staff. The CABE Report makes no specific reference to co-education and this omission has been criticized. It may have been due to the presence on the Board of a number of Muslims, who, at that time, if they are not still, were strongly opposed to co-education.

Turning from the organizational pattern to the question of what should be taught in secondary schools and how it should be done, the Commission agreed with the CABE that the medium of instruction should be the mother-tongue, but added, as an alternative, the regional language. Developments since 1947 have given the regional languages an importance which were not attached to them previously. It also recommended that linguistic minorities should be cared for on the lines suggested by the CABE.

The Commission's next proposal is of particular interest, also in the light of what has happened since Independence. It is that at the middle school stage—which may be taken in the context to mean junior secondary and not senior basic—every pupil should be taught at least two languages, Hindi and English being introduced at the beginning of this stage. Since the question of how many and what languages should be included in the secondary curriculum has been a live and, at times, a controversial issue since the Republic was established, it may seem curious that the Commission offers no clear guidance as to what should be done to find room in the curriculum for Hindi and English in those schools where the mother-tongue of the pupils is not Hindi. The evolution of what is called the "Three Language Formula" and its curricular implications will be dealt with later in this book.

Both the Commission and the CABE agreed that, in addition to languages, all pupils in secondary schools, whatever academic, technical, agricultural or other diversified courses they might choose in their last two or three years at school, should have a common core of subjects like mathematics, general science and social studies. There was also substantial agreement in listing the optional subjects from which schools might make a selection suitable to their character, situation and resources. It is good to note that prominence is given in these lists to subjects like art, crafts, music and physical training, which, because they were not included in examination syllabuses, were unpopular in the old days.

Two divergencies between the two reports should be recorded. The first is that the CABE, with a six-year course in mind, would allow diversified courses to start at class IX, whereas the Commission, with a seven-year course, would start them at class X. The second is that the CABE, with the object of keeping schools reasonably small and economizing on equipment, favour different types of school rather than diversified courses in the same school.

The Commission was, not surprisingly, concerned about finding a solution to the long-standing problem of ensuring a supply of reliable, up-to-date textbooks for use in schools. Little is said about this in the CABE Report but a year after its publication the Board did appoint a committee to look into this matter. It is not known whether any steps have yet been taken to implement its suggestions. It is outside the scope of this chapter to inquire why the production of textbooks in India should have been, for so long, at the worst a racket and at the best a means of supplementing teachers' salaries. Nor is it possible to examine in any detail the Commission's proposals for reform. That they took a serious view of the current situation is evident from the fact that they advised the setting-up by each State of a high-powered Textbook Committee, the prescribed membership being a judge of the High Court, a member of the Public Services Commission, a vice-chancellor, a headmaster, a headmistress, two distinguished educationists and the Director of Public Instruction. The Commission's final recommendation in this connection is also enlightening; frequent changes in textbooks and other books prescribed for study should be discouraged. If this advice has been acted upon, some teachers' incomes will have suffered.

The report then goes on to deal with dynamic methods of teaching, the education of character, guidance and counselling, the physical welfare of pupils and a new approach to examinations and evaluation. Since this section is concerned with structure rather than methodology, discussion of the many interesting suggestions made in regard to the matters listed above must be deferred for the moment. The same applies to the final proposals in the report, which relate to the improvement of the teaching personnel and various problems of administration.

It may be well, before concluding this section of the present chapter, to emphasize the fact once more that just as thinking and planning about Indian education did not begin with the CABE Report, so thinking and planning about the all-important secondary stage did not end with the Mudaliar Commission. A great deal has been thought, written and done in the secondary field since 1953. Limitations of space, if no other reasons, have made it necessary to confine this survey to the two most authoritative pronouncements that have been made during the last twenty-five years. If, however, the Education Planning Commission produces its report before this book has to go to press, it will be reviewed in a final chapter.

UNIVERSITY EDUCATION

It is clear from the tone of its chapter on universities that the CABE was seriously concerned about the existing situation. The Sapru Committee's Report in 1935 had called attention to the alarming extent of unemployment among university graduates. Even for minor posts in the Government services there were often as many as sixty or seventy applicants with university degrees.

The CABE, while attributing the major share of the blame for this to the economic system, could find little evidence that universities were making any systematic attempts to adjust their output to the capacity of the labour market to absorb it. In addition to the shortage of openings in industry for graduates at that time, the lack of adequate financial resources led universities to give preference in enrolment to students of art subjects, who would be much cheaper to educate than those choosing science, technology or medicine. In other ways also, despite many admirable features and achievements, Indian universities, as a whole, were far from fulfilling the true function of a university, as defined by Cardinal Newman 100 years before. He wrote :

> A university aims at raising the intellectual tone of society, at cultivating the public mind, at purifying the national taste, at supplying true principles to popular aspiration, at giving enlargement and sobriety to the ideas of the age, at facilitating the exercise of political power and refining the intercourse of private life.

In order to raise standards all round, the CABE proposed that the conditions for admission should be revised with the object of ensuring that students were capable of taking full advantage of a university course. To promote this object, financial assistance should be available for students of promise who might otherwise be debarred by poverty. Following the Sadler and anticipating the Mudaliar Commission, the Board advised that the intermediate course should be abolished. Ultimately, in its opinion, the whole of this should be covered at the secondary stage, but for the time being the first year should be transferred to the high schools and the second to the universities. This meant that the minimum length of a course leading to a first degree would be three years. The need to set a high standard in postgraduate studies and, above all, in pure and applied research, received special emphasis. To ensure closer personal contacts between teachers and students, the tutorial system should be widely extended.

The Board then made a new and important proposal that to prevent overlapping by co-ordinating activities and to allocate such additional funds as might be forthcoming from government or other sources, a University Grants Committee should be constituted. To allay inevitable suspicions as far as possible, it was laid down that this body, in the beginning at any rate, should be purely advisory and have no executive or financial powers. As was only to be expected, Indian universities were anything but enthusiastic about the new idea, but a visit to India a year or so later by Sir Walter Moberley, then Secretary of the UGC in Britain, did much to reassure them that no serious invasion of their autonomy was threatened. The very valuable work done by the UGC since Independence will be described in a later chapter.

The first action of real importance to be taken by the Government of the new India in the sphere of education was the appointment at the end of 1948 of a University Commission. Its chairman was Dr. S. Radhakrishnan, until recently President of India. As an eminent scholar, a former Vice-Chancellor of Benares University, Spalding Professor of Eastern religions and ethics at the University of Oxford and a man of wide human sympathies, he was an admirable choice for the post. Associated with him were nine other men of distinction in the university world, including two Americans and one Briton. Among the Indian members was Dr. A. L. Mudaliar, chairman subsequently of the Secondary Education Commission whose report has been dealt with at some length in the previous section. There was no woman on the University Commission, an omission that was to be repaired later in the case of the Secondary Education Commission.

The terms of reference of the Commission could hardly have been more comprehensive. They covered not only such pedagogical issues as standards of admission, length and content of courses, the relation between teaching and research, examinations and student discipline, but also administrative and financial problems with special regard to the need for more places and more money. No time was wasted and in August 1949 the Commission produced its report of 747 pages, which included 207 recommendations. This was supplemented by a second volume of evidence and statistics. No attempt will be made here to explore the whole of this vast store and the best course may be to concentrate on those recommendations that either go beyond or conflict with those of the CABE.

Many people, both inside and outside India, have expressed surprise that the new Government, in planning its approach to the urgent problem of educational development, should have begun with the top storey rather than the basement but the explanation is supplied by the Commission itself, when it writes :

> Our leaders have drawn up ambitious plans for the industrialization of our country. . . . If these schemes are to be realized, we have

to increase the number of professional colleges, agricultural, medical and engineering, to produce the requisite number of graduates and set up throughout the country technical schools, which will supply the much larger number of technicians needed for the purpose.

The first series of recommendations is concerned with the question of making university teaching more attractive by improving the conditions of service and widening the avenues of promotion. This, of course, is in harmony with the views expressed by the CABE. The next five chapters examine *in extenso* the various subjects or faculties which should find a place in the programme of a modern Indian university, and the methods to be used to make the teaching of them as realistic and effective as possible. A special chapter is devoted to professional education, which includes agriculture, commerce, engineering and technology, law, medicine, education and new professions. This part of the report ends with a chapter on religious education.

To return to the early part of this section, the heading of the first chapter of the report, "Standards of Teaching", is rather misleading, as it contains several important recommendations, which cannot be regarded as strictly pedagogical. The first of them, for instance, lays it down that the standard of admission to a university course should correspond to that of the current intermediate examination, i.e. after the completion of twelve years' study at a school and an intermediate college, and this leads to a further recommendation that in each province a large number of well-staffed intermediate colleges with classes IX–XII or VI–XII should be established. The use of the word "intermediate" here is rather confusing, for it is clear that what the Commission had in mind is not more two-year intermediate colleges of the existing type but something on the lines of the higher secondary school, favoured later on by the Mudaliar Commission.

There is, however, no indication that the University Commission shared the hope both of the CABE and the Secondary Education Commission that the first year, if not both years, of the intermediate course could be covered in up-graded high schools with classes XI and XII.

The Commission next proposed the opening of numerous occupational institutes, to which pupils who, presumably, are not cut out for or cannot afford a university career, can be diverted after ten or twelve years of schooling. These institutes should provide both full-time and part-time instruction in a large variety of subjects and at different levels.

Of the remaining recommendations in this chapter two or three must have come as considerable shocks both to the authorities and the students of the Indian universities of the day. One is to limit the number of students in the arts and sciences of a teaching university to 3000 and in affiliated colleges to 1500. Another is to increase the number of working days to a minimum of 180 in the year, exclusive of examination days, while a third proposes that there shall be no "prescribed" textbooks for any course of study. Less controversial are the proposals for a big extension in the use of tutorials and a great improvement in libraries and laboratories.

The next three chapters, which deal comprehensively with the content and duration of the courses leading to various degrees, call for no comment at this stage, but the last chapter in this section, which is about religious education, deserves mention, if only because it copes with a subject which defeated the CABE. The Board first appointed a committee with a neutral chairman, on which Hindus and Muslims had equal representation. After several meetings the committee reported to the Board that it had failed to arrive at any agreed recommendation. The Board reconstituted the committee with a few changes of personnel and asked it to try again. After several further meetings the committee had to tell the Board that the only suggestion, upon which it could agree, was that colleges and schools should start the day with a brief period of silent meditation. When this came up at the next meeting of the Board, an amendment was moved and carried that during this period there should be no obligation upon any pupil or student to meditate upon religion! In view of the CABE's experience, which was, of course, before Partition, it is interesting to find that the first recommendation of the University

Commission reads: "All educational institutions should start work with a few minutes for silent meditation." It then goes on to suggest that in the first year of the degree course the lives of the great religious leaders of the world should be studied, in the second year selections from the principal scriptures and in the third the central problems of the philosophy of religion.

The next main issue to be tackled was the thorny question of the medium of instruction in universities and other institutes of higher education. As the Commission observes: "No other problem has caused greater controversy among educationalists. . . . The question is so wrapped up in sentiment, that it is difficult to consider it in a calm and detached manner." The fact that the new India must have a federal language is accepted, and Hindi is preferred to the other Indian languages, which can claim a literature of their own. Although English can no longer be officially employed as a lingua franca, its importance as a means of intercommunication in a rapidly changing world is fully recognized, and its study must be maintained at a high level both in high schools and universities. Other recommendations to be noted are those relating to the development of the federal language by assimilating words that have entered Indian languages from various sources; the adaptation to Indian phonetics and scripts of the international technical and scientific terminology; the use for the federal language of a revised form of the Devanagri script. The Commission advocated the teaching, in all higher secondary schools, of three languages, the regional, the federal and English. At all the higher stages instruction is to be imparted through the regional language, with the option to use the federal language for some subjects or for all subjects. It is not clear, however, what is to happen when the mother-tongue of a student is not the same as the regional language.

The many useful things which the Commission has to say about the need for improving the technique of examination and making them less restrictive on progress as well as its proposals in regard to university administration and finance will be examined later.

TECHNICAL, COMMERCIAL AND ART EDUCATION

The policy of rapid industrialization upon which the new India has embarked, and the manpower and other problems involved in it make the chapter in the CABE Report which deals with technical instruction of more than usual interest. The Board was fortunate to have at its disposal not only the Abbott–Wood Report of 1937—Mr. Abbott was the Chief Inspector of Technical Institutions under the Board of Education in England—but also the report of a special committee which it had appointed to study this subject two years before. In approving its recommendations, the Board stated : "In view of the prospective needs of post-war industry and commerce for skilled technicians and in order to cater for those who will derive greater benefit from a practical course, the establishment of an efficient system of technical education at all stages is a matter of great urgency."

The committee, which duly acknowledged its indebtedness to the Abbott–Wood Report, made twenty-one recommendations and most of them are sufficiently relevant to current problems to merit quotation here. Technical education, it says, should be regarded as an integral part of any educational system and as in no way inferior to education of the academic type. It should include commercial subjects and art in relation to industry. Agricultural education should also be treated as one of its essential branches and both senior basic and secondary schools in rural areas should have an agricultural bias. In order to provide suitable training for the different grades of workers required, the following main grades of technical institutions should be available, viz. (a) junior technical or industrial or trade schools, (b) technical high schools and (c) senior technical institutions. Of these (a) and (b) will normally provide full-time instruction preparatory to employment, while (c) will also provide part-time instruction for those already in employment. The type and duration of part-time courses should be settled in consultation with employers and in accordance with the needs of the locality. In Indian conditions it may be desirable that part-time classes should be held in the day rather than in the evening. Wherever circumstances permit, polytechnics are to be preferred to mono-technics. One external examination at the end of the course should be sufficient; other examinations should be conducted internally. There should be an adequate system of scholarships and maintenance allowances to ensure that no one having the necessary aptitude and ability should be prevented, by lack of means, from pursuing a course in a technical institution. Hostels should be provided wherever necessary.

The committee's most significant recommendations in the light of what has happened since, are those relating to the administration of technical education. Technical high schools, junior technical, trade and industrial schools should be administered by provincial governments, but all technical education beyond this stage, other than that given in the technological departments of universities, should be placed under the control of a central body, which should have on it representatives of all the interests concerned. This body should be set up as soon as possible. Another argument put forward in favour of central control is that while for obvious reasons technical and commercial institutions should be located in or near industrial and commercial areas, students from other areas should have an equal opportunity of admission. Though the Board does not say so, parochial hurdles in the educational field are not confined to India. As a help to co-ordinating technical education on an all-India basis, the Board welcomed the recent formation of the Association of Principals of Technical Institutions (APTI) and suggested that it should have adequate repesentation on the proposed central controlling body.

Then follow two recommendations which, in the circumstances of the time, were certainly courageous. The first is that as a corollary to technical education in its higher stages being administered by a central body, the cost of it should be borne by the Central Government. The second is that all technical education, except that provided by universities, should come under the Education Department of the Central or Provincial Government, as the case may be, but it should maintain close contact with the other departments concerned with industry and commerce.

The remaining recommendations relate to the types, content and duration of the courses to be provided and the qualifications and conditions of service of technical teachers. It is laid down that all teachers of technical subjects should have had some first-hand experience of some branch of industry or commerce. They should also be encouraged, while teaching, to keep in touch with the relevant branch of industry or commerce, and, with this object in view, they should be permitted to undertake consulting practice or commissions, subject to approved conditions.

It is a significant sign of the changing attitude of the Central Government towards its educational responsibilities that instead of being shocked at the audacity of some of the Board's proposals, it proceeded to act upon them. By 1946 the central controlling body was in existence and functioning. It was called the All-India Council for Technical Education (AICTE). To meet the suscepti-bilities of the provincial governments it was given purely advisory duties in the first instance, but, under the inspiring chairmanship of Mr. N. Sarkar, at one time Education Member of the Viceroy's Executive Council, it soon began to gain their confidence and to exercise a powerful influence over major developments in the technical sphere. With the aid of the APTI it set about formu-lating a national policy in this field, with national standards in all the major branches at the degree and diploma levels.

One of the earliest, and probably still the most valuable of the projects sponsored by the AICTE, was that put forward for the establishment of four technical institutes of the highest grade. The fact that they were often referred to at the time as the Indian MITs (Massachusetts Institute of Technology) will give those familiar with that famous institution some idea of what the Council was aiming at. They were to be situated in Bengal, Bombay and Madras, and though the location of the fourth was left open, Kanpur has since been selected. What has happened since Independence to them and to technical development generally will be described in some detail in a later chapter.

ADULT EDUCATION

Apart from a few literacy campaigns, launched by Congress Ministries in the decade before 1947, the permanent results of which hardly repaid the time and enthusiasm expended on them, adult education in the fuller sense was the least cultivated of all the sectors of the education field. Even at the top, the universities showed little interest in extra-mural work, and their so-called extension lectures were mostly opportunities for some professor to display his talents before an admiring audience of personal friends. Consequently, when the CABE came to formulate its proposals for adult education, the practical experience at its disposal was of little value and it had to depend, as in other cases, on the report of a committee which it had appointed as early as 1938 to survey this field. After a careful reconsideration of its proposals, the Board embodied most of them in its plan.

The first problem to be tackled was obviously that of illiteracy, and not merely of illiteracy alone but of what steps should be taken to see that adults, once made literate, had both the inducement and the opportunity to remain so. To create a reasonably educated population within a reasonable time, the introduction of a free and compulsory system of elementary instruction must be complemented by the provision of facilities for adult education on the widest possible scale. In view of recent depressing experiences, the Board issued a warning that literacy must be treated as a means to further education and not as an end in itself. It goes on to urge that whatever subjects are included in the curriculum and whatever the teaching methods adopted, the form in which instruction is given must be intelligible and interesting to an adult student; it should be closely related to his occupation, his personal interests and the social and economic conditions under which he lives.

Before turning to teaching techniques, the Board defined what it meant by an adult. Boys under the age of 12 should not be admitted to an adult centre in any circumstances, and boys attending a day school full-time should not be encouraged to attend evening classes as well. It is unnecessary to fix any age limits in the case of girls who may wish to join adult classes for women.

In view of the wider connotation given in the new India to adult education, it is interesting to find the Board advising that every effort should be made to enlist the aid of voluntary agencies, including those whose primary objects are not educational, since adult education, fully interpreted, is one branch of social reconstruction. There must, of course, be proper safeguards against the movement being used for religious or political propaganda. Universities should expand and popularize the work of their extra-mural departments. The committee had suggested that universities should also provide opportunities for adult students of exceptional ability to go on to take a university course, but the Board doubted whether this idea would commend itself to the university authorities.

The Board recognized that as things are in India, it is even more important to provide adult education for women than it is for men, but, in their case, the approach must be more varied and less formal.

Mechanical aids to learning, such as the radio, cinema, gramophone and magic lantern—this was before the television era—can be used with great effect in adult education. To enable these to be employed more widely, steps should be taken to increase the supply and reduce the cost. A library is an essential adjunct to every adult centre.

There were two other suggestions by the committee about which the Board had some doubts. While agreeing that in attacking illiteracy in urban areas the co-operation of employers of labour and associations of workers should be enlisted, it could not see its way to put them under any legal obligation to contribute towards the cost. The other was that students in universities and pupils in the upper forms of high schools should be required to do a period of social service before leaving, though this idea might deserve further examination.

As in the case of compulsory basic education, the Board considered the time factor. Even if it was possible to start on this in the immediate future, there would still be 90 million illiterates under 40 to be dealt with. The Board planned to do this in twenty-five years. The peak of the literacy campaign would be reached about the fifteenth year, and thereafter an increasing amount of money and teaching power would be available for post-literacy work.

The Board's recommendations in regard to the supply and training of teachers for adult classes and the way in which the movement should be administered will be found under the relevant headings in the next chapter.

CHAPTER 6

Prevalent Assumptions—
the Essential Services

THE SUPPLY AND TRAINING OF TEACHERS

AN OBVIOUS assumption about any education system, formal or
otherwise, is that, if it is to succeed, it must be able to rely on an
adequate supply of competent teachers at all levels. Few people
would dissent from this, and yet there is hardly anywhere in the
world, even today, where good teachers receive rewards and
recognition commensurate with the debt which society owes
them. This applies with special force to teachers in the lower
storeys of the educational structure. Whatever may be the position
in the more advanced countries today, the result in underdeveloped countries like India is that many teachers at the
elementary and junior secondary stages fall below what may be
regarded as the essential minimum, so far as academic background and professional training are concerned. In India, in
1941, out of just over half a million teachers in primary and
junior secondary schools over two-fifths were untrained and a still
larger proportion had finished their own schooling before reaching matriculation standard. It is, therefore, of fundamental
importance to assess the efficacy of the steps that have been taken
since then, not only to improve the quality of the staffs in existing
schools but also to attract into the profession the vastly increased
numbers of competent young men and women that the attainment of the objectives set out in the Constitution will demand.

The first step in this direction was taken in 1942, when the
CABE appointed a committee to consider what should be done
about the recruitment, training and conditions of service of

teachers below the university grade. The findings of this committee formed the basis of the Board's recommendations two years later. So far as output was concerned, it was found that the existing training institutions could do little more than meet normal wastage and possibly provide some training for teachers, already in service, who were untrained. There were also serious defects in the organization and methods of these institutions. Apart from being generally out of line with modern requirements, there was a lack of uniformity in the duration and content of courses and, in many cases, little or no attention was paid to co-ordinating theory with practice.

In order to inaugurate a more up-to-date and uniform system, it was proposed that there should be three separate types of training institution for (a) pre-primary teachers, (b) basic, i.e. primary and middle teachers and (c) non-graduate teachers in high schools, and that the normal periods of training should be, for pre-primary teachers two years, for primary or junior basic two years, for senior basic or middle three years and for non-graduates in high schools two years. These proposals follow those of the Wardha Committee for basic teachers, the extra year in the case of senior basic teachers being to enable them to receive special training in crafts.

For graduate teachers in secondary or high schools one year of professional training was suggested, though a longer course would be needed for those undertaking research or aspiring to special degrees in education. The Board did not recommend the setting up of institutions to train technical teachers, as they would get their practical training in industry and their pedagogical training in the institutes themselves. The question of what should be done to train teachers for pre-primary schools and special schools for handicapped children was deferred for the time being.

In its report the Board supplemented the proposals of its committee with two useful suggestions. The first was that to increase the supply of women teachers, every encouragement should be given to married women and widows to enter or re-enter the profession. The second was that to induce more matriculates to take up teaching, suitable pupils, who showed some inclination in that direction, should be picked out during the last two years of their secondary career and given the chance of visiting other schools and trying their hands at actual teaching under the eyes of their heads and the local inspectors. Those who needed them should receive liberal stipends. This method might also be used to sift doubtful cases at an early stage and so help to ensure that intending teachers, before being admitted to training schools or colleges, were prima facie likely to make good.

The Secondary Education Commission devoted a long and important chapter to the "Improvement of the Teaching Personnel". It agreed with the CABE that there should be only two types of training institution for teachers in primary, middle and secondary or high schools, one for those whose academic qualification was matriculation or the school leaving certificate and the other for graduates. It also agreed that the period of training for the former should be a minimum of two years and for the latter one year, though this might be extended with profit to two years in due course. Further recommendations common to both bodies are that there should be no fees in training colleges, that maintenance allowances should be available for those who need them and that it should be a normal part of the activities of training institutions to provide facilities for research and refresher courses, as well as residential accommodation, wherever necessary. The Commission made some useful suggestions that are not to be found in the CABE Report. One was that to help meet the shortage of women teachers, special part-time courses should be organized, and another that the syllabus for all intending teachers should include training in one or more of the various extra-curricular activities. It also proposed that no trained graduate should be allowed to sit for the degree of Master in Education until he or she had done three years actual teaching. Another rather novel but potentially fertile idea was that there should be a free exchange between professors in training colleges, heads of schools and inspectors.

The Commission was deeply impressed by the urgent need to

attract more and better recruits into the teaching profession. For this purpose it drew up improved scales of pay. It may be well to defer details of the actual salaries proposed until both they and those proposed by the CABE can be compared not only with those in force today but also with those recommended by the EC. This will be done in Appendix B. In order that the effect on remuneration of rises in the cost of living and other relevant factors might be kept in sight, the Commission proposed that the States should set up reviewing committees with arbitration boards to look into appeals and grievances. In the teachers' interest, States were also urged to introduce what was called the "triple benefit system", which combined pensions, provident funds and insurance. Teachers should also enjoy free education for their children, free medical attention and treatment and liberal arrangements for travel and study leave. In return for these concessions teachers must be prepared to give up private tuition.

In the chapter about University education in the CABE Report there is a somewhat cautious recommendation that steps should be taken to improve the conditions of service, including the remuneration of university and college teachers, where those then in operation were not attracting men and women of the requisite calibre. The reason why no more definite proposals were forthcoming was probably that in the case of this branch, unlike that of most others, the Board had no specific report of a committee at its disposal. Subsequent to the publication of its Report the CABE did appoint a committee to consider the recruitment, training and conditions of service of teachers in universities. Its recommendations in regard to salaries and those of the Universities Commission four years later will be reviewed in Appendix B in relation to the present situation. Very little, however, is said about professional training for university teachers. It seems to be assumed in India, and, indeed, in other parts of the world, that the respective values to be attached to teaching ability and academic qualifications vary inversely, as one ascends the educational ladder. Yet many graduates may well feel that they might have got better degrees if some of their lecturers had had even a rudimentary acquaintance with the art of imparting knowledge.

THE HEALTH SERVICE

Poverty, ignorance and low hygienic standards, both personal and public, make this service unusually important in India. In the earlier years of this century spasmodic attempts were made in most provinces to provide medical inspection for school children, but, in most cases, these were limited to the larger towns, and, owing to the dearth of doctors and nurses, they only touched the fringes of the school population. More attention was given to secondary than to primary schools, where, for obvious reasons, this work should start. With rare exception girls were left out of these schemes altogether.

At last, in 1941, the CABE and the Central Advisory Board of Health set up a joint committee to report on the "Medical Inspection of School Children and the Teaching of Hygiene in Schools". On the findings of this committee the recommendations in the CABE Report are for the most part based. After expressing its grave concern that so many earlier schemes had been abandoned owing to financial stringency, official parsimony or other reasons implying indifference on the part of those in authority, the joint committee dealt, in turn, with medical inspection, treatment and follow-up, nutrition, personal and environmental hygiene, the teaching of hygiene in schools, training schools and colleges, physical education and corporate activities. It also outlined the administrative set-up that would be needed to stage a successful attack along the whole front. Its conclusions and recommendations were enumerated under fifty-six headings; all that can be done here is to select a few of these to illustrate the sort of service that was contemplated.

It was estimated that at least half the children attending school would be found to require medical attention or observation. It was desirable that the necessary inspection should begin at an early age, and for this reason, the committee was in favour of school life starting at 5 rather than 6. It deprecated, too, many inspections, and felt that one at admission, one at 11 and one at 14 should suffice; pupils in secondary schools should have a final inspection before leaving. Medical inspection should only be carried out by a qualified doctor with special training; it should take place during school hours and, if possible, the parents should be present with the physical instructor, if any. All children should have medical record cards, which should go with them if they moved from one school to another.

Medical inspection is clearly of little use without proper arrangements for treatment and follow-up, and it reflects on the poverty prevalent in India that the committee felt it necessary to lay special emphasis on the provision of supplementary nourishment. All children should have a midday meal, either brought from home or supplied at the school; parents able to pay should be required to contribute.

The recommendations about personal and environmental hygiene are of considerable interest in the light of the conditions which then obtained—and may still obtain—in many primary schools, both in villages and in the poorer urban districts. Few will disagree with the committee when it says that the practice of personal hygiene by school children depends largely on the example set by the teacher but it may have been expecting too much in existing circumstances when it prescribes for all teachers good physique and sound general health as well as high standards of cleanliness.

Turning to environment, the committee advised that where schools are housed in buildings not designed for the purpose, the local health officer should be consulted as to their suitability. No one familiar with schools of this type in India will question the wisdom of this advice. The next proposal related to the appointment of a body of experts to determine proper standards of lighting, ventilation and heating, with particular reference to new schools. One member of the committee recalled the surprising results of such an investigation in another and more advanced country. Other points raised were the importance of ensuring an ample and wholesome supply of water for drinking and other purposes, and seeing that latrines are maintained in a sanitary state. It was hoped that every encouragement would be given to the children to take a pride in keeping their school and its surrounding area clean.

The next section dealt with the teaching of hygiene. So far as children are concerned, this should begin as early as possible; at the outset it should be on strictly practical lines and devoted mainly to personal cleanliness. Hygiene should be a compulsory subject in all training schools, and intending teachers should be taught by demonstrators to recognize common defects in children and to give elementary treatment. Textbooks dealing with hygiene in Indian conditions and embodying the fundamental principles of nutrition should be made available in all the main Indian languages.

The Secondary Education (Mudaliar) Commission devotes a chapter to the physical welfare of pupils. Its recommendations in regard to medical inspection and treatment and the maintenance of proper nutritional standards, particularly in residential schools, are in line with those of the Joint Committee. It goes beyond them in suggesting that secondary schools, wherever possible, should help not only in keeping their own buildings and grounds in good order, but also in improving the sanitation of the surrounding area and thereby learning to appreciate the dignity of manual labour. It also takes a wider view of the part which physical education can play in the general life of a school and gives a warning that physical activities should be made to suit the individual and his or her capacity for physical endurance. Facilities for training teachers of physical education need to be greatly expanded, and these teachers, when trained, should have the same status as other teachers with comparable qualifications. The Commission, possibly, is expecting a little too much when it prescribes that all teachers below the age of 40 should actively participate in the physical side of the school programme.

The University (Radhakrishnan) Commission, whose report had appeared four years before that of the Secondary Commission, had already laid down in considerable detail what universities ought to do to promote the physical welfare of their students. Although its advice about such things as medical attention, feeding and lodging arrangements, games facilities and so on are in line with what one would expect to find in a good modern university in most parts of the world, to implement some of the proposals, e.g. that each university should have its own hospital, would put a considerable strain on the resources of many institutions before the days when substantial help could be expected from the Central Government through the good offices of the UGC.

Although there is little specific reference in any of the official reports to health services for technical students, it may be assumed that what has been recommended for pupils in secondary schools will also apply to those in junior technical schools and technical high schools. Similarly, students in full-time attendance at senior institutions may look forward to being given the same advantages as their co-evals in ordinary universities. How far recreative facilities are required for part-time students in polytechnics will depend, in most cases, on the extent to which employers in the industrial areas of the new India recognize their obligation to their employees in this respect.

Little need be said about health services for adult students for, in regard to medical attention, they will be dependent for a long time to come on what is available for the general public in their districts. There is, however, great scope for classes in all aspects of health education and physical training and these may well be popularized by the high priority now given to family planning.

THE EDUCATION OF THE HANDICAPPED

Few people in these days would deny that provision for those children who are physically or mentally handicapped should form an essential part of any national system of education but, as the CABE points out, governments in India, whether central or provincial, had shown little interest in this subject and had left it almost entirely to voluntary effort. Chapter 9 of the CABE Report, therefore, represents the first official attempt to analyse the problem, estimate its extent and suggest ways of dealing with it.

Physically handicapped children fall into three main categories, viz. (a) those who are deficient in one or more of the senses like the blind, the deaf, the blind and deaf, deaf-mutes and so on, (b) those who are retarded by motor deficiency, including respiratory, heart and orthopaedic cases and (c) those who are defective in speech. Mentally handicapped children may be broadly classified under two main heads, viz. (a) those born with intelligence below the average and (b) those who are "backward", owing to some form of maladjustment or physical ailment which causes temporary retardation.

If intelligence tests may be accepted as a fairly reliable index of the educability of a child, those born with subnormal intelligences may again be subdivided into three groups, viz. (i) those with IQs between 85 and 70, usually termed "dull", (ii) those with IQs between 70 and 55, the "feeble-minded", (iii) those with IQs below 55, the "imbeciles". For psychological and other reasons it is not advisable to separate the dull from the brighter pupils, though they may need special attention, and the same applies to those of the feeble-minded who will not be a disturbing influence in class. Imbeciles, for obvious reasons, will need special care either at home or in institutions. "Backward" children may be more simply divided into those who try and those who do not. The Board investigated in some detail the many possible causes of backwardness.

In outlining ways and means of dealing with the various types of handicap listed in the report, the Board was guided by the fundamental principle that the handicapped should not, if it can possibly be helped, be segregated from normal children. Only when the nature or extent of their defect makes it necessary should they be sent to special schools or institutions. It agreed, however, that the blind and deaf need special educational arrangements with specially trained teachers. Another important point is that care should be taken to train the handicapped, wherever possible, for remunerative employment and to find jobs for them, which makes the provision of after-care essential.

There has been no official inquiry or action specially directed to this particular problem since 1947. This has been mainly because the necessary funds and trained personnel could not be produced in the face of more urgent claims, but it is clear that the need to do something about it as soon as possible has been in the minds of those concerned with health problems generally, and there is every reason to believe that it will receive the attention which it merits in the report of the EC.

RECREATIVE AND SOCIAL ACTIVITIES

Although the CABE recognized the value of these activities for those at school or college, for adolescents, who had left school and, at a later stage, for adults in the wider sphere of social service, they were rather at a loss to suggest how best to adapt to Indian conditions methods that had been tried with success in many Western countries.

So far as the school and college period was concerned, the information before them indicated that the importance of extra-curricular activities as a means of developing the social impulses of growing boys and girls, was being increasingly recognized by Indian educators, and that plenty of clubs and societies, as well as organized games, were to be found in most high schools and universities.

The real problem was how best to provide recreation and social guidance for young people in the age-group of 14–20, who were no longer receiving formal education. Much had been done in this direction in recent years in the more advanced countries, but the Board was not satisfied that the kind of youth club or youth movement which had proved successful elsewhere would suit Indian conditions, especially in the remoter rural areas. Nevertheless, the importance of providing friendly and unobtrusive guidance for young persons no longer under school discipline and exposed to new experiences, problems and temptations, was so patent that the Board finally concluded that there ought to be an Indian Youth Movement under the auspices of an All-India Council for Social Service. A major difficulty was where to look for leaders with the rather rare combination of qualities required for success in this work. The Board thought it possible that after the war, suitable recruits for this service might be found among demobilized officers and NCOs. Up to 1947, however, little or nothing was done either to cater for the recreational needs of adolescents or to make a start in the larger field of social service for the adult population, although the latter had been explored by a committee appointed by the Board in 1941.

Fortunately, as has been noted in the section about adult education, the whole approach to the educational problems of the adult population has been greatly widened since 1947. Apart from the needs of young people at school or at college, which have been closely examined by both the Mudaliar and Radha-krishnan Commissions, the many schemes for local devolution, rural and urban, which have appeared since 1947, have not over-looked the part to be played by recreative activities not only in broadening the outlook of the poorer classes but also in brighten-ing their lives. There is great work to be done in this connection by all those concerned with Block Development.

EMPLOYMENT BUREAUX

Prior to 1944 a few careers masters had found a place on the staffs of the more progressive high schools but otherwise very little indeed was being done by Indian educators to find a market for their output, either by guidance to parents or by contact with potential employers. This was all the more serious because at that time openings to progressive and remunerative employment were scarcer in India than in many other countries.

The CABE regarded the establishment of employment bureaux as an integral part of its plan for future development and sum-marized their main functions as follows :

(a) To establish contact with all schools, from which, on completing the course, boys and girls normally enter employment, and to advise parents and head teachers in the light of school records, aptitude and other tests and the openings for employment available in the area, as to the occupations, which leavers should seek to enter.

(b) To establish contact with employers of labour in the area with a view to (i) ascertaining what openings are likely to be available and the essential qualifications for filling them, (ii) persuading employers to use the employment bureaux and (iii) minimizing, as far as possible, blind-alley occupations.

(c) To place in employment those leavers who have not already obtained posts for themselves.

(d) To arrange for the after-care of young workers in order to deal with misfits.

(e) To establish and supervise, in co-operation with employers, regular systems of apprenticeship in those trades for which these are suitable.

Here, as in the case of the other services, the Board laid emphasis on the need to employ only trained experts. Subject to proper contacts with other departments concerned, employment bureaux should be administered by the Department of Education.

The Mudaliar Commission fully shared the views of the CABE that guidance at the secondary stage was of great importance and that it deserved much greater attention on the part of the responsible authorities. It realized, however, that it would take time to provide all schools with trained guidance officers and careers masters and that to help the States, the Centre should take the initiative in opening, in the different regions, centres for the training of these people. In the meantime, much could be done to broaden pupils' understanding of the scope, nature and significance of various occupations if films could be prepared of industries at work and these could be supplemented by actual visits, wherever possible.

Although national planning was still in an embryonic stage, when the Radhakrishnan Commission began its work, the members could have been in no doubt as to the effect which rapid industrialization and its demand for skilled manpower was going to have on universities and other institutions of higher education. A long and important chapter is devoted to professional education, which covers agriculture, engineering and technology, commerce, law, medicine, education and the new professions likely to come into prominence as national development proceeds. Universities are urged to adjust their courses to the requirements of the new age and to establish such contacts with the professional world as will bring home to students not only the opportunities which the new era has to offer, but also the social obligations implicit in a professional career. The need for all universities to have employment bureaux with experts in charge is fully recognized, but special emphasis is laid on impressing on students from the day they enter and through their course what they can and should contribute to the welfare of their country.

An important assumption, which has led in recent years to the appointment, by Government, of a number of manpower and other committees, is that the university output, which comprises or should comprise the pick of the nation's brains, should be kept as closely in line as possible with the present and prospective openings in the employment market. This may seem an obvious proposition to those who live in countries with a reasonably stabilized economy, but it is not so simple in India, where a fluctuating economy and conventional attitudes towards certain types of employment combine to complicate the issue.

Administration and Finance

The last chapter in the CABE Report is, in some respects, the most important of all, not merely because the best schemes will fail if badly administered, but because educational administration in India involves most of the problems common to large countries as well as some of its own.

Since, as was said earlier, success, especially in the lower stages, must depend very largely on the establishment of satisfactory personal relations between teachers, parents and children, it is a local and intimate affair which calls for a wide delegation of authority, so far as circumstances will permit. On the other hand, since education is an expensive business, particularly at the higher stages, the need to avoid overlapping and other forms of waste calls for some degree of centralized control. To effect a workable synthesis between centrifugal and centripetal trends is a problem which has worried, and still worries, some of the most advanced countries, and it was complicated in India in the British period by the existence, in the educational field, of a variety of authorities claiming autonomous rights. Apart from the Central Government there were the provinces, the princely states, the universities, the missionary schools and a host of privately owned and managed institutions at different levels.

Perhaps the best way to illustrate the situation as it was in 1944 is to summarize the main conclusions contained in the CABE Report. These were :

(a) The provinces should remain the chief units for educational administration, except in regard to university and higher technical education, the activities of which should be co-ordinated on an all-India basis.

(b) In the event of the (princely) states taking part in educational development on an all-India scale, it may be necessary, in order to form economic units, to group the smaller ones or attach them to larger states or contiguous provinces.

(c) A national system of education will demand much closer co-operation, financial and otherwise, between the central and provincial governments.

(d) Provincial governments should be left to make such changes in their administrative arrangements as the carrying out of education developments on the scale now contemplated may require : experience suggests that they would be well-advised to resume all educational powers from local bodies, except where these are functioning efficiently.

(e) In order to enlist local interest in education, school managing bodies, school boards and district education committees may be constituted, if and when sufficient people of the right type are available to serve on them.

(f) An Education Advisory Board for the whole province may be desirable.

(g) A strong Education Department will be required at the Centre and the scope and functions of the CABE should be enlarged.

Chapter 4 will have shown that these recommendations have had their influence on the administrative structure of education in the new India, particularly with regard to the amalgamation of the former princely states with one another or with adjacent provinces, to the delegation of authority to local bodies and to the need for much greater help being given to the states by the Central Government. Whether the EC has new or different ideas in this connection will be examined in the final chapter.

So far as the financial assumptions underlying educational programmes since 1944 are concerned, some tables illustrating what the educationists have asked for and what governments have been able to supply since that date, will be found in Appendix A. The CABE estimated that their plan, when in full operation, would involve a net annual expenditure to be met from public funds of approximately Rs. 280 crores, which would have to be multiplied several times to bring it into line with the present cost of living. As the total expenditure on education from public funds in 1940–1 was Rs. $17\frac{1}{2}$ crores, it is not surprising that the CABE's estimate came as a considerable shock not only to government finance departments but also to public opinion. One critic even went so far as to suggest that it had been deliberately inflated in order to give the authorities a good excuse for doing nothing about it. Appendix A will show that it was not, after all, so very fantastic. At any rate, the CABE, in defending its plan, appears to have anticipated the assumption on which national planning in the new India would be based. The last page of the Report contains these words :

> The cost of education, like that of other essential services, must ultimately be met out of current revenues and this will not be possible, unless the taxable capacity of the country is increased many times. For this one can only look to an all-out development of the national resources through a rational expansion of industry on the one hand and the improvement of agriculture on the other. The Board believes that neither of these will be possible without a wider extension of educational facilities and the spread of enlightenment and expert knowledge, which this will promote. . . . Indeed the development of India's economic resouces and the expansion of her social services are inseparably connected and must proceed side by side.

Appendix A will also show that a recent criticism of the Board's estimate on the ground that it takes no account of the increase of population, while the scheme was being implemented, is not justified.

When the CABE Report appeared, the question was raised as to how it arrived at an estimate so vastly in excess of current practice and experience, and it may not be out of place here to say a few words about the broad lines upon which education estimates are constructed. They are, in fact, easier to frame than those of most other public services, because the determining factor, teachers' salaries, will normally account for from two-thirds to three-quarters of the total. This item will be highest at the lower stages—the latest figures show that in Indian primary schools it accounts for four-fifths of the bill—and will decrease in the higher, as the amount and cost of equipment and other supplies gets larger. There is one factor that may reduce the ratio of salaries to other expenditure and that is if any large outlay on sites and buildings has to be met out of revenue. In Britain and some other countries substantial capital items are usually met by loans over thirty to sixty years, the interest and sinking funds for which do not, as a rule, exceed 10 per cent of the annual budget. For various, no doubt sound, reasons, the loan system for capital expenditure so far as education is concerned, has not found favour with the finance experts in India. Other items in the budget which may be expected to remain fairly stable are the special services at 10 per cent and administration at 5 per cent of the total.

In conclusion, a word about the fundamental assumption which should inspire and determine the approach to constructing a national system of education. Indian educationists rightly insist that any such system as will suit their country must be in harmony with the inherent genius and ethos of its people. As a criticism of education under the British Raj this has some validity, but in the light of what the Constitution prescribes and of the impact on traditional sentiments and ideas of an era of rapid political and economic evolution, it is not easy to be sure how far or in what ways the ethos of India today differs from that of other nations which have faced or are now facing similar changes in their social structure. Possibly this will become explicit in the report of the EC. In the meantime, however, the safest assumption on which to work may be that Indian parents, like parents all over the world, look to education to help them to make their children physically fit, mentally alert and morally sound.

CHAPTER 7

The Existing School
and Formal Education System

IN THE preceding chapters an attempt has been made to review
the assumptions or basic principles by which it has been suggested
that educational development in the new India should be guided.
Considerations of space have made it necessary to concentrate
almost entirely on the conclusions reached by the Wardha Committee and by official bodies since 1937. This does not imply that
wisdom and initiative are qualities which only official bodies
possess. Much has been thought and still more written by non-
official persons during the period in question about India's
educational problems, but it would take a very large volume to
summarize, let alone analyse, the views which they have expressed. Anyone, however, who looks at the lists of bodies and
individuals consulted by the University and Secondary Education commissions, will see that they spared no pains to seek the
advice of knowledgeable persons in their respective fields. If to
them are added the members of the CABE and its various committees, the result can fairly claim to represent an impressive
assemblage of expertise.

The main aim of this chapter will be to give an objective
account of the present position in the different branches and to
show how this has come about. Achievements, setbacks, existing
gaps and current controversies will be mentioned, but a detailed
discussion of the more important ones will be reserved for the
next chapter. Since such a record will entail at least a minimum
of statistics, attention must again be called to the fact that figures
for years prior to 1947 relate to an unpartitioned India. It

appears, however, from the latest figures supplied by the Registrar-General that the increase in the population of India since 1947 has just about replaced the number who went to Pakistan, so that the numbers in the 1946–7 and 1965–6 age-groups will be roughly comparable.

PRE-PRIMARY EDUCATION

If 3–6 is taken as the normal age-range for nursery schools or classes, there were over 40 million children in this group in 1960–1 and the number will be approaching 50 million by 1965–6. Owing to more urgent calls on the national resources since 1947, it has not been possible to plan any comprehensive development at this stage. Nevertheless, even if the number now enrolled is small in proportion to the total in the age-group, substantial progress has been made. The CABE had no information as to the number of nursery schools and classes in existence at the time of its Report but thought that there were only a few and those mostly in private hands.

Since Independence the number has grown from 303 in 1951 to 1909 in 1961, and is expected to reach 3500 by 1966. The enrolment has risen from 22,000 in 1951 to 121,000 in 1961. In addition, there are a good many children below the age of 6 in ordinary primary schools.

In the same ten years the number of teachers has gone up from 866 to just over 4000, of whom 3600 are women. The percentage of these who are trained has remained steady around 65 but it is not known how far the training they have received has been specially designed to fit them to deal with very young charges. It is generally agreed today that the nursery teacher needs to have special qualities of temperament as well as special training.

PRIMARY OR JUNIOR BASIC EDUCATION

In dealing with India it is important to make clear the distinction between what is now called primary or junior basic and what used to be called elementary education. The primary or junior basic stage covers the age-group of 6–11, whereas in Britain elementary used to comprise the whole range from 5–14 in schools other than secondary.

Soon after Independence, as has been already mentioned, the new Government decided on the advice of their Planning Commission that the limited funds available for the lower stages of education should be assigned in the first instance to develop primary schools and that the implementation of the directive in the Constitution that free and compulsory education should be provided for all children up to the age of 14 should be postponed until easier times. The effect of this decision on educational development as a whole will be discussed in a later chapter.

In 1946–7 the number of primary schools was 172,661, of which 21,480 were for girls. By 1950–1 the total had risen to 209,671 but the girls schools had fallen to 13,901. This was very largely due to the inclusion in Pakistan of so many Muslims, who prefer separate schools for girls at all stages. In the ten years from 1950–1, which are covered by the first two Five-year Plans, the total number of schools, including those for girls, increased by almost exactly half. It is estimated that by the end of the third plan the total will reach 400,000. The official tables do not reveal how many of these schools contain pupils below and above the primary age-range.

The enrolment, in 1946–7, in primary or junior basic schools was just over 13 million and there were probably another million in the preparatory departments of secondary or high schools. This meant that about 35 per cent of all the children between 6 and 11 were at school but only just over 17 per cent of the girls. Since then the numbers on the roll have risen at an increasingly rapid rate, until at the end of second Five-year Plan 35 million or over 62 per cent of the age-group were in attendance and 41 per cent of the girls. By the end of the third plan it is hoped that 78 per cent (56 per cent of the girls) will be at school.

Impressive as this growth certainly is, the persistence of serious wastage is still causing grave concern. On the figures before it when it was preparing its Report, the CABE found that only one out of every four children admitted to class I stayed on as far as class IV, the earliest possible stage at which anything like permanent literacy could be expected. If the wastage figures today are less disturbing than they were in 1944, they are still formidable, for the official tables show that from 1950–1 onwards the percentage of enrolment in class V to the total population between 10 and 11 has remained steady at about half the similar percentage for the whole primary age-group. It is true that legislation to make attendance compulsory has been enacted for a number of areas in most states but in the absence of any effective machinery for enforcing it the practical results have been negligible.

With regard to the all-important matter of teaching power, the number employed at this stage has risen from just over 400,000 (55,575 women) in 1946–7 to 742,000 (127,000 women) in 1960–1, and is expected to pass the million mark by 1966. The percentage of those who have been trained has remained steady at about 65 per cent for men and 70 per cent or a little over for women. No figures are available as to the percentage of primary teachers in 1947 whose academic background was below matriculation standard, but it is satisfactory to know that the very high percentage of nearly 90 per cent in 1951 had fallen to 64 per cent in 1961 and may be down to 54 per cent by the end of 1966. There would seem to be little or no difference between men and women in this respect. The pupil–teacher ratio, which was 32 in 1947, had risen to 36 in 1961, and will become 38 if the expectations of the Third Plan in regard to increased enrolment are fulfilled.

The total expenditure on primary education has gone up about four times since 1947, and in 1961 stood at Rs. 73·4 crores; by 1966 it may exceed Rs. 100 crores. To ascertain how far this increase has been due to better pay for teachers and how far to a steady rise in prices and the cost of living generally would call for a detailed analysis beyond the scope of this book. It is, however, worth noting, in view of what has been said earlier about the normal share of teachers' salaries in the education budget, that of the total expenditure on primary education in 1961 over 88 per cent was attributable to this item. The implications of this in relation to the amount provided for buildings, equipment and other essential services will be examined later. The cost per pupil rose from Rs. 14·2 in 1946–7 to Rs. 27·6 in 1960–1.

MIDDLE SCHOOL OR SENIOR BASIC EDUCATION

Here again it is necessary to define what is meant in India by the middle stage. It covers both senior basic schools and the older type of elementary schools with classes VI to VIII as well as the three lowest classes in secondary or high schools, the normal age range in each case being from 11 to 14. Although the aim of the instruction given in senior basic or old middle schools is different from that of lower secondary classes, the former being a finishing school for most pupils, while the latter is preparatory to further study, it is convenient, so far as statistics are concerned, to take them together. A caution is, however, necessary, for at the moment there is considerable fluidity at this stage. In some states the conversion of the old type of middle schools into senior basic schools is proceeding more rapidly than in others, while priority is being given by some to upgrading middle schools to the secondary level.

In 1946–7 there were 12,843 schools covering this stage, of which 1653 were for girls. By 1951 the corresponding figures were 13,596 (1674 for girls) and thereafter a welcome acceleration to 21,730 (3337 for girls) in 1956 and 49,663 (4666 for girls) in 1961. The objective for 1966 is 78,000 (8000 for girls). The total enrolment at the middle stage in 1947 was just over 2 million, of whom 320,000 were girls; in 1951 this rose to $3\frac{1}{3}$ million (534,000 girls), in 1956 to nearly 4 million (867,000 girls) and in 1961 to $6\frac{2}{3}$ million (1,630,000 girls). It is hoped that these totals will be at least half as big again by 1966.

When it is remembered that it has been the policy of Government since the First Five-year Plan to concentrate on the primary branch and leave a full-scale attack on the middle stage until easier times make it feasible to find the necessary resources, the rate of growth which the above figures record is surprising. At the same time, even if the 1966 goal is reached, less than a third of the age-group will be in school as compared with over three-quarters in the case of the primary group.

The number of teachers employed in middle schools or classes in 1945–7 was 72,413 (10,619 women). By 1961 this had risen to 345,288 (83,532 women) and is expected to pass the half-million mark by 1966. Between 1947 and 1961 the percentage of trained teachers improved from 59 per cent to 66·5 per cent in the case of men and from 63·5 per cent to 73·4 per cent in the case of women. A small number of graduate teachers now makes its appearance, but the number of those with academic backgrounds below matriculation remains unduly high, though over the last ten years it declined from 62·8 per cent to 46·8 per cent. In the same period the pupil–teacher ratio increased from 24 to 31.

While the actual enrolment at the middle stage went up by over 3½ times between 1947 and 1961, the total expenditure increased more than eight times and stood at Rs. 42·9 crores at the end of the second plan. Here also, as in the primary stage, the percentage attributable to teachers' salaries, viz. 85 per cent, is higher than experience elsewhere would lead one to expect. It is also rather surprising that the cost per pupil per annum only appears to have gone up from Rs. 37·1 to Rs. 40·5.

HIGHER SECONDARY EDUCATION

This stage comprises, in the main, those pupils who are in classes IX, X and XI in high schools. It is the present policy to add another class—perhaps later on two more—in those high schools which are fit or can soon be made fit for upgrading, but the progress so far made in this direction has not been sufficient to require any substantial modification in the official statistics.

In 1946–7 there were 5298 high schools, including 725 for girls. In 1950–1 there were 7288 (1064 for girls), in 1955–6 10,838 (1583 for girls) and in 1960–1 17,257 (2521 for girls). It is anticipated that by the end of the Third Plan in 1966 the total may have reached 27,000 (4000 for girls). In addition to upgrading selected high schools by the addition of an extra class, it is proposed to convert a number of existing middle schools into high schools.

The total enrolment in 1946–7, in classes IX and above, was 871,000; no separate figures are available for girls. In 1950–1 it was 1,220,000 (girls 163,000), in 1955–6, 1,878,000 (girls 320,000) and in 1960–1, 2,887,000 (girls 541,000). It is hoped that the 1960–1 total will have been nearly doubled by the end of the third plan. As a percentage of the whole population in the age-group between 14 and 17, the enrolment in classes IX and above rose from 5·4 per cent to 10·6 per cent in the case of boys and from 1·5 per cent to 4·1 per cent in the case of girls between 1951 and 1961.

With regard to staffing, the pupil–teacher ratio has been constant at 25 during the period, and, consequently, the total number of teachers has increased at the same rate as the number of pupils, but the proportion of women has become much larger than it was, as the following figures will show. In 1946–7 there were 87,862 teachers, including 11,643 women, while, out of 296,056 teachers in 1960–1, no less than 62,293 were women. Over the whole period the percentage of trained teachers increased from 51·6 per cent to 64·1 per cent in the case of men and from 67·1 per cent to 73·9 per cent in the case of women. No comparable figures are available for 1946–7, but between 1951 and 1961 the number of teachers with graduate or postgraduate qualifications rose from 41·8 per cent to 49·7 per cent, while those with less than matriculation fell from 17·4 per cent to 10·1 per cent.

The total expenditure on education at this stage rose from Rs. 12·2 crores in 1946–7 to Rs. 68·9 crores in 1960–1 and the cost per pupil per annum from Rs. 55·7 to Rs. 91·8.

New features of interest in the secondary branch which have appeared since 1947 are the multi-purpose schools and "merit" or "quality" schools for specially able pupils, as recommended by the Mudaliar Commission, which include the few "public" schools in existence before 1947. Not much has happened about technical high schools. Two other matters which are the subject of discussion at the moment are the "Three Language Formula" and the need for more scholarships and other forms of assistance for poor pupils. These, however, may be reserved for examination later, as it is probable that the EC will have a good deal to say about them.

UNIVERSITY EDUCATION

When one gets beyond the sphere of secondary or high school education, differences of organization as well as variations of nomenclature make it difficult to present either a coherent picture or really comparable statistics. One thing, however, is plain, and that is that at the university level there has been a remarkable expansion since 1947 both in the facilities provided and in the number of students in attendance. To take a few figures, which are comparable, the number of universities has gone up from seventeen in 1946–7 to forty-five in 1960–1 and is expected to reach sixty-six by 1966. Then, in regard to constituent or affiliated colleges, there were 420 of these, including 59 for girls, in 1946–7, while by 1960–1 there were 1039 (165 for girls). Nearly a 50 per cent increase on these figures is expected by 1966.

The enrolment in university teaching departments, arts and science colleges, research institutions and other forms of general, i.e. not professional or vocational, higher education has risen from about 200,000 in 1947 to 800,000 in 1961 with a projected 50 per cent addition by 1966. The 1961 figure includes 150,000 girls.

The total expenditure on the above services amounted to Rs. 4·4 crores in 1946–7 and to Rs. 21 crores in 1960–1. The cost per student remained fairly steady at between Rs. 220 and 230 per annum from 1947 to 1956 but rose to Rs. 300 in 1961, and will probably be about the same in 1966.

As is natural in a country as large as India, there is a great variety in the size, organization and standards of its universities. The number of students ranges from a few thousand in those which are unitary and mainly residential to well over 100,000 in the case of Calcutta. In organization some are unitary, some affiliating and others a mixture of both. Although there are common features in regard to the administrative and academic arrangements, there is a considerable variation in functions between one place and another. Thanks to their economic importance since 1947 and to the co-ordinating influence of the UGC, a good deal has been done to reduce the disparity in standards which was prevalent in the British period. There has been a considerable increase in the number of students taking science and technical courses, but according to the Fourth Plan the swing away from arts is not going fast enough either to cope with industrial requirements or to stop the rise in the educated unemployed. This is one of the problems to be examined in the next chapter.

To illustrate the increasingly important role played by the UGC with the backing of the Central Government in stimulating university development, it distributed, in 1962–3 a total of Rs. 10·68 crores for both plan and non-plan projects. Of this sum, Rs. 2·72 crores went to the Central universities. Of the balance shared among the other universities just over a crore was earmarked for implementing the three-year degree course and just under a crore each for their engineering and technological departments and for improving salary scales.

Soon after 1947, the federal or the regional languages began to supersede English as the medium of instruction, but in 1963 twelve out of the fifty-five universities were still using English for this purpose.

TECHNICAL EDUCATION

As was pointed out in the last chapter, both the Abbott–Wood and the CABE Reports anticipated substantial developments in the technical sphere after the war, but neither realized how big and rapid they were, in fact, going to be. Since 1947, the progress made in this branch has been impressive both in quantity and quality. This has been largely due to the priority given to it, for economic reasons, in the national plans and to the need for defence preparedness in view of the strained relations with Pakistan and China.

It is interesting that, in spite of the great importance attached to technical development since Independence, it has not been found necessary to set up any special commission as was done for both secondary and university education. Government has been content to act upon the advice tendered to it by two bodies set up before 1947, the AICTE for general policy and the Sarkar Committee for action at the highest level. A number of committees have been established to examine special sectors of the technical field and, to mention only the more recent ones, there have been reports by the Working Group on Technical Education and Vocational Training (1960), the Committee on Postgraduate Engineering Education and Research (1961) and the Committee on Commerce Education (1961). In addition, the Institute of Applied Manpower Research has issued twelve reports during the last few years and has also held two seminars on collaboration between industries and technical institutions. The careful watch being kept by this Institute is of first importance in the existing circumstances, for although, up to the end of the Third Plan, results have not fallen far short of what was projected, it is clear from the forecasts of the Fourth Plan that they have not kept pace with actual requirements, whether based on economic expansion or investment ratio. With such rapid growth on both sides it is hardly surprising that it has not been practicable to strike an accurate balance between supply and demand. Although it does not seem to be imminent, the risk that supply may outstrip demand, either in the country as a whole or in any given area, has to be guarded against.

The Sarkar Report deserves notice because it has been responsible for what most observers will regard as the most striking achievement at the top level and that is the creation of the Indian Institutes of Technology (IITs). In view of the time at which the Sarkar Committee was appointed, its terms of reference are worth noting. It was asked to consider, with a view to ensuring an adequate supply of technical personnel for post-war industrial development, whether it is desirable to have (a) a central institution, possibly on the lines of the Massachusetts Institute of Technology, with a number of subordinate institutions affiliated to it, or (b) several higher institutions on a regional basis, or (c) any other organization. In the light of its conclusions it was asked to suggest the scope, size and situation of the proposed institution or institutions, the arrangements for control and management, the qualifications and conditions of the staffs and the best way to recruit them, the preparation of plans and specifications for buildings and equipment with an estimate of the cost involved. The committee finally decided that not less than four higher technical institutions would be necessary, one in the east, one in the west, one in the south and one in the north, and that the one in the east should be set up in or near Calcutta at an early date, to be followed as quickly as possible by the one in the west in or near Bombay. Places were to be provided in each for 2000 undergraduate and 1000 postgraduate students. The estimated cost in each case amounted to just over Rs. 3 crores and the recurring annual charges to about Rs. 70 lakhs with an offset in the way of income of about Rs. 13 lakhs. There is no room here to record the Committee's recommendations in regard to the other issues submitted to it but it did make one that has not always been followed in more advanced countries, which was that to ensure the proper planning of buildings, equipment and courses of study, the principal and heads of the main departments should be appointed and the services of an architect with experience in the planning of technical institutions should be secured at a sufficiently early stage.

The new Government accepted the recommendations of the Sarkar Committee, and, considering the many difficulties which it was facing, acted with commendable promptitude. The first institute, at Kharagpur in West Bengal, was opened in 1951, followed by Bombay in 1957, Madras in 1959 and Kanpur in 1960. A fifth at Delhi was started in 1961 and five more existing colleges are to be upgraded to IIT status during the next ten years. Each of them is designed to cater for 2000 undergraduate and 500 postgraduate students. Kharagpur has now reached that strength and visitors to it have been so impressed by the work being done there that even at the risk of giving too much space to the technical branch, some details about it can be justified. It stands on a site of 1500 acres, which it owes to Mr. Sarkar's influence with the Government of West Bengal. The layout is spacious and the administrative and laboratory blocks are well planned and equipped, and a first-class library is being built up. There are ten hostels for students, nine for men and one for women. The number of societies catering for literary and artistic interests are a welcome indication that technology is not the sole interest of the inhabitants.

The Institute provides courses for undergraduates on the science side in chemistry, geology, geophysics, physics and mathematics; on the technological side in aeronautical, agricultural, chemical, civil, mechanical and electrical engineering, as well as electronics, mining and metallurgy. There are also undergraduate courses in architecture and naval architecture. Postgraduate courses are also provided in these subjects, and in city and regional planning and psychology. At the moment there are about 100 students doing research. An important contribution towards the solution of an urgent problem is a special course for the training of technical teachers.

The Institute owes much to its two directors, who, between them, afford an interesting link between the old dispensation and the new. The first of them was Dr. J. C. Ghosh, who, in the last years of the British régime, was Director of the Bangalore Institute of Science, at that time and probably still the premier scientific research institution in the whole of Asia. His successor, Dr. S. R. Sen Gupta, who, in 1946, was in charge of the technical branch of the Central Ministry of Education, was Secretary both of the AICTE and of the Sarkar Committee.

The attention that has been given to the Kharagpur Institute must not be taken to imply that it is unique. It was the first in the field but the others, established later, have already made their mark and those still to be added will no doubt further strengthen the provision for higher technical education.

When the policy of five-year planning was adopted by the new Government, it was recognized that a balance between the demand for and the supply of manpower was essential, and that this applied particularly to technical education and training at the post-secondary level. In arriving at an output figure for existing and new institutions, an estimate, necessarily tentative at first, was needed to decide how this output should be divided between degree and diploma holders. In the light of the experience gained during the first plan this was provisionally fixed at one graduate to two diploma holders. So far the output of diploma holders per graduate has not risen beyond 1·5 but if the steps now contemplated to stop wastage among diploma holders are successful, there may be no need to modify the present ratio in admissions to the respective courses. In comparing admissions with outputs it must be remembered that the length of the degree course is usually five years and that of the diploma course three.

A few statistics will illustrate the development which has taken place in the technical field since Independence. In 1947–8 admissions to degree courses numbered 2940 and the output 1270; to diploma courses the admissions were 3670 and the output 1440. By the end of the first plan (1955–6) admissions to degree courses had risen to 5890 and, in the case of diploma courses, to 10,480, the corresponding outputs being 4020 and 4500. By the end of the Second Plan the totals were degree courses; admissions 13,870, output 5700 and diploma courses; admissions 25,800, output 7790. It is estimated that at the end of the Third Plan, degree admissions will have risen to 24,000 and the output to 10,500, while, for diploma courses, admissions will reach 44,000 and output 17,000.

To keep pace with this growth in the number of students it has been necessary both to increase the size of existing institutions and to establish many new ones. In 1947–8 there were thirty-eight institutes offering degree courses and fifty-three diploma courses, the latter being mostly of the polytechnic type. By 1965 there were 130 degree colleges and 264 polytechnics. In addition to what has been done by the central and state governments, there has been a useful contribution from private agencies, assisted by government grants. Plans for opening eight large regional colleges were included in the first two plans and others are now on the way.

In spite of these impressive achievements at the higher levels, much still remains to be done lower down if two essential aims are to be fulfilled. The first is to supply the higher institutes with an adequate supply of entrants with the requisite ability and preparatory training. The second is to fill the lower ranks in industry with competent supervisors and technicians. Much help in this direction may be expected from the polytechnics, old and new, which, in most cases, will cover a wide range of subjects at varying levels. Technical high schools of the kind recommended in the CABE Report have hardly appeared on the scene as yet and it is too early to assess what may be expected from the technical courses in the multi-purpose schools. Junior technical schools are making slow progress, partly because ministries of labour, who have an enrolment of 38,000 in their own industrial training institutions, have not so far agreed to recognize junior technical qualifications as adequate for entry to industry under the Apprenticeship Act of 1961.

SOCIAL EDUCATION

Those people who may have an uncomfortable feeling that education in the new India has become the slave of industry may find some consolation in what has been happening in what is now known as the social branch. The extension of adult education to hasten the enlightenment of the illiterate masses, who are in theory and may become in fact the political masters in a new democracy, was a wise decision, and even if the implementation of the programmes for this purpose has been slowed up by force of circumstances, the lines laid down for the new approach are both sound and imaginative. As an item in the First Five-year Plan the National Fundamental Education Centre, following UNESCO advice, drew up a five-point programme for social education. This comprised literacy, education in health and hygiene, vocational training, citizenship and recreation. This centre, which has now become part of the NCERT, not only does research and evaluation of social programmes, but also trains social education organizers for the districts in the present system of local government. The Ministry of Community Development, Panchayat Raj and Co-operation also trains organizers for block and district work. The CABE also has a standing committee for social education.

Literacy, for obvious reasons, is the focal point in plans for social betterment in a country like India, but it is satisfactory that it is no longer regarded as an end in itself. Little was done about this before 1947 apart from a few campaigns by Congress Ministries, which failed to produce any permanent results, largely because literacy was treated as an end in itself. The less accessible rural areas were almost totally neglected. A good deal has been done since, but according to the Fourth Plan forecasts it needs more attention than it has so far received. Owing to the spread of education at the primary stage the total percentage of literacy in the population of 5 years and above has increased from 19 per cent in 1951 to 28 per cent in 1961 but during this period, due to population growth, the number of illiterate persons rose by over 5 million. The planners' comment is worth quoting. "Adult education", they say, "is a crucial sector, where all studies have shown that it is possible to get a quick return in economic terms. Its neglect, therefore, has seriously affected the development effort of the country."

THE ESSENTIAL SERVICES

For several reasons not much need be said here about these services. The present position in regard to the supply and training of teachers for the different branches has already been dealt with and there will be a good deal more to be said about this vital problem in the concluding chapters. So far as the health service is concerned, both schools and colleges have benefited from the increased attention which this has received since 1947, but so far the object has been to enlarge facilities for the people at large, and since doctors, nurses, hospitals and clinics are still in short supply, it has not yet been possible, except in a very few of the larger cities, to create a special school medical service. Steps have been taken in some training colleges to give student teachers some knowledge of hygiene and first-aid. More encouraging is the liberal provision now being made in many areas for school meals and for physical training, games and other recreational activities. Education for the physically and mentally handicapped still remains largely in the hands of private agencies but the national obligation in this respect is clearly recognized and suitable action will no doubt be taken as soon as the necessary resources become available.

Vocational guidance is another service the importance of which is appreciated, but where, for similar reasons, progress has been slow, and it may be some time yet before the recommendations of the commissions already mentioned can be made effective. It is, at any rate, an indication of things to come that employment bureaux were operative in all the states but two in 1964.

ADMINISTRATION AND FINANCE

Unlike the Constitution of the U.S.S.R., which reserves education for the Central Government, the Constitution of India puts it on the Concurrent List, which means that the responsibility for administering it, where it is maintained or aided out of public funds, is shared between the Centre and the States.

At the Centre, soon after the new Republic was established, it was decided, for reasons which can only be surmised, to set up a separate ministry to deal with scientific research and cultural affairs. Whether it fulfilled or failed to fulfil the purpose for which it was set up is not officially known, but it has now been merged with the Ministry of Education, so that responsibility for the system as a whole is no longer divided.

The Minister of Education has at his service, in addition to the staff of the department, a number of advisory bodies. The functions of the CABE, UGC and AICTE have already been described, and they are, in virtue of their membership, all-India rather than central government bodies. Other bodies of similar range associated with the Ministry are the All-India Councils for Elementary and Secondary Education and the National Council for Women's Education. Another valuable auxiliary is the NCERT, which was created comparatively recently and has absorbed several smaller institutes concerned with specific aspects of educational development. The CABE itself, as already mentioned, has five standing committees which deal with (a) basic, primary and pre-primary education, (b) secondary education, (c) higher education, (d) social education, and (e) general purposes. The Minister and his department, therefore, do not lack people to whom they can turn for advice.

At the State level the administrative pattern resembles that at the Centre, though the statutory powers and personal influence of state ministers of education naturally vary from place to place. On the staff side there have been proposals for setting up an All-India Education Service. From the point of view of integrating effort and widening experience this has attractions, but if it is ever to be implemented, it must wait for quieter times. Another proposal which deserves consideration in view of the delegation of powers to local authorities is that each State should have an advisory board to facilitate regular contact between the bodies responsible for administering education in its area.

Details as to the present expenditure on the education service and its apportionment between the Centre, states and private bodies will be found in Appendix A. These will show the extent to which it has grown since 1947, the amount which is likely to be available during the Fourth Plan and what further increases the EC contemplate during the next ten or twenty years.

CHAPTER 8

Current Problems, Including Adaptation
to Technological, Social,
and International Change. I

THE preceding chapters have attempted to indicate some of the assumptions and general principles which should determine the establishment of a national system of education for a new democracy like India, and then to describe what has so far been done to give effect to them. It is now time to consider both the obstacles which have held up their implementation and the problems which progress to date has revealed. It cannot be too strongly emphasized that any suggestions now put forward for resolving these problems are made with due appreciation of what has been achieved in the face of adverse circumstances which may continue to operate for some time to come. Grave as these circumstances admittedly are, those who have watched, with mingled anxiety and admiration, how India has faced up to them, will see no reason to share the pessimistic outlook which has been characteristic of some recent books by both external and internal observers. The relevant issue today for all who believe that efficient social services are a *sine qua non* for national prosperity is not what might have been but what is and what can be.

The main problems which have confronted India since 1947 may be roughly classified as (a) political, (b) economic, (c) emotional integration, and (d) population. Each of these has had a direct or indirect influence on education and the social services in general.

Prominent among the political issues have been the tensions

137

with Pakistan, and, since 1962, with China. The Tashkent Agreement raises hopes that India–Pakistan relations may improve before long. These tensions have meant the diversion to war preparedness of large sums, which, in more peaceful times, might have been available for social development. They have also made a serious inroad on the supply of technicians at all levels and to that extent have handicapped the industrial and agricultural programmes. A further matter, which has made an inescapable claim on government attention, has been the influx of refugees and other legacies of Partition. The moral, as distinct from the material, rehabilitation of these unfortunate people has presented the social services with a new and complex problem.

One can appreciate the force of the political and economic arguments that convinced Nehru and his colleagues that the best and quickest way to enable India to hold its own with other large and more advanced countries was a new industrial revolution. This was, of course, a break with the Gandhian conception of an agricultural society based on an enlightened peasantry and sustained, in the main, by a wide expansion of small cottage industries. But Gandhi was no longer there and big business, stimulated by the prospect of foreign aid, had the last word. It naturally followed that in the earlier Five-year Plans a high priority was assigned to industrial and agricultural development. The following resolution, adopted by the National Development Council at its meeting in September 1965, makes it clear that there is to be no change in this policy for some time to come :

The Council realizes that the large investment made in the last three Plans has not improved the standard of living of the mass of the people in the measure that was required or anticipated. This has been due in part to a more rapid increase in population and in part to an inadequate increase in agricultural and industrial production. Together with the additional burdens of defence expenditure imposed on the nation since the emergency of 1962, these factors have caused internal prices and the cost of living to rise to levels which are proving onerous to large sections of the community. These problems have to be tackled resolutely in the Fourth and succeeding Five-year Plans. One of the urgent problems . . . is the effective control of population growth. The Plan allocations accordingly provide for the maximum possible effort for educating the country on the subject of family limitation and for organizing an effective programme to achieve the object of a rapid reduction of birth rates.

The Council thereupon decided that in the field of social service, priority should be given to family planning, technical education and the supply of drinking water in both rural and urban areas. Apart from these, consolidation, a comfortable if sometimes slightly ambiguous term, is to be the watchword during the Fourth Plan. Here again the official policy in the economic as in the political sphere involves not only a severe restriction on the funds available for social development but also, in the case of education, a concentration on the higher branches which is making the system as a whole even more top-heavy than it was when the British handed it over.

No one who knows India will question the importance of what is now termed "emotional integration" in a country comprising such a mixture of races and cultures. The struggle for Independence and Gandhi's pervasive influence over the people from one end of the country to the other did a great deal to promote Indian unity, but signs have not been lacking since 1947 that local patriotisms are by no means dead and that unless they are tactfully handled, fissiparous tendencies may develop. This presents a challenge which education must take up. The contributions towards a solution, which may be expected from social education on a broad front and from language teaching at the post-primary stage, will be examined later.

The population problem, unlike the others so far mentioned, can hardly be ascribed either to external pressures or to government policy nor can it be regarded as a legacy from British rule. Between 1931 and 1951, the population increased in round figures by 82 million; during the next ten years it grew by nearly as many. In 1961 the total was approaching 450 million, so that the population lost to Pakistan at Partition had been replaced. The official estimate for the end of the Fifth Plan in 1976 is 625 million, and mathematicians can work out for themselves what the position will be in A.D. 2000 if the present rate is maintained. Although the outlook may not be as menacing as some foreign observers appear to think, it is having a serious impact on the planning of national prosperity. By the end of the Third Plan it is estimated that the national income will have risen by more than a half but the income per head will not have risen by more than one-fifth because of so many more heads. To make matters worse, this will hardly keep pace with the rise in the cost of living. So far as the education system is concerned, the need to cope with increasing numbers is intensifying the strain at all levels. It is not, therefore, surprising that a high priority has been assigned to family planning in the Fourth Plan. What, however, is to be done about it?

In the experience of most advanced countries the spread of public education has proved to be an effective contraceptive, but it is a long-term process for which India cannot afford to wait. With regard to the two factors that determine growth of population, rise in the birth rate and fall in the death rate, the latter will obviously be accelerated by a progressive public health policy. There has been a commendable advance in this respect since 1947 but the average expectation of life in India is still not much more than half that in most Western countries. No reasonable person would wish to rely once more on war, famine, pestilence, flood and other natural calamities to put a brake on population growth. A vast increase in food production may provide one part of the answer but the real solution must lie in finding a permanent means of curbing the birth rate. The principal methods now being used are Family Planning Centres, of which 18,000 have already been set up all over the country, and advocacy of all known forms of safe contraception and sterilization. So far, these, admittedly, have only touched the fringe of the problem and according to a recent article in *India News* at least 100 million married couples must adopt family planning devices in order to make a decisive impact on the rate of increase.

There is a clear opportunity for social education to do useful work here through special classes, especially for women in rural areas, during the day, and by providing various forms of recreation, as an alternative to procreation, for both men and women in the evenings. The importance of electrifying villages for this and other purposes has already been stressed. A more difficult question is how far the schools can be enlisted in this crusade. Whatever may now be done to teach boys and girls at the higher stages something about the facts of life, it must not be forgotten that two-thirds of those on the verge of adolescence are not in school and these, for the most part, live in places where the need for birth control is most urgent. A current debate in Britain today is about the earliest age at which such instruction can profitably begin. An increasing number of people, both teachers and doctors, maintain that the earlier it can be done the better, and that it should be given directly and not through the old "bee and pollen" approach. However rapidly taboos and other conventions may be disappearing in the new India, there is still room for doubt whether average parents, particularly in the remoter districts, would react favourably to the introduction of sex teaching even in the mildest form into the curriculum of the primary school. A still graver doubt arises as to how many of the existing teachers would be competent to teach it properly. The fact that, as a rule, marriage still takes place earlier in India than in the West is a strong argument for bringing under educational influences the adolescents now out of school. It also emphasizes the need for giving their teachers a thorough and up-to-date course of training. There does not appear to be any religious obstacle in the way of family planning, for Hinduism, unlike some other faiths, does not definitely frown on birth control. The real difficulty lies in the apathy or antipathy of the Indian villager and this can only be overcome by a tactful and sympathetic approach on the part of all those agencies which are concerned with rural development. The problem is not so acute in the towns, if only because they are better served in regard to medical advice and facilities.

After this brief survey of the national problems facing India since 1947, attention may now be turned to what may be called domestic issues within the educational field. In many cases, of course, these are the direct outcome of what has been decided at the top level and embodied in successive Five-year Plans. The imperative need for more and more technologists and other experts which the political and economic situation has created, and the diversion to meet this demand of what, in normal circumstances, might be regarded as a disproportionate amount of the educational budget and other resources, has caused—to use a word popular with the planners—a serious "imbalance" within the educational system itself. The expansion at the university and higher technical stages has not been paralleled by a similar expansion at the lower stages, on which they depend for recruits. That this necessarily entails a progressive deterioration in the standard of entrants for the higher stages, the Fourth Plan frankly admits, though it holds out no early prospect of the normal balance between the various branches being restored.

Accepting the limitations imposed by national policy on what educationists might consider the logical method for constructing a democratic system, one may still ask whether the best use is being made of such financial and other resources as are left over for the less fortunate branches, in particular for the lowest stages. Previous chapters will have shown how much has been done since 1947 to give India the social services which a progressive democracy must have if it is to survive. At the same time, Indian thinkers and sympathetic foreign observers recognize the need for some reorientation of present trends if the possible anti-social effects of over-rapid industrialization are to be countered, or at least mitigated. The aim must be not only to align social with economic development but also to ensure that the welfare of the community as a whole is not unduly subordinated to sectional interests.

The really crucial issue arises at the elementary level. The new Government, although it generally endorsed the CABE Report, decided, and put it in the Constitution, that universal and free education should be provided for children up to the age of 14 in ten years, whereas the CABE had given chapter and verse for showing that it could not be done properly in less than forty. It is not easy, in the absence of any official explanation, to understand what prompted this optimistic decision, since the difficulties in the way of securing the necessary teaching power and other essentials were even greater after 1947 than the CABE had anticipated in 1944. Perhaps an intelligible patriotic urge to catch up with the so-called advanced countries, together with pressures from radical elements in the political field, may be the answer. It now seems to be accepted that the goal will not be reached in less than the time forecast by the CABE.

While it would be unfair to blame Government for failing to give effect to their over-optimistic decision, it is open to question whether the approach to the final fulfilment, which has so far been followed, is the one best calculated to meet the urgent requirements of the overall national policy. This has been to concentrate on the primary (6–11) age-group in the first instance and leave the 11–14 year-olds until easier times. As a result, it is expected that at the end of the Third Plan in 1966 over three-quarters of the 6–11's will be in school but less than one-third of the 11–14's.

This decision has set up a chain of reactions which are having an unfortunate effect both inside and outside the educational field. In the first place, it means that two-thirds of the 11–14 age-group are not getting the finishing course, which, in most cases, would be their last formal training for life, livelihood and good citizenship. In the second place, it largely accounts for the comparative failure of the basic system. This was conceived by Gandhi and worked out by the Wardha Committee specially to meet the needs of children who would go out to work at 14. The Committee realized, as did the CABE, that to derive maximum benefit from the scheme, children must complete the course by staying at school until 14. It is only when they get beyond the age of 11 that they begin to master their tools, to understand the relation of their craft or crafts to the other subjects and to think of themselves not merely as so many individuals but as units in a society. The fact that wastage at the primary stage, if not as bad as it was, is still very serious, is an indication that many parents are not impressed with the value of the schooling which their children are now getting. In the third place, the appropriation to the primary stage of the bulk of the money left over when economic demands on the highest branches have been satisfied, has meant that not only the senior basic or middle stage is suffering but the secondary stage also. In spite of the increased numbers now in attendance at secondary schools, there is still less than one place available for every six children in the age-group, while the CABE prescribed a minimum of one place for every five. It is also probable that a lot of the existing places are being filled by pupils who are there because their parents can afford to pay the fees and not because they are capable of taking full advantage of a secondary course. What, however, is more serious from the national point of view is that scholarships and maintenance grants are only available, as things now are, for 2·8 per cent of those at the middle stage, for 8 per cent at the secondary stage and for 18 per cent at the post-matriculation stage. This means that the doors of higher education are practically closed to the able children of poor parents and the opportunity of tapping the latent resources of brainpower, which the economy so badly needs, is not being taken. This applies not only to industrial requirements but also to the recruitment of the additional teaching power, which is now in such short supply.

The present effect of this policy is that the top-heavy structure handed over by the British has been replaced by something resembling a lady of the Victorian era with plenty round the legs and a wasp waist surmounted by an imposing display of bodice, cape and bonnet. The consequent bottleneck—if a sudden change of metaphor may be forgiven—means that the flow of suitable students to universities and higher technical institutions, which cater today for three or four times as many as they did before 1947, is running down and threatens to dry up. The principals of these institutions are mostly agreed that the intellectual standard of new entrants is steadily deteriorating.

That this should be so is not far short of a mathematical certainty.

Is there any remedy which it is still not too late to apply? One may perhaps be found in the CABE Report. The Board recognized that to build a national system of education and so to integrate its parts that a broad highway would be opened for those able and willing to use it, would be a long-term process. The controlling factor, the supply and training of the body of competent teachers required, enabled it to estimate how long it would take to cover the whole country if the build-up started from the foundations. But it also recognized that if an independent India went in for industrialization on a big scale, as it probably would, some means must be found for providing the new economy more quickly with the expertise which it would urgently need, for it would clearly demand much more in the way of talent and brainpower than the existing educated classes could possibly produce. Since, therefore, there was neither the time nor the money to build one broad highway for the whole country, the alternative was to provide a number of smaller highways in selected areas which would, in about twelve years, begin to supply the highest stages with recruits of the calibre which the national economy was seeking. In other words, the progress towards an overall system of national education should be from area to area and not from age to age.

For obvious reasons, the number of areas to be selected in the first instance would have to be determined by the amount of money available and they would have to be distributed as evenly as possible over the States and Union Territories. They would also have to be large enough to justify the provision of the adequate variety of schools at the secondary stage, so that at least one child in five of the appropriate age-group could be given the chance of higher education, however poor his or her parents might happen to be. If the areas chosen could be mixed, i.e. partly rural and partly urban, it would facilitate experiment in the way of providing diversified institutions and courses at the secondary stage. Priority might well be given to areas where parents had already shown their interest in education and where there were persons who could be entrusted with the responsibilities of a local education authority. Valuable help in this connection could be expected from the block development system as it spreads.

A few figures may illustrate, very approximately, a convenient size of area in respect of population. Official estimates indicate that in 1966 about one-eighth of the total population will be in the 6–11 age-group. On this basis, an area containing 800,000 people should produce 100,000 children at the primary stage. Owing to deaths there will, of course, be more between 6 and 7 than between 10 and 11, but to avoid complicated calculations let it be assumed that the number in each year will be 20,000. Accepting the CABEs recommendation that there should be places in secondary schools for at least one in every five, it means that 4000 children would enter such schools each year. So, with a six-year secondary course, places would be required for 24,000 pupils, with a seven-year course for 28,000. The number of schools needed to accommodate so many pupils would be enough to afford opportunities for a wide range of diversified courses, whether in multi-purpose schools, technical high schools or high schools of the conventional type.

Beyond the secondary stage the CABE assumed that, as a minimum, one in every fifteen secondary pupils would be found fit to go on to a higher stage either at a university or institution of similar grade. Owing to the steps already taken to meet the requirements of the national economy there has been a large increase in the facilities at the post-secondary stage and probably, by now, the one-in-fifteen ratio could be reduced to one-in-eight, even at the risk of a lower average standard of ability than the CABE had in mind. This would give an annual entry of 500 or a total of 1500 for the three-year course for a first degree. Since there are now nearly sixty universities as well as a number of higher technical institutions scattered over the country, it should not be difficult to see that the university students from any selected area secured admission to a higher institution where the language issue would not be a serious problem. With regard to the areas themselves, it would be advisable to see that their boundaries coincided as far as possible with those of the development blocks established, or to be established, in them. This would prevent overlapping and promote co-ordination of the social services. It will be seen from what has just been said that if the areas initially selected for intensive development are already reasonably well-equipped with primary schools, they should be able, in little more than ten years, to send a steadily increasing flow of graduates into the employment market, which is what the economy is looking for.

It may be argued that area-to-area progress, inasmuch as it means, at any rate in the earlier stages, giving certain sections of the population better facilities than others, conflicts with the ideals of social justice explicit in the Constitution. On the other hand the policy of concentrating in the beginning on the primary (6–11) age group, which has so far deprived two-thirds of the 11–14s of what most people would regard as the minimum training for good citizenship, is not immune from a similar criticism. Moreover, the failure to open the gates of higher education to poor children of ability through an adequate provision of scholarships could be cited as a form of discrimination against a certain class, which is also forbidden by the Constitution. No doubt some politicians may have felt that if their constituencies were not among the areas first selected, they would find themselves in trouble with their constituents, but those familiar with how a democracy works, particularly when money is short, will know that popular agitation, if kept within bounds, is a useful lever for moving the administration to action. Since the Fourth Plan envisages a period of consolidation rather than one of rapid expansion, would it not be possible to take a few promising areas and complete in them the whole of the proposed educational structure up to the university stage? These would then exhibit *in parvo* the integrated fabric of a national system and make clear what Government intends to do as soon as circumstances permit.

It is now time to turn from the consideration of what is the best expedient for building a national system in the face of present obstacles to problems which are confined to particular branches of it. It is proposed to leave to the end of this chapter the fundamental problem on which the solution to the success of education in India, as in every other country, must ultimately depend, which is the supply and training of an adequate body of teachers of all grades.

The first, and probably the most critical of what may be called the domestic issues, is the future of Basic Education. It was described earlier as a "comparative failure" at the present time. The reason then given was that the policy of concentrating on the primary stage gives less than a third of the children in the 6–14 age-group a chance of completing the course as set out in the Wardha Scheme. This is undoubtedly the main reason but it is not the only one. Although the basic system has had the official blessing of Government since Independence, the percentage of basic schools in the total number at the elementary stage has only risen from 15·1 in 1951 to 26·5 at the present time, and according to a memorandum by the education division of the Planning Commission, the majority of these differ little from the ordinary or older type. It adds that although 75 per cent of the teacher training institutions are to be converted to the basic pattern by 1966, programmes, buildings and equipment will need considerable improvement before their output will be up to the necessary standard. One explanation of this unsatisfactory state of things, apart from the truncation of the course, is that most of the so-called basic schools fall far short of what Gandhi had in mind. He realized that the correlation of as many subjects as possible with a basic craft would demand a high standard of teaching, and, for this reason, prescribed a minimum of two years' training. As the outcome of the present urge for quick results, very few of the teachers in the converted schools have had more than six months' training—in some cases only three or even less—and, to make matters worse, the majority are not new entrants to the profession ready to try out new ideas but teachers already in service, who do not find it easy to master a new technique. In addition to trained teachers, basic schools need better premises and more expensive equipment than the old type, and, for these, it has not yet been possible to find the money.

It is not easy to suggest changes in the present approach that will be acceptable to politicians or others looking for quick dividends from a limited investment. The basic system itself, sensibly interpreted in regard to the choice of a craft or crafts suited to local conditions and the correlation of other subjects therewith, is in harmony with approved modern principles and there seems to be every reason to share Gandhi's opinion that it is well suited to meet the needs of Indian children, above all of those in rural districts. It would, therefore, be a pity to abandon a scheme, sponsored by a man to whom India owes so much, before it has had a fair trial in favourable conditions. The obvious suggestion would appear to be that no more basic schools, new or converted, should be established unless they can cover the whole eight years, can be staffed with fully trained teachers and can be provided with suitable premises and equipment. No existing teacher should be accepted for training who is too old or too set in his or her ideas. In the first instance, it might be wise to take for basic training young teachers already marked out for promotion and then send them either to run new schools or to staff demonstration schools at centres in selected areas.

Other problems at the lower stages are referred to in the preliminary memoranda for the Fourth Plan. The first one, that expansion is not uniform over the whole country is that some States lag behind others and the scheduled castes and tribes are not taking advantage of the facilities available, is not surprising. In many parts of the world local authorities, whether large or small, vary considerably both in enterprise and efficiency. Given time, things in this respect will no doubt improve, as they did in England from 1870 onwards. More serious are the disparity in enrolment between boys and girls and the persistence of the heavy wastage which was one of the most disquieting features of elementary education under the old régime.

In 1950–1 the proportion of girls in classes I to V was 28·1 per cent, and in classes VI to VIII, 17 per cent; it is estimated that in 1965–6 the percentages will have risen to 38·3 and 26. The urgent need to narrow the gap still further is generally accepted, though it may take time to convert the Muslims still in India to the fact that, in a small village, co-education is unavoidable.

The latest figures about wastage, which are given in the memorandum for the Planning Commission, indicate that 60 per cent of the children admitted to class I fail to reach class IV and that this figure has remained steady over the last ten years. The reason suggested in the memorandum is that the education provided in most elementary schools makes little contribution towards agricultural improvement or the running of panchayats or co-operatives and so fails to impress parents with its value or to train pupils for life in a modern democracy. If this is so, it shows how far the current intepretation of the basic pattern differs from Gandhi's original conception. It is true that most States have passed legislation making attendance at school compulsory up to the age of 11 and, in some cases, to 14, but the machinery in the way of attendance officers to enforce it has still to be provided. Better and more realistic teaching may do a good deal to enlist the co-operation of parents, but until the peasant is much more prosperous than he is at present, it will not be easy to persuade him to leave his children at school once they reach the age when they become valuable as workers in the home or the fields.

At the secondary stage, in spite of the increased enrolment since 1947, there remains an urgent need for many more places if poor children are to be given their chance and the demands of the higher branches for better recruits are to be satisfied. The problem is how to do this within the present limits of money and teaching power and without some reconsideration of existing priorities. Apart from this main issue, there are a number of interesting problems within the secondary sphere, about the solutions to which educational opinion is by no means unanimous.

It may be advisable to list these before examining them. They are (a) nomenclature, as defining the length and content of courses, (b) age of entry, (c) methods of selection for admission, (d) diversified courses, where and how they can best be provided, (e) the addition to selected schools of classes XI and XII to cover one or both years of the old intermediate course and (f) the "Three Languages Formula" or policy.

Nomenclature is important to the extent that it should enable one to distinguish between the different types of course which should follow immediately on the primary stage, at any rate until secondary education for all becomes a practical proposition. It may be well to retain the term "middle" to cover the three top classes in those schools, whether senior basic or old type, where the course ends at class VIII. It is true that "middle" is a misleading term in that it suggests something still to come but it is less misleading than "junior" or "lower secondary" would be, as this might imply that the middle school is a minor type of high school and not the finishing school for the great majority, who will clearly need a very different kind of curriculum from that of their co-evals in the lower forms of the normal secondary or high school. There would seem to be no need for any special designation for the 11–14 age-group or classes VI to VIII in those schools, where the course extends to class X or beyond. Perhaps "secondary" might be used to denote those which end at class X, and "higher secondary" those which include classes XI and XII. There is no reason why those which prefer to call themselves "high schools" or even "public schools" should not do so, provided that their range and intention are made clear. The name "merit schools" has been suggested for institutions to which specially gifted pupils may be drafted, but it might avoid a possibly invidious form of intellectual discrimination if the money such schools would cost were diverted to equipping the higher secondary type to cater for pupils of the calibre in question.

The length of the secondary course and its content is tied up with the current debate as to whether there should be a separate stage between it and the university course proper. It will be convenient to consider this a little later in conjunction with the alternative proposal to add classes XI and XII to selected schools in order that they may cover the work which used to be done in the old intermediate colleges.

With regard to the age of transfer from the primary to the middle or secondary stage, it seems to be agreed at the moment that this should remain at about 11. After that age the question of how best to facilitate transfers between one kind of post-primary school and another and so to safeguard the interests of late-developers will need more consideration than it has hitherto received.

As to methods of selection for admission, the Secondary Education Commission recommended that these should combine previous school records with written and, where desirable, oral examinations on modern lines. Few people would disagree with this, provided that the actual machinery of selection is elastic and sympathetic enough to reduce undeserved casualties to a minimum. A side issue is what should be done for those children whose parents wish them to have a secondary education but who fail the admission test. The CABE suggested that places might be found for them so long as no cost fell on public funds, but did not specify how this was to be done.

Another issue connected with the age of admission is whether all pupils should complete the course at a senior basic or middle school before going on to the secondary stage. Until these schools are much more numerous and efficient than they are at present, this will remain largely a theoretical question. Arguments in favour of it are that it would give a more democratic look to the national system and would meet the objections of those who, in India and elsewhere, regard the age of 11 as too young for the hiving off of the intellectual élite. It would also make it easier to deal with the late-developers. On the other hand, in view of the inevitable handicaps in the way of size, staff and equipment, under which middle schools are likely to labour for some time to come, it could accentuate the difficulty, experienced even by the most fortunate high schools, of providing a sufficiently varied curriculum for pupils of differing aptitudes and abilities and often with future objectives which will determine the age at which they will want to leave school. Whatever may be decided about these questions and whether or not the secondary stage should be provided under one roof or two or even three, there would seem to be something like general agreement that boys and girls aspiring to a first degree should have been under instruction for at least fifteen years, five primary, seven secondary and three at a university.

The next point of importance that arises at the secondary stage is the variety of courses required and how far it is desirable and feasible to provide these under the same or different roofs. The need for a considerable reorientation of secondary objectives, if the new economy is to be well served, will be seen from the fact that, in 1966, the number of pupils in schools with a vocational bias is likely to be about 150,000 as compared with 5,200,000 in those of the general type. An interesting experiment with the object of bringing the secondary curriculum more into line with industrial requirements, which is being tried in several States, is the multi-purpose school. Its aim, as explained in a previous chapter, is to provide, in some cases after class VIII, in others after class X, in addition to a common core of basic subjects, diversified courses in the humanities, science and technology. In theory the idea is attractive, at any rate where the funds to secure the requisite staff and equipment are to hand. It is perhaps too early to form any definite conclusion as to whether this will prove the right answer, but doubts are already being expressed in India as to whether these diversified courses, as now planned, are really fitting pupils either for jobs on leaving school or for entries to higher studies. As a general pattern to be followed in the future organization of secondary education, the multi-purpose school is open to certain criticisms which apply mainly to the technological course. In the first place, with regard to staff, since higher technical institutions and polytechnics are finding the greatest difficulty in engaging and keeping, against industrial inducements, teachers of the necessary calibre, what are the chances of schools with lower salaries to offer being more fortunate? Then as to equipment; this, if up to date, is beyond the resources of all but a very few opulent schools, and pupils who had been trained on obsolete machines, often surplus war stores, are not likely to fit in to a modern factory without a lot of reconditioning. Leading manufacturers are already expressing a preference for young people with a good grounding in general science over those who have taken a technical course largely unrelated to modern industrial practice.

The right answer may be that secondary schools, multi-purpose or otherwise, should confine themselves to two courses in the arts and the sciences, and that a limited number of technical high schools should be established in or near industrial areas. It will not be easy, as things are, to find, for even a small number of such schools, the staff and equipment that will make them really worthwhile from the industrial point of view, but it will do more to conserve limited resources than the multiplication of the multi-purpose type. If as many technical high schools as possible can be located near higher technical institutions or polytechnics, they may benefit from the contiguity in many ways. In view of the supreme importance of the agricultural industry, it is important that an appropriate number of schools of this type should be in rural areas and have the necessary accommodation for boarders.

How long the secondary course should be is another issue about which there is a considerable divergence of opinion. This is closely linked up with the proposal, originally put forward by the Hunter Commission and subsequently endorsed by the CABE and Secondary Commission, though not by the University Commission, that the intermediate colleges should be abolished, their first year being transferred to the secondary schools and the second to the universities. The CABE, indeed, was optimistic enough to hope that, with rising standards at the secondary level, these schools should, in time, be able to cover both years. It was, however, agreed that during the time required to upgrade high schools by the addition of class XI, and, where possible, class XII as well, a special one-year course should be provided for pupils going on to a university. Until a few years ago the university authorities appeared to be satisfied that the high schools so far upgraded were succeeding in covering the first year of the intermediate course and might, given the necessary staff and equipment, be able to cover both years before long. Naturally, the schools first upgraded were the best equipped, and doubts have since arisen as to the possibility of finding the wherewithal to bring all schools up to the same standard. So far, only five States have followed the advice of the Secondary Commission and extended the length of the secondary course, while its necessary corollary, a three-year course leading to a first degree, has not been adopted by universities in Bombay and Uttar Pradesh. The fact that many States are proceeding—perhaps too rapidly—with the conversion of middle into secondary schools, has lent support to the argument in favour of retaining some form of intermediate stage, at any rate for the present. The result is that many Indian educationists today advocate the provision of a two-year course of pre-university instruction in what are now to be called "Junior Colleges".

Apart from the question as to who should administer these new colleges and what steps should be taken to make them more effective links between secondary schools and universities than their predecessors, there are things to be said on behalf of the higher secondary schools, which possess both the staff and equipment to do justice to classes XI and XII. Experience elsewhere suggests that secondary education will lose much of its value as a preparation both for further study and for entry into employment if the normal course is limited to five years. It will also add to the curricular problems presented by the "Three Languages" policy, of which more later. It has, however, wider implications. It was in 1902 that the State in England first began to take an interest in the provision of secondary education. For some years the new municipal and county high schools contented themselves with a five-year course ending about the age of 16, after which most of their pupils entered employment. The few who aspired to a university career were either transferred to a neighbouring grammar school or were given private tuition. By the end of the First World War, however, many of the state schools began to emulate their older rivals, the "public" and grammar schools, by adding on what are known in England as "sixth forms". This meant another two years at school for those going to universities or entering occupations for which a higher school certificate, now called A-level, was required. These sixth forms, therefore, correspond closely both in age range and intention to classes XI and XII in Indian schools. An expert inquiry in the 1930s found that sixth forms had not only met the needs of senior pupils but had also raised standards of work throughout the school. There is little reason to doubt that classes XI and XII can provide a similar stimulus in India.

Another advantage of having some older boys and girls in a secondary school is that they can be entrusted with minor responsibilities with benefit to the staff but with greater benefit to themselves. Very few Indian schools have a monitorial or prefect system and its absence may partly account for something that is causing concern to the authorities in some universities and that is indiscipline among students. The average Indian student is quite as intelligent as and often more industrious than his co-eval in a Western university but he is, as a rule, less mature in some ways, as well as less conscious of his social obligations. Some training and practice in shouldering some of these obligations before he leaves school might prove, later on, to be both to his own advantage and to that of the community which he joins. The idea has often been mooted that all university students should do a period of compulsory social service before being granted their degrees, but apart from the disturbance to studies which this would involve, the self-discipline imposed by a voluntary acceptance of obligations towards the less fortunate is likely to be a more lasting influence in the way of good citizenship.

The next problem in the secondary field which, owing to its political implications may turn out to be a crucial one, arises from what is now called the "Three Languages" policy. When it was laid down in the Constitution that Hindi should be the national language, it meant that children going beyond the primary stage whose mother-tongue was not Hindi would have to learn it as well. It was further decided that when English ceased to be the administrative language, its vogue as an international medium justified its inclusion as a compulsory subject in the curriculum of all secondary schools. As a result of these decisions, pupils in non-Hindi speaking areas were faced with the task of learning three language in from five to seven years. In order that they should not be at a disadvantage with their fellows in the Hindi areas, the latter were also required to study a third language. The intention, no doubt, was that to promote a consciousness of national unity and to facilitate migration from one part of the country to another, this third language should be another modern Indian tongue. It has worked out, however, that many Hindi area schools have chosen Sanskrit, while others have preferred a modern foreign language like Russian, German or French.

This policy, in spite of its apparent equity, has been described by cynics as one of equal handicaps for all. In the years following the Revolution a somewhat similar linguistic problem existed in the U.S.S.R. Lenin's view was that "the demands of the economic cycle will always force the nationalities living in one State—as long as they want to live together—to study the language of the majority" and it is often claimed that even in the outlying states of the Union, Russian is superseding the local languages and dialects as the mother-tongue of the rising generation. Whether or not this claim can be justified in the U.S.S.R., there is little prospect of Hindi ousting the other major languages and becoming the common speech of all Indians. In fact, linguistic differences and the local patriotisms inspired by them seem to be stronger today than they were before. The people of the south may welcome "emotional integration" and other measures designed to promote national unity, but not to the extent of sacrificing their traditional Dravidian culture.

Apart from its political angle, the "Three Languages" policy is creating no small problem from the purely educational standpoint. This is whether, even if the teaching of the languages is highly efficient, normal pupils, during their secondary career, can secure a sufficient mastery of them to justify the time spent. By mastery is meant not merely the ability to read a book in a foreign tongue, but to be able to communicate freely with foreigners. It is generally admitted that such a mastery has not yet been achieved except in a few schools rich enough to engage expert teachers, in some cases from abroad, or where a disproportionate amount of time has been allotted to languages at the expense of other subjects. Here, once more, the crux of the problem is the teacher, and it must also be remembered that quite a lot of the pupils now occupying places in secondary schools are not there by virtue of a high IQ.

Concern about the present standard of language teaching in secondary schools has caused some States to start foreign languages in the primary school, usually at class III, but since the real difficulty facing secondary schools is to find competent language teachers, the chances of their being available at the lower level are not very bright, and if the foundations are badly laid, the task higher up will only become more arduous. An experiment which may help to relieve the linguistic pressure is the "staggering" of the school-leaving examination, so that pupils may dispose of certain subjects in their penultimate year and thus have some time to spare in their last year to concentrate on those subjects, e.g. languages, which require more attention. Alternatively, the Junior Colleges, if they come into existence, might give a reasonable priority to teaching the language that will be the medium of instruction at the neighbouring university, particularly for the benefit of those students for whom it will be a foreign tongue.

Before leaving the secondary stage, attention may again be drawn to its supreme importance to a large, new and ambitious democracy like India. It alone is the channel through which urgent economic requirements in the way of manpower can be satisfied. It is both the door to higher studies and to entry to employment. The need for high-grade technologists and other experts must not obscure the importance to industry of people with education to fill supervisory posts below the top level. These will usually enter employment on completing the secondary course. A nineteenth-century philosopher once said that it was the function of higher education to train an élite not for its own sake but for that of society. No modern nation stands in greater need of such an élite than India, and it is the business of a truly national system of education to seek out its future members not in one section of the community but wherever they may be found.

CHAPTER 9

Current Problems. II

As THE earlier chapters will have shown, the developments which have taken place at the university and higher technical levels since 1947 have been outstanding, and this has been mainly due to the fact that national economic planning, from the beginning, has called for a special effort by these branches. It naturally follows that expansion on such a scale has produced its own problems, many of which have arisen since the University Commission and the Sarkar Committee presented their reports. Here, due credit must be given to two All-India bodies, the UGC and the AICTE, for their success in persuading both State Governments and university authorities to accept not only their advice but also their assistance in the more concrete form of financial aid. The CABE also continues to provide a valuable forum for the discussion and investigation of educational issues on a national basis and it now has—and this is true of the whole educational system—an ally in the form of the NCERT, which is equipped to supply expert guidance in regard to any issue that may be submitted to it.

In spite of the services rendered by these and the other advisory bodies set up since 1947, a number of problems remain to be solved. The first of these, which the Fourth Plan regards as serious, is primarily a quantitative one. Although the question of adjusting the output of educational institutions to economic requirements has received attention from Manpower and other committees, the figures given in the preliminary memoranda show that enrolment at the post-matriculation stage in arts has increased from 34·2 per cent in 1950–1 to 52·2 in 1962–3, while that in science and professional courses has decreased from 65·8 per cent to 47·8 per cent in the same period. One result of this has been that the number of educated unemployed on the live registers of the labour exchanges has risen from 160,000 in 1953 to 739,000 in 1963. While these figures may not be entirely reliable, they do suggest that in spite of the attractive prospects offered by industry today, Indian parents of the upper and middle classes still prefer their children to enter "black-coated" occupations. To supply the needed corrective, steps should be taken to give secondary education a much stronger vocational bias than it has at present and then to open its doors, and those of the still higher stages, to the able children of parents who see no objection to industrial employment.

This problem also has a qualitative aspect, to which the tapping of latent reserves of brainpower would again appear to give the right answer. This is the generally admitted deterioration in the standard of entrants. More than 50 per cent of the candidates fail at their examinations and of those who get degrees, the majority are in the third class, which is below the standard for which progressive firms are looking. Even in the popular technical branch failures are 25 per cent at the graduate and 50 per cent at the diploma level. It stands to reason that unless the catchment area is continuously refreshed to meet ever increasing demands, standards must fall.

It is not only the waste of time and money involved in this high percentage of failures that is causing concern today. University authorities in many places are much exercised about the prevalence of indiscipline among students. Though the forms which this takes and the circumstances which give rise to it may vary from place to place, fear among the less able students that they may fail to make the grade and the feeling of frustration arising from this may be a common factor underlying the current unrest. There are, of course, other causes. Reference has been made already to the lack of opportunities, at the secondary stage, for the older pupils to undertake social obligations. Too large colleges, too little residential accommodation and too few personal contacts between teachers and students are other reasons why some Indian students fail to appreciate the need for the self-discipline which membership of a corporate body should entail. It is significant that the Vice-Chancellors of the smaller universities with residential colleges or halls are much less concerned about student indiscipline than those the great majority of whose students live in lodgings, often of a very poor kind. There is general agreement as to the desirability of delimiting the size of new universities and colleges and of effecting reductions, wherever possible, in that of some of the older ones, of which Calcutta is a formidable example. In this case, action is already being taken. New colleges of a reasonable size are being built on the outskirts to relieve the pressure on those in the centre of the city and, at the same time, new universities are being established in different parts of the State of West Bengal which will absorb the colleges in their areas at present affiliated to Calcutta University.

No more need be said here about the possible effect on universities, and indeed on all types of post-secondary education, of the changes in contemplation at the secondary stage, and in particular the impact on the first degree course of the junior colleges, if and when created. There are, however, some matters concerning organization, standards and contents of courses, which call for some comment. In the first category is the question of preventing wasteful overlapping, which the rapid increase in the number of universities and other institutions of higher study makes especially urgent. The UGC has done a lot of useful work in this connection but it has to be remembered that the bodies directly responsible are, in many cases, jealous of their autonomy and that the recent resurgence of regional and linguistic patriotisms does not make things any easier. It might be a good thing to encourage the new universities, while remaining true to the meaning of the word university, to pay special attention to those subjects which have a direct bearing on the character of the area in which they are situated.

On the academic side there is the trite but still live issue that Indian students should be encouraged to think rather than to memorize. It is not surprising that many of them found this difficult in the old days, when the medium of instruction was a language in which they were not accustomed to think. This difficulty has been largely removed today through the super-session of English by the mother-tongue or the regional language, but both students and examiners still need reminding that reliance on lecture notes and nothing else should not be the passport to a good degree.

Another matter which has received some attention in recent years but still requires a lot more, is the securing of greater uniformity of standards between different universities and between the different faculties in the same university. Not long before 1947, one university made a formal request that, in connection with the award of certain central government scholar-ships, its second-class degrees should be accepted as equivalent to the first-class degrees of any other university and the request, even if it was not acceded to, was not without some justification. It would also help Indian students wishing to study abroad if they could have definite information, before they set off, as to how far Indian university qualifications would be accepted for admission to the institution or course which they wanted to join. It is understood that the Commonwealth Universities Associa-tion has taken this matter up, but it is not known what agreement has so far been reached.

In view of the success which it has already achieved, it would seem desirable that both the executive functions and the funds at the disposal of the UGC should be enlarged so that it may be in a position to give effective help, not only in regard to existing problems, but also in regard to those which the proliferation of universities is bound to precipitate in the near future.

A tribute has already been paid to the admirable build-up of the four IITs, the foundation of which was one of the first projects sponsored by the AICTE after its inception in 1946. Those who have visited them will probably agree that they do credit to the famous institution on which they were originally modelled, the Massachusetts Institute of Technology. If the fifth institute recently established at Delhi and others now projected attain to the same standard, these, with the National Research Institutes set up since Independence and the enlargement of similar facilities at universities, will give India a provision in the higher ranges of technology of which any country could be proud.

On the instructional side there is little to criticize so far as the degree and research courses provided in these institutes are concerned. The former cover five years as a rule and are carefully aligned with changing requirements as industrial development proceeds. It is, however, recognized that the three-year diploma courses need some revision. They are, for the most part, too academic—they have, in fact, been described as anaemic versions of the degree course—and do not adequately prepare students for the sort of posts which diploma-holders should be expected to fill in any industrial organization.

Below the highest level the present picture is not quite so impressive. As was recorded earlier, a lot has been done to increase the meagre supply of polytechnics that was available in 1947. Many of the new ones are well housed and equipped and provide courses covering a wide range of subjects varying from those which, if more practical in content and treatment, approach degree standards down to part-time classes for ordinary craftsmen. The fact, however, that there is rather a high rate of wastage among their students would seem to indicate that what they are doing is not sufficiently in line with contemporary requirements. It may be that a closer contact with local industries is needed. This would give teachers a better idea of what employers are looking for and students a stronger claim on employers' interest. A practical way of promoting both these aims would be a wide extension of the "sandwich" system, which so far has hardly taken root in India. It would also be a good thing if a polytechnic could house a day school, such as a technical high school or a junior technical school, but as evening classes are not popular in India, there is not usually much space vacant during the day in an Indian polytechnic.

A technical need, important everywhere but specially urgent in India today, is the production of a sufficient supply of people to fill the supervisory grades like foremen and chargehands. The essential role to be filled in an army by competent NCOs has long been recognized; the same type is no less essential in large works today. Where are such people to come from? Since the products of the higher institutes are likely to remain in short supply for some time to come so far as the more senior posts are concerned, there is no prospect of any surplus, e.g. of diploma-holders, being available. Moreover, in an industrial system organized mainly on a horizontal basis, incentives are lacking for those who might have otherwise been ready to work their way up. It seems, therefore, that the supervisory grade will have to look for recruits to those pupils in technical high schools who do not go on to further studies and to the abler pupils from schools of the junior technical type. This emphasizes the need for many more schools of both kinds. Valuable reinforcements may also come from labour-training camps, ITIs and other schemes for producing skilled workmen which are now in operation. Their output will contain many young men who, with some practical experience at work, could soon be fitted to fill responsible positions. To tie up loose ends, it is advisable that all schemes of this kind should be put under the Department of Education. The present shortage, not only of supervisors but also of skilled craftsmen, may also be ascribed to the comparatively slow expansion of middle and senior basic schools, where such people would normally receive their preliminary education.

The importance of agricultural education as a vital sector of the technical branch is fully recognized in India, but it is doubtful whether commercial and art education is yet receiving the attention to which its potential contribution to the success of modern industry entitles it. Probably, the explanation lies in the priority so far assigned to heavy industry. Design here is, of course, of supreme importance, but the value of machinery depends more on its functional efficiency than on its aesthetic appeal. In the case of consumer goods the scale of values changes and appearance becomes more important. So, also, do various problems of distribution, not excluding the art of salesmanship. This points to the desirability of including departments of commercial and art instruction both in polytechnics and at the higher levels as well.

What was said earlier about enlarging the authority and resources of the UGC applies with equal force in the case of the AICTE. In fact, the case for it may be even stronger because the interests that have to be both satisfied and co-ordinated in the technical sphere are more complex than in the case of universities. In view, however, of the size of the AICTE and the infrequency of its meetings, it might be well to have a much smaller body like the UGC.

One of the wisest decisions so far taken in the Indian educational field has been the enlargement of the conception of adult education to include training in a wide range of social activities for those over the normal age for formal instruction. As has been pointed out earlier, adult education under the old régime meant little more than enthusiastic but spasmodic and short-lived campaigns to combat illiteracy. Literacy for all under 40 will continue to be the primary objective, but it is now recognized that literacy by itself is not enough. Newly made literates must be convinced that it is worth their while to stay literate, and this can best be done by relating the training given to their interests both as individuals and as members of a community. The importance now attached to the Panchayati Raj and the spread of the Block Development system will be of great help in social education.

Mention has already been made of the contribution which social education may be expected to make towards the solution of a national problem of great urgency, viz. family planning. Other important matters now within its sphere of influence are agricultural improvement, sanitation and the supply of clean

water, health precautions and the preservation of the countryside. On what may be called the lighter side, it is within its
scope to provide facilities which may make life more interesting
and enlarge contacts with the outside world. Among these are
village institutes and libraries, informal classes and demonstra-
tions for those with time off in the daytime and, for evenings, all
the healthy forms of recreation and entertainment likely to
appeal to adults after their day's work is over. The very few
travelling cinema projectors that were available in the old days
enjoyed an enormous and occasionally embarrassing popularity,
particularly in the remoter rural districts. Let us invoke yet once
more the aid of that indispensable ally, electric light.

What has been said so far about social education may give
the impression that it is very largely a rural problem. This would
be misleading, for the policy of rapid industrialization has
already shown the need for it not only in the fast-growing towns
but also in the new residential areas attached to the larger
development projects like the one at Durgapur. Much has been
said and a good deal has been done about India avoiding the
social evils associated with industrial revolutions in other parts
of the world, but it is by no means certain that all Indian
employers realize their obligations to their employees or that
Government will bring pressure to bear on those who do not.
Hence, there is ample scope for social education in the towns as
well as the villages.

While it is satisfactory that the right lines are being laid down
and that certain aspects of social education, e.g. family planning
and local sanitation, may look forward to special attention during
the Fourth Plan, a lot remains to be done if the necessary army
of teachers and other helpers is to be enlisted. To get the right
kind of teacher here is even more difficult than it is in the case
of the more formal branches, because what is wanted is not so
much classroom techniques as human sympathy and an adaptable
mind. Also, the qualities which may make a man or woman a
good instructor of youth are not always those that make for
success with older people. India, like other countries which have

tackled adult education in a big way, will have to depend to a large extent on the professional teacher from primary or middle schools, though in towns, perhaps, secondary school teachers may also feel the urge to serve in the social sphere.

Experience elsewhere shows that adult education, even in the more limited sense, heeds the help of agencies and persons outside the education service. The lines which development is now following in India makes this still more essential. The officers concerned with Block Development and other aspects of local administration will, of course, be invaluable allies, but any help that they may be able to give outside their immediate duties will need to be supplemented by a host of other workers, paid and unpaid. To secure enough of these will be a difficult matter in any case and it has to be remembered that very many of the Indian villages most in need of social education are remote and, at some seasons, hard to reach. Whatever aid may be forthcoming from travelling "squads" and other mobile units, social workers, for the most part, will have to be on the spot. The fact that some of the most urgent problems, like family planning and domestic hygiene, can best be tackled by women does not make things easier. If the experimental educational settlements already mentioned become widespread, they could also prove focal points for social as well as general education.

It will no doubt be some time before India produces as many voluntary agencies in the social field as are to be found in Western countries. Splendid work is being done by some of the existing ones, like the Ramakrishna Mission, but there is one body which might do more than it is doing to help the cause of social education; that is the university. Now that there are some sixty universities, most parts of the country have one within reasonable reach. Some of them have extra-mural departments but few, if any of these, are staffed to do the kind of work in the social field that India so badly needs. What is wanted is not extension lectures, addressed to more or less educated audiences in the towns, but full-time trained lecturers, who would go about starting and watching over all sorts of educational activities from popular talks to serious study groups, wherever the soil was found to be fertile. Such people could be of considerable help in connection with Block Development and other forms of rural reconstruction. They might also, in the course of their labours, bring to light quite a lot of hitherto undiscovered talent. If it is objected that to provide a service of this kind on the scale required would cost money, one answer is that, at the moment, universities are in a better position to find it than most of the other branches of education.

The suggestion has often been made—it goes back in fact to pre-1947 days—that university students, and even the senior pupils in high schools, should have to undertake a period of social work before receiving their degrees or leaving certificates. Reasons were given earlier in this book for thinking that to make such service compulsory would defeat its own object, though to encourage rather than to compel young people to go to the help of those less fortunate than themselves is a good thing everywhere. Many colleges and schools do have their social societies and programmes but if more students would voluntarily undertake, either as individuals or as members of some organization, the kind of social work that appealed to them, it would probably do them as much good as it would the intended beneficiaries. "Servants of the People" is a title of honour in India.

Before we come to what is undoubtedly the most urgent of the essential services, viz. the supply and training of teachers, some reference must be made to what is being done and what remains to be done in the case of the others.

Thanks to some enlightened administrators, a lot has been done since 1947 to develop the public health service, even if one result has been to accentuate the population problem. Pupils and students are clearly benefiting by the overall growth of the state medical services but so long as doctors, nurses, clinics and equipment remain in short supply, a special school medical service will have to stay on the waiting list. The same applies to special provision for the mentally and physically handicapped. The lines to be followed in developing all branches of the medical service were authoritatively laid down in the Bhore Report, a monumental contribution towards post-war reconstruction which made its appearance before 1947. It is rather surprising that so little notice seems to have been taken of this important document by those engaged in health planning since Independence. It is, however, good to know that nearly all States are now making provision, on a reasonably liberal scale, for school meals, especially at the elementary stage.

Increased attention is now being paid to vocational guidance in schools, and most universities have their employment bureaux, the immediate object being to meet the insistent demands from industry for more recruits with some scientific or technical training. There is, however, some risk that efforts for what may be called mass conversion for this purpose may ignore individual aptitudes and ambitions. It is highly desirable that some training in up-to-date methods of vocational guidance should be given to the officers concerned with the new units of rural reorganization. The modern approach to agriculture contemplated by the planners opens many new avenues of employment to the villager.

A good deal has already been done to bring administration, in theory at any rate, into line with the new political and economic dispensation. The schemes for Block Development and Panchayati Raj and the importance attached to the devolution of administrative authority on local bodies generally will directly affect the social services. At the Central and State levels there is certainly no lack of boards, institutes and standing committees to look after them but whether the district boards, to which it is proposed to delegate so much responsibility in the education field, will be able to enlist the services of enough men and women of intelligence and goodwill to make them effective administrative units is a matter about which one may have some doubts.

So far as the professional side of social administration is concerned, the need for strengthening ministerial staffs both at the Centre and in the States is generally recognized, and the proposed reconstitution of the IES on a sounder basis should do much to help this. Two small but not unimportant suggestions may be offered. In the first place there should be closer contact between the inside and outside staffs. Inspectors and other district officers should be brought in frequently for consultation with headquarters. The projected devolution of authority makes this increasingly necessary. In the second place—and this applies particularly to education—administrative officers should have first-hand experience of teaching problems, especially at the lower levels. It would be interesting to know how many of the senior members of the Central or State Departments of Education have ever taught in a primary school. Would it be possible to take more successful teachers into administration and to second for periods of teaching administrative officers who lack experience in that respect?

All-important as the question of the best way to finance the social services indubitably is, very little will be said about it here, and for two good reasons. The EC Report, when it appears, is certain to contain elaborate calculations as to the cost of the proposals which it has in mind, either at once or spread over a period of years. On the other hand, the Fourth Five-year Plan is equally sure to explain in detail how much money it can find for the various branches of the social services during the period with which it is concerned. When these figures are available, it may be justifiable to suggest reallocations or even reconsideration of priorities; all that can be usefully done at the moment is to reaffirm the view, expressed by the CABE Report and subsequent inquiries, that if development is to take place on the scale which the new India requires, substantial financial aid from the Centre to the States will be indispensable.

When individuals or nations find themselves confronted by grave difficulties, it is wiser to treat these as problems challenging solution than as crises creating apprehension. So far, the use of the word crisis has been avoided except in regard to the growth of population, which is only indirectly an educational issue. There is, however, a matter of direct concern to the education service which may soon become a crisis, if it is not one already. This is the serious shortage of teachers in all branches and at all levels. At the risk of ending this chapter on a pessimistic note, it is essential to examine the causes of this and to explore possible remedies.

If any profession is to attract enough entrants of the right calibre, it must offer reasonable remuneration and conditions of service; it must also confer a status indicative of the estimation in which it is held by society. A good deal has been done since 1947 to improve conditions all round and to reduce the glaring disparity that used to exist between teachers in universities and those in primary schools, but that it has not been enough is clear from the fact that grave shortages exist even in the highest branches, which have been receiving preferential treatment. A recent official estimate shows that so far as teachers of science and technology are concerned, between 30 and 40 per cent of the approved posts remain unfilled. The higher their reputations, the more difficult colleges are finding it to secure and still more to keep teachers with first-class qualifications. Since the pay offered by industry to top graduates is often half as much again as the average salary of a lecturer, any idea that a remedy can be found by a further raising of salaries is not within the bounds of practical politics. This is implicit in the memorandum, already referred to, by the Education Division of the Planning Commission, which states that while Rs. 20 crores should be included in the Fourth Plan for improving the salaries of teachers, this should be "utilised for linking improvements in emoluments to upgrading of qualifications. No provision has been made in the Plan for a general rise in the salaries of teachers, as that is not a development expenditure and should be separately examined outside the Plan." In the existing financial circumstances it would be unduly optimistic to anticipate any early examination of this kind.

In addition to the fact that the number of teachers now forthcoming is inadequate to meet existing, let alone prospective, requirements, it is admitted that the expansion which has so far taken place, especially at the primary level, has outstripped the capacity of the training institutions to satisfy its demands. The result has been a steady deterioration in standards all round, and temporary expedients to step up the supply, like shortened training courses, have only made it worse. The disfavour with which the basic system is coming to be regarded in some quarters is almost entirely due to the fact that the right kind of training is not being given to the right kind of teacher. That this is not simply a pessimistic opinion on the part of the writer may be seen from the memorandum quoted above; it states that "the rapid expansion of educational facilities has outstripped the resources of trained teachers . . . the number of untrained teachers has been increasing" and then, a little later on, "the quality of training has considerably deteriorated".

It is by no means easy to find a solution or solutions to this fundamental problem. So far as its qualitative aspect is concerned, it was hoped to do a lot during the Third Plan to improve training institutions, in particular those for future basic teachers. How much has actually been achieved is not known at the moment, but it is at any rate satisfactory to know that steps are being taken. The more disquieting feature is the quantitative one. To translate into action existing assumptions about a national system of education and to provide for growth of population, between 2 and 3 million teachers will be required. Where and how are they to be found? Although, in view of the present economic policy, the shortage of teachers in the highest branches causes immediate concern to the planners, the outlook is, in some respects, more serious at the primary and middle levels. In spite of the spread of modern amenities to many rural areas through the various development schemes, one can hardly regard the life of the village teacher today as a very attractive one, except to the few dedicated spirits. It is not so much poor pay and prospects as intellectual loneliness that repel young people, above all those from urban homes. Some States have been experimenting with schemes for dealing with this, and this may be the place to say a little more about the new Educational Settlements which have already been mentioned. The West Bengal plan is to form, at some reasonably accessible centre, a kind of colony where quarters are provided for the teachers in the neighbouring village schools as well as those actually working in the settlement. It has its own shopping centre and other facilities. Some primary and middle schools will be located there and the children brought in daily from their homes. In other cases teachers will go out to their schools and return to the settlement at night. In the larger ones there may also be a secondary school and possibly a training institution as well. There would seem to be no reason why people engaged in other kinds of social work should not also find a home in a settlement. From the purely educational point of view, this new scheme has much to commend it but the social drawback is that it deprives villagers of the cultural advantage of having a school on their doorstep and teachers as their neighbours.

There can be little doubt that the main source of supply must be sought in the primary and middle schools themselves. Here again, British experience may not be irrelevant. When, as a result of the Act of 1902, the new county and municipal high schools opened their doors to boys and girls likely to benefit by the education provided and not simply to those whose parents could afford to pay for it, many able children from poor homes, who were thus given their chance, found teaching in elementary schools a career not without its attractions. H. G. Wells, the author, a critical observer of the social scene, expressed the opinion that the spread of secondary education among the masses had resulted, among other things, in the elementary schools of the country being staffed by the élite of the lower classes. Those in close contact with these schools at the time will probably agree that Wells' comment was not unjustified.

Is it unrealistic to look for a similar result in India, if Government can be persuaded to convert the present structure into a more pyramidal shape, or, in other words, to stop further expansion at the primary stage and devote the money so saved to more middle schools and more places at the secondary stage for poor children of ability? This would open two promising avenues for augmenting the supply of teachers. In the first place,

at the end of the middle stage, boys and girls who were attracted
by the idea of teaching might be drafted to institutions somewhat
on the lines of the former pupil–teacher centres in England,
where a special three-year course would prepare those who
showed promise for entry to a training college. In the second
place, pupils in secondary schools who would otherwise leave
after class X might, in suitable cases, be offered inducements to
stay on at school until those considered likely to succeed as
teachers were ready to take a course either at a training college
or at a university.

Some readers may feel that too much stress has been laid on
the need for more attention to those branches which follow
immediately on the primary stage so that poor children of ability
may be given their chance and latent resources of brainpower
may be tapped. The answer must be that of all the social problems facing India at the moment, this is the greatest. It is not
merely a question of ensuring social justice for all and so obeying
the Constitution; it is the only way of giving the political and
economic life of the country the fresh infusion of lifeblood without which it cannot continue to flourish. Of the two Indias that
exist today, the educated and the uneducated, the former class
is too limited both in quantity and in quality to go on carrying
the burden, even if it were desirable that it should attempt to
do so.

It is true that India differs from most of the newly enfran-
chised countries in that it is the source of streams of culture,
which neither foreign conquest nor internal anarchy have ever
dried up and which the association, over many years, of Indian
with Western intellectuals, both at home and abroad, has in
many ways enriched. Nevertheless, it would be wise to pay heed
to some words of wisdom uttered a few years ago by a shrewd
political philosopher. He said :

> The future of education in the new societies is by no means a
> cloudless one. What many of these countries have learned is that
> education *per se* does not solve fundamental economic and social
> problems. The rising tide of nationalism does not necessarily carry

along with it the mechanism designed to meet the rising expectations of the people. The impact of change is so sudden and great that many of the leaders are bewildered by the contents of the Pandora's box which they have opened. The problems emerging under this impact, such as the growth and rise of an uprooted and dislocated proletariat, the presence of steadily increasing population, the insistent demand for more educational facilities, dissatisfaction with the existing social and political order and the substitution of new and conflicting value systems, establish conditions, which make the future of education seem bleak in many areas. The fact that these societies are now free has not eliminated these problems. (Gruber, F. C., *Education and the State*, Martin G. Brumbaugh Lecture OUP, 1960.)

CHAPTER 10

The Report of the Education Commission and the Fourth Five-year Plan

IT IS impossible, in a single chapter, to do justice to the proposals contained in the draft outline of the Fourth Plan for developing education and the social services. This was published in August 1966 and as, at the time of writing, it has not yet been approved by the Governments concerned, it is subject to final revision. Unless, however, there are dramatic changes in the economic or political situation as a result of the forthcoming elections, it is unlikely that the proposals which it contains will be materially altered. It is even more impossible to attempt to analyse or digest all the ideas put forward in the 692 pages of the EC Report. All that one can hope to do in the time and space available is to summarize its main conclusions and to call attention to those which go beyond or differ from the views expressed by previous commissions or those set out in the earlier chapters of this book.

THE REPORT OF THE EDUCATION COMMISSION

The EC was established by a Government resolution issued in July 1964, and its personnel included not only some of the most distinguished Indian educationists but also experts from a number of foreign countries. In the course of its labours it also consulted many people eminent in various sectors of the education field. It is not surprising, therefore, that the outcome of such a consortium of wise men is a weighty and impressive volume. The

EC defines its objectives in the foreword to the report, which says :

> We need to bring about a major improvement in the effectiveness of primary education; to introduce work-experience as an integral element of general education; to vocationalize secondary education; to improve the quality of teachers at all levels and to provide teachers in sufficient strength; to liquidate illiteracy; to strengthen centres of advanced study and strive to attain, in some of our universities at least, higher international standards; to lay special emphasis on the combination of teaching and research and to pay particular attention to education and research in agriculture and allied sciences.

Later in its report the EC lays down what it calls a "strategy of development", by which is presumably meant the best way of giving effect in existing circumstances to the objectives outlined above. It states :

> The capacity of society to expand educational facilities in terms of real resources sets up minimum targets, whereas the maximum targets are suggested by the public demand for secondary and higher education or the need to develop the available pool of native talent. The gap between these high and low targets can be bridged by considerations, which emerge from the necessity to relate the output of the educational system to manpower needs and to equalise educational opportunities. These will indicate the priorities to be adopted, the different courses of study to be developed, the extent to which facilities should be provided in the different courses and the manner in which enrolments in them could be made to include, after equality of access is provided for all, at least the best students in the community.

It will be clear from these statements of aims and methods that the EC was expected to undertake an exhaustive exploration of the existing system at all levels. The resolution which set it up exhorted it to survey every square inch of the educational field, with a small reservation in regard to legal and medical training. "What is needed", it said, "is a synoptic survey and an imaginative look at education considered as a whole." It also held out definite hopes that specific recommendations by the Commission would be implemented, for "the nation must be prepared to pay for quality in education and from the value attached to education by all sectors of the people it is clear that they will do so willingly". One cannot help wondering whether the Ministry of Education consulted the National Planning Commission before issuing their resolution, for its optimism is hardly justified by the present wastage at most stages and the allocation of funds in the Fourth Plan to national education considered as a whole.

Before considering the ECs more general recommendations in regard to organization and method, it may be well to summarize its principal proposals for development in the various branches.

The pre-primary branch, as was to be expected, is to be left very largely to private enterprise, but it is hoped that by 1986 there will be places in nursery schools or classes for 5 per cent of the 3–5 and 50 per cent of the 5–6 age-groups.

At the primary stage, the "strategy" prescribed raises some doubts. It is laid down that "each State and District should be assisted to go ahead at the best pace it can and the progress in no area should be allowed to be held up merely for want of essential facilities or financial allocations". But since the main essentials, teachers and money, are, as the EC frequently admits, in short supply, what exactly does this mean? It is explicit elsewhere that seven years of effective education for all children cannot be provided before 1985–6. Here, again, there is some ambiguity, for the EC does not seem to have made up its mind whether the full primary course should cover seven or eight years, nor does it seem to be unduly concerned by the fact that, by 1966, only a little over one-third of the 11–14's will be at school as compared with three-quarters of the 6–11's. All it has to suggest for the former is that part-time education, $4\frac{1}{2}$ hours a week for one year, should be provided for those not at school.

The EC attaches great importance to work-experience and describes this as a redefinition of Gandhi's educational thinking in terms of a society launched on the road to industrialization. The essential principles set out in the Wardha Scheme should guide and shape education at all levels and no single stage should be designated as basic. Work-experience at the lower primary stage should take the form of simple handwork, and at the higher primary stage of a suitable craft. Concern will no doubt be felt in some quarters that the EC sees no prospect for a long time to come of reducing the maximum size of classes below fifty at the lower and forty-five at the higher primary stage. A proposal which may not commend itself to everybody is that where classes I and II have more than sixty pupils they should be split into two shifts of three hours a day, with suitable overtime pay for the teachers.

Turning to secondary education, the EC lays down as the main objectives the improvement of standards, the vocationalizing of courses and the suitable location of new schools. On economic grounds, the optimum size for schools should be between 360 and 450 and steps should be taken to convert public opinion in favour of co-education both here and lower down. The size of classes should not exceed forty in either lower or higher secondary schools. A new idea is that part-time courses, conducted by secondary teachers out of normal school hours, as well as correspondence courses, should be provided for children who have completed the primary course but are unable to attend a secondary school.

Unfortunately, there is no room here to refer to the many useful proposals in regard to such matters as curricula, textbooks and examinations but it is worth noting that the EC differs from the Mudaliar Commission and some protagonists of the multi-purpose school by declaring that there should be no specialization until after class X. With regard to language teaching, it is not satisfied with the "Three Language Formula" as it operates at present. It suggests as an alternative (i) the mother-tongue or the regional language, (ii) the official language of the Union or the associate official language, i.e. English, as long as it exists, and (iii) a modern Indian or foreign language not covered in (i) or (ii) and other than that used as the medium of instruction. The scripts for future use should be either Devanagri or Roman. The EC also feels that the starting of English in class III is undesirable and that Sanskrit should not be included in the Three Language Formula.

Before passing on to the post-matriculation stage, to which

some people may think that the EC has devoted a disproportionate amount of attention, some reference must be made to proposals that affect most of the lower branches. For the raising of
standards generally, the EC attaches great importance to the
establishment of "quality" schools to act as pace-setters in their
districts. To these, the best pupils and teachers will be drafted.
For this purpose 10 per cent of the primary schools and one
secondary school in each block should be raised to the optimum
level during the next ten years. Pupils in "quality" schools are to
cost twice as much per head as those in ordinary schools. To
promote the discovery and development of talent "enrichment"
programmes are to be introduced in selected schools. Further
recommendations are for "school complexes", consisting of a
secondary school, with which all the lower and higher primary
schools in the locality will be closely linked, and for "neighbour-
hood schools"—in some ways not unlike English comprehensive
schools—which all children in the district will be required to
attend. The increased number of scholarships to be awarded at
the secondary stage is to be confined to pupils attending
"common" schools, i.e. not independent private schools. The
general policy for the grant of scholarships, which the Report
proposes at all stages of education, will be discussed later, as will
the question of fees.

There is an important recommendation in regard to the provision of vocational instruction at the secondary level. By 1986
20 per cent of the enrolments at the lower secondary stage and
50 per cent of those beyond class X should be in full-time or
part-time courses of this character. The number of ITIs should
be increased and the age of entry lowered to 14. The present
junior technical schools should be converted into technical high
schools.

Finally, the EC deprecates any attempt to upgrade all
secondary schools and would be satisfied if one in four were
raised to higher secondary status. It agrees with the CABE and
the Mudaliar Commission that pre-university courses of all kinds
should be transferred to higher secondary schools by 1985.

When it comes to education at the post-matriculation stage, whether in universities or technical institutions, the EC deals so meticulously with all aspects of organization and methods of instruction that it will only be possible here to call attention to those recommendations which either go beyond or differ from what the Radhakrishnan Commission proposed. The reason for the exhaustive treatment of education at this stage is no doubt mainly due to its current importance to the national economy, but it may also be partly due to the fact that so many of the Commission and its consultants are specialists in this sector of the educational field.

With regard to the expansion needed to meet manpower demands and employment opportunities, enrolments in under-graduate and postgraduate courses will have to increase from 1 to 4 million during the next twenty years. To lessen the accommodation problem, one-third of this increased enrolment should be catered for by correspondence courses and evening colleges. Each State should have at least one agricultural university at which the first-degree course should normally be five years after ten years' schooling. Faculties of agriculture should also be established in the IITs and in some of the ordinary universities. Large polytechnics with about 1000 students should be attached to the agricultural universities.

The EC makes two new proposals, which may not receive an enthusiastic welcome from the existing university authorities. The first is that in the interest of pace-setting six of them should be made into "major universities". These, like the "quality schools", will have special advantages in the way of teachers and students through better emoluments for the former and more liberal scholarships for the latter. The second proposal is that outstanding affiliated colleges should be given autonomous status but the future administrative relation to the parent university is not very clearly defined. The UGC is to have the possibly invidious task of making the selection in both cases.

With respect to student welfare, the EC feels that if present discontents are to be allayed and a university career made more attractive than it now is in many places, more should be done to provide the amenities that are usual in the more advanced countries. Apart from more generous financial assistance for those who need and deserve it, there should be better health and guidance services, more residential facilities, closer personal relationships between teachers and students and the various kinds of recreational activities that appeal to young people.

The Report has a lot to say about the qualifications, methods of appointment and interchangeability of university staffs from Vice-Chancellors downwards which calls for no special comment, and its proposals in regard to emoluments and conditions of service will be examined later in common with those suggested for teachers in other branches. Other points of interest are that in view of the large number of additional functions which the EC wishes the UGC to undertake, that body should not be expected, for the time being at any rate, to deal with technical, agricultural and medical education. It is stated, by the way, that the UGC was established on the recommendation of the Radha-krishnan Commission but, in fact, the original idea of such a body is to be found in the CABE Report. Another interesting point is that all degrees granted by a statutory university or by an institution "deemed" to be of university status should receive automatic recognition by other similar bodies in India and the Inter-University Board should confine itself to securing recognition by foreign universities of the degrees, diplomas and examinations of Indian universities. Even more important, perhaps, is the proposal that to relieve the pressure on State resources the Central Government should become almost entirely responsible for post-graduate education and research.

The proposals in the Report which relate to fees and scholarships are interesting and progressive. With regard to the former, the objective is to abolish them by stages. So far as primary schools are concerned, this should be achieved by the end of the Fourth Plan, and at the lower secondary level, by the end of the Fifth Plan. In the case of the higher secondary and university stages the main effort during the next ten years should be to extend tuition-free education to all needy and deserving students, and, as a first step in this direction, free studentships should be provided for 30 per cent of those enrolled as soon as possible. The EC rightly calls attention to the fact that, as things are now, the other costs of schooling, e.g. books, stationery and so on, are even more burdensome to poor parents than fees, and it recommends that these should be made free at once at the primary stage and progressively reduced higher up. It is by no means easy to assess the cost of these proposals, particularly in a country like India, where so many schools and colleges are still under private management. The CABE made a rough estimate that about one-third of the cost of general education would be met from non-governmental sources. Government contribution to the total education budget is, of course, more considerable today than it was in 1944, but it still looks as if the ECs recommendations under this head will make a substantial inroad on such funds as may be available during the next ten or twenty years.

With regard to scholarships, the EC agrees that the present provision, especially at the lower stages, is quite inadequate, and further recognizes that the increase which it hopes to see by 1986 will still leave India some way behind the more advanced countries in this respect. With regard to the main proposals in this connection, scholarships should be provided for 2·5 per cent of the enrolment at the primary stage by 1975–6 and for 5 per cent by 1985–6. At the higher primary stage, this should cover 15 per cent of the children in the age group, and 10 per cent of the top pupils in class VII or VIII should go with scholarships to a "quality" school in each development block. At the university stage, scholarships should be available for 15 per cent of the undergraduates by 1976 and for 25 per cent by 1986, while for postgraduates there should be 25 per cent by 1976 and 50 per cent by 1986. In vocational education 30 per cent of those at the school stage should be eligible for scholarships and 50 per cent of those at the collegiate stage. For study abroad there should be 500 scholarships annually, which continues or renews a practice that goes back as far as 1943. That many of the proposed scholarships will take the form of loans has already been mentioned and calls for no further comment. Preferential treatment in the matter of scholarships is to be given to girls at all stages. The cost of the scheme is to be borne mainly by the Central Government at the higher education stage and by the States at the school stage, but the EC thinks that the latter will need some help from the former at any rate during the next two plans. In addition, it is proposed that a national scholarship scheme with a placement programme should be set up to ensure that the "major" universities are filled with talented students.

Vocational, technical, engineering and agricultural education, in view of its direct relation to current economic necessities, naturally occupies a prominent place in the report. The EC endorses, in the main, the recommendations made by various experts from the Abbott–Wood Report onwards. It is right in laying more emphasis than its predecessors on the twofold aspect of modern technical instruction; it can either be institution-based with training completed within industry, or industry-based with part-time education or retraining provided by institutions. It also stresses the need for more and better middle-level technicians, who should come from ITIs and technical high schools, into which, as already mentioned, existing junior technical schools should be absorbed. The contribution towards closer links between education and industry to be expected from sandwich courses is another earlier recommendation which the EC strongly endorses. It is typical of the new Indian outlook that the provision, in polytechnics, of special courses for girls receives special attention. The EC shares the common concern about the present shortage of teachers in all types of technical institutions.

The EC leaves one in no doubt about the place it assigns to agricultural education in the technical sphere. The fact that 85 per cent of the 60 million farm families in India are illiterate speaks for itself. It is, however, noteworthy that the EC does not attach any great importance to specific agricultural courses below the matriculation stage. It agrees that agriculture is a suitable craft for basic schools, but is doubtful about the value of introducing it as a course subject at the secondary level. At the post-matriculation stage on the other hand, it strongly advocates not only the establishment of special agricultural universities and polytechnics but also the development of agricultural faculties in ordinary universities, both at the undergraduate and postgraduate levels. To co-ordinate extension work in this connection the Indian Council for Agricultural Research (ICAR) should be converted into a UGC-type of body and put in general charge of agricultural education. With a similar object, the Report recommends that all institutions engaged in fundamental scientific research which at present are functioning outside the university system should be brought within it.

One cannot help feeling that when it comes to dealing with the complex issue of adult or social education, the EC has its feet less firmly on the ground. It is, of course, right in insisting that in a country like India, where 70 per cent of the people are unable to read or write, "strategy" involves a frontal attack on illiteracy, since to rely only on the spread of compulsory education for all up to 14 to solve the problem would mean that the goal could hardly be reached before A.D. 2000. It is also right in roping in all available agencies, official and private, including universities, not only to follow up literacy campaigns but also to enlarge the whole concept of social education. It is when it comes to the mobilization of forces to implement this strategy that the report may appear to stray into the realm of idealism. Is it wise or even feasible to compel all teachers and students to take part in the campaign? Will present resources allow all institutions to be equipped with the necessary mechanical aids? Is it practicable to make all industrial and commercial concerns legally responsible for making all their illiterate employees literate in three years? In view of all that has been said in this book about area-to-area progress it is interesting to find the EC recommending this method so far as social education is concerned. It is hoped that by the adoption of all the means suggested, the percentage of literacy will be raised to 60 by 1971 and 80 by 1976.

The task of bringing India into line with the more advanced countries so far as the special services are concerned is a very difficult one, partly because comparatively little was done to provide these before 1947 and partly because the need for them in a country like India is exceptionally large. The services in question are health facilities, education for the mentally and physically handicapped, recreational amenities and vocational guidance. Issues of more general import, like the supply and training of teachers, administration and finance, will be left for later discussion.

On the health side, as already recorded, the EC has a good deal to suggest for the benefit of students, i.e. boys and girls beyond the matriculation stage. At the school level it agrees broadly with the recent recommendations of the School Health Committee, whose chairman was Mrs. Renuka Ray, one of the signatories of the CABE Report. Subject to existing limitations in the way of doctors, trained nurses, rural clinics and, in some areas, suitable types of food, the general aim is to give Indian pupils the regular medical inspection and treatment and the nourishing school meals which are now common practice in many other countries. So far as adults are concerned, it is hoped that one of the ancillary effects of the family planning campaign will be an improvement in the calorific value of the dietary of poorer families both in rural and urban districts.

In regard to the education of the handicapped, whether mentally, physically or socially, the last of which categories includes members of the scheduled tribes and classes, the EC admits that the problem is too complex to justify hopes of any early solution. In the first place, it is difficult to form even an approximate estimate of the numbers suffering from various forms of handicap. Then there is the question of producing, in anything like the requisite numbers, teachers with the special training necessary in most cases and thirdly, how far can governments be expected to help shoulder the burden which, hitherto, has been mostly borne by voluntary agencies. These and other reasons explain why what the Report proposes may seem rather modest. This is that by 1986 educational facilities should be provided for about 15 per cent of the blind, deaf and ortho-paedically handicapped children and for about 5 per cent of the mentally retarded. The EC endorses previous views that handicapped children should not be isolated from normal ones unless the nature of the handicap makes this inevitable, but feels at the same time that the whole matter requires more expert investigation than it has hitherto received. The NCERT should have a special "cell" for this purpose.

The Report, while recognizing their importance, has nothing very novel to suggest about the provision of recreational facilities. The same applies to guidance, vocational and in other connections. Universities and higher technical institutions are doing more in this way than they did, but in secondary schools progress so far has been slow; in 1966 only 13 per cent of them were in a position to give real help in this matter.

An encouraging feature of the Report is the attention which it pays to school buildings. It not merely condemns the unsatis-factory premises in which so many schools are housed, it also suggests that in many parts of India climatic conditions and the building materials available afford opportunities for scientific research to design not only better but also cheaper structures. This is a matter well worth pursuing. The same applies to all kinds of equipment needed in educational institutions where standardization of design and large-scale production could do a lot to reduce costs.

The increases in enrolments at all stages, which the EC would expect to see by 1986 if its proposals are carried out, are set out in tabular form in Appendix A. It will be seen that the grand total assumes an overall increase of between 300 and 400 per cent but at the post-primary levels of more than 600 per cent. It will be a splendid thing for India if anything approaching this estimate can in fact be achieved during the next twenty years.

When one comes to what most people will regard as the most important section of the Report—and indeed the most important

section of any report about any national system of education—
namely the supply and training of teachers, it would take a
captious critic to cavil at most of the things which the EC has
to recommend.

It has been the aim of this book not to burden the reader with
more statistics than are absolutely necessary, but, in this case, a
few are unavoidable if one is to show how the monetary attractions of the profession have risen or fallen since 1950–1, when
national planning began. Table 1 in Appendix B will illustrate
what has happened. The Table shows that although there has
been a considerable increase in salaries so far as some categories
of teachers are concerned, increases over the whole profession
have been far from uniform. What is more serious, the effect of
the increases has been offset by the rise in the cost of living which
has taken place during the period—the increases in the various
categories have gone up by 18–92 per cent, while the cost of
living has risen by 65 per cent. On the whole, there was some
improvement in the remuneration of teachers in real terms up
to 1960–1, but this has been almost completely neutralized by
the sharp increase in prices that has taken place in the last two
or three years. To make the profession as a whole even less
attractive, there are considerable variations in scales between
States and between institutions under different managements in
the same State. The total effect in the ECs opinion has been to
lower the morale of teachers generally. A contributory cause has
been government sanction, in order to meet economic demands,
to higher scales in certain branches of higher education. This has
further widened the gap between them and the teachers at the
lower stages.

The EC accordingly expresses the opinion that the most urgent
need is to upgrade the remuneration of teachers substantially,
particularly at the school stage, and with this object in view
proposes revised scales, the main features of which are sum-
marized in Table 2 of Appendix B.

To remove existing disparities it is recommended that there
should be national scales at the school stage with local allowances

to meet different living costs and other varying factors, rather like the original Burnham Scales in England. Teachers with equivalent qualifications should have similar pay and conditions of service, whether working in government or private schools. To relate salaries to changes in the cost of living, there should be reviews at regular intervals. Finally, if salaries are to be raised on the lines suggested, financial aid from the Centre to the States will be essential, and this should preferably be included in the plans. This, of course, is at variance with the line taken in the Fourth Plan.

So far as the training of teachers is concerned, the ECs proposals are much less controversial and follow generally what previous commissions have suggested. There should, for instance, be no teacher at the primary stage who has not completed the secondary school course and has not had two years of professional training. Graduate teachers, whether in primary or secondary schools, should have one year's training. Fees should be abolished in all training institutions. The EC, however, does make one new and valuable proposal, even if some considerable time must elapse before full effect can be given to it. This is that all teacher training institutions should be upgraded to collegiate status and become integral parts of universities. If this proves feasible—and the obstacles in the way are not inconsiderable—it will do a great deal to unify the teaching profession and to remove the inferiority complex from which teachers at the lower levels have always suffered. Another step in the same direction is that official recognition and encouragement should be given to teachers' organizations. Educationists in England will gladly acknowledge how much elementary education has owed to the influence exercised by the National Union of Teachers during the last fifty years.

A particularly interesting and possibly controversial part of the Report is the section which deals with administration. Few people who have watched educational development in India since 1947 will disagree with the EC that there has been too much emphasis hitherto on the achievement of targets in enrolments and expenditure and that the time has now arrived to pay more attention to improving quality and determining priorities in the light of national economic needs. It is in regard to the actual recommendations for the structural pattern of future educational administration that some doubts may arise. As a general principle, the EC endorses the view, already expressed in this book, that education is too personal a service to be run successfully from a remote centre, whether in New Delhi or a State capital, and that devolution is essential. The query here is how far and how soon. The EC is apparently satisfied that the effective control of all forms of education at the school level should be handed over to district education boards and that the role of the Central and State governments should be to provide leadership and funds. This, of course, is in line with the importance attached in the new India to the Block Development system and the Panchayati Raj. Sound as this idea undoubtedly is in theory, in practice care must be taken, as the EC admits, to see that the efficiency and integrity of local bodies have improved sufficiently since British times to justify their being entrusted with such an important responsibility. To give a lead to these local bodies as to the lines which they should follow, it is suggested that all states should have an Education Act and the need for a National Education Act should also be considered. For the same purpose the CABE should be functionally strengthened.

Within the district board areas every school should have its own committee or board of managers, half the members to be elected by the local panchayat or municipality and half to be nominated by the district board. Whether, in fact, there are, at present, enough competent people available to enable these bodies to function efficiently is a matter that remains to be seen. The EC recognizes that its proposals for the progressive abolition of fees at the school stage seriously involves the future of the many private institutions now in existence. The good ones, which will be unable to carry on without this source of income, will be recognized and given state aid, while the others, which do not seek or deserve recognition, will remain outside the national system.

The EC clearly has its doubts as to how far the delegation proposed, unexceptionable as it may be in theory, will work out in practice. It recalls the emphatic view expressed by the Kher Committee that education should not be made "a guinea-pig on the altar of democracy or decentralisation" and records that almost all the teachers' associations have represented to it that the local authorities should not be placed in charge of educational institutions. While sticking to its opinion that school education should be regarded as a Local–State partnership and higher education as a Centre–State partnership, it concedes that there is no immediate need for a uniform policy about the local administration of education and that each area should be allowed to progress at a pace and in a manner suited to its growth.

Turning to the actual planning and organization to be carried out by the responsible bodies, the EC reaffirms its conviction that resources should be concentrated on a few crucial problems. The list of these, however, is a formidable one and although most of the items have already been dealt with, it is worth repeating here, if only because it makes one wonder whether the EC ever worked out in detail how far the resources in money and personnel likely to be available during the next twenty years would make it possible to deal comprehensively with these "few crucial problems". Here they are: improvement of the quality of teachers, development of agricultural education, provision of good and effective primary education for all children, liquidation of illiteracy, vocationalization of secondary education, establishment of major universities, expansion and improvement of postgraduate education, increase in the number of scholarships and the development of about 10 per cent of the institutions at each stage to optimum levels of quality. The main issue in many of these cases is not to decide what should be done or how it should be done, because the EC is often only elaborating what former commissions have proposed, but to find the personnel and money with which to do it. Since the number of people with the ability and experience to implement large schemes is admittedly very inadequate, it is rather surprising to find the EC frequently recommending the setting up of special boards, committees and institutes to deal with various aspects of education, to which the experts in question will have to devote a good deal of their time. On the administrative side, the State directorates of education are to have State institutes of education as their academic wings, corresponding to the NCERT at the Centre. In addition, there should be State evaluation organizations and State boards of school education. Moreover, since various branches of education at the State level are administered by a number of departments and it is not considered feasible at present to bring them all under the Department of Education, a co-ordinating agency, to be called the Council of Education, should be created in each State. This should deal with all education below the university stage. There would seem to be a real risk here of important projects being strangled at birth by red tape.

When one comes to the question of administrative personnel, it is easier to agree with the EC, though its condemnation of the existing state education departments may be a bit too sweeping. It strongly supports the view, originally expressed by the CABE, that the Secretary to the Ministry of Education, both at the Centre and in the States, should not be a member of the IAS but should be an experienced educationist on a tenure appointment for six years with a possible extension for another three or four. It approves the proposal to reconstitute the Indian Education Service (IES), provided that due emphasis in recruitment is placed on previous teaching experience. There is much to be said in favour of relieving DPIs of the routine administration which now occupies so much of their time, but whether, in view of the dearth of competent executives, the proposal to transfer most of their responsibilities to the district inspectors will work well, is another matter about which those familiar with Indian education may have some doubts.

The ECs estimate of the total cost of its proposals up to 1985–6 will be found in Appendix C, Table 2. It should be noted that the anticipated increase in expenditure over the next twenty years is roughly 50 per cent higher than the forecast of enrolments in Appendix A. It also assumes that the percentage of the national income allocated to education will be doubled during the period.

It may well seem ungracious to try to pick holes in a Report, to which so much time and thought have obviously been given by so many distinguished educationists, but anyone who has read it with care and high expectancy can hardly fail to ask the question, To whom is it addressed? To the educational intelligentsia of the world as a whole, to the Central Ministry of Education, which was the *primum mobile*, to the Members of Parliament at the Centre and in the States, who alone can give full effect to it or to the people of India, whom it is designed to benefit? One can rule out the first and the last of these classes, because the approval of the first, while desirable, can hardly be dynamic and the last, because four-fifths of its members will be unable to read, still less to understand, the Report. This leaves the Ministry of Education at the Centre and the Members of Parliament both at the Centre and in the States. However influential the Minister of Education may be, his department, like those in the States, is only one of many competing for a share of the available resources and must depend on the will of Parliament before any of his plans which involve substantial expenditure can be implemented. This leads one to the conclusion that while proposals that are mainly pedagogical may be left to the pandits to settle, those for expansion or qualitative improvement must be approved by Parliament.

Is this Report, then, presented in a way most likely to secure this approval? There can be no doubt that for many years to come it will be a gold mine for writers of doctorate theses or others interested in educational theory as applied to modern India, but what is the average Member of Parliament going to make of it? In the first place it is too long, as the Chairman of the EC himself admits, to receive the intensive study it deserves from busy men, whose interests may lie in other directions than education. Nor can one feel that the language in which much of the Report is written is such as to make it easy for the layman, even if he has time to study it, to disinter from this mass of erudition the salient points which call for a decision if anything is to be done in a big way. One has to recognize that in a changing world new discoveries in the sciences and elsewhere call for an enlarged vocabulary, but in a report designed for common consumption, jargon should be avoided as far as possible. How many people know what is meant by a "heterogeneity of cohort" in the lowest classes of a primary school? This comment is not as frivolous as it may seem to some. "In the multitude of counsellors there is safety" is a precept that has often appealed to governments anxious to justify inaction on the ground that the advice which they have received from the experts has been either conflicting or incomprehensible. No one, however, could bring this charge against the present Ministry of Education in India, because it is clear from the terms of their resolution that they have got what they asked for.

Apart, however, from the use of language which may baffle the layman, the arrangement of the Report, in places, does not make for clarity. In Chapter 9, for instance, teaching methods, textbooks, class sizes, school buildings, school health services, guidance, the search for talent, the education of the backward and methods of evaluation all jostle one another. It might have been more helpful to people not directly concerned with teaching techniques, such as the average Member of Parliament, if proposals for major changes, reforms or developments in the structure of the national system had been kept separate from pedagogical issues, which might well have formed a special section of the Report. Moreover, the EC lays much stress on flexibility to meet the requirements of a changing world, and since the earliest date at which it expects most of its more important proposals to become operative in 1986, there is the risk that too precise directions may, by then, be inapplicable. There may well be revolutionary changes before that time in the educational and social complex of the Indian community.

A more serious question arises as to whether the Report takes the right line in its approach to what everyone would agree is the fundamental problem in Indian education today, and that is how to expand at all stages as fast as possible and, at the same time, not merely to maintain but also to raise the quality of the instruction provided. The Commission is undoubtedly right in insisting that there must be pace-setting but is it better to do this by having model or quality institutions at each level or by developing selected areas in each of the States and Territories which will exhibit an integrated structure or pyramid of educational facilities from the lowest stage to the highest and can be expanded, as resources become available, to cover the whole country? This, it is true, would mean that in the beginning, certain areas would be getting more than others, but the Fourth Plan accepts the necessity, in such important matters as agriculture development, of progress from area to area. Moreover, the development of an area, if regarded as the prototype of the future national system, should obviate or at any rate reduce the need for preferential treatment of students and teachers in "quality" schools or "major" universities or any of the other model institutions which the Commission has in mind. These run the risk of creating a new caste system within the educational field. Admittedly, the areas first selected would have to have some kind of preferential treatment if they were to be patterns for future progress but this should take the form of fully trained teachers, smaller classes and up-to-date buildings with the essential equipment for work-oriented instruction, to which the Commission attaches so much importance. There would, however, be no need to pay the teachers special salaries, and if the areas were big enough, they would produce their own supply of talent. Furthermore, by co-operation between the Centre and the States such areas should do much to reduce the disparity between educational standards in different parts of the country, to which the Report calls urgent attention.

THE FOURTH FIVE-YEAR PLAN, 1966–71

Turning from the EC Report to the Fourth Plan is rather like a transition from some Utopia or Erewhon to that Somewhere with which those who have spent their lives in the service of education are only too familiar. It follows, in general, the lines indicated in the preliminary memoranda prepared by various exploratory committees set up by the NPC. Although the projected outlay on the social services is by no means illiberal, even if it represents a smaller proportion of the total outlay than in the previous Plans, it is clear that the aim for the next five years is to devote the greater part of the funds available to increasing the output of technologists and technicians and decreasing the output of children. Anything left over will go, as before, to expanding the lower primary stage and the 11–14 age-group will still be left out in the cold. The provision for opening the doors of opportunity to poor children of ability falls far short of what the EC thinks necessary for the discovery and training of latent talent in the national interest. There are to be no more universities during the period but what is much more serious, no prospect is held out of any general improvement in the salaries and conditions of service of teachers at all levels, which alone could replenish the present depleted cadres and attract into the profession the large additional numbers that projected developments will require.

The main object of economic planning is defined as the achievement of self-reliance, which means not only freedom from dependence on foreign aid but also involves the establishment of an acceptable minimum standard of living for the masses and a continuing rise in this standard. To bring this about predicates a decisive change in the social and cultural climate. "The inherited culture", the Plan states, "has in it strands of idealism and fellowship as well as embedded privileges and discriminating practices. In daily life the latter choke the former." This supports the ECs view that there are "growing and dangerous symptoms of social disorganisation", which must be promptly dealt with. It is clear from this and similar comments that the planners recognize that to create the Socialist State contemplated by the Constitution is not going to be an easy or a short-term business. The same applies to self-reliance, which they regard as a condition precedent to the achievement of the ultimate object. According to the Third Plan, self-reliance was to be attained by the end of the Fifth Plan in 1976, but things have happened since then which make it unlikely that it will in fact be achieved by that date.

The Fourth Plan is frank about the results of national planning up to date. Those of the First Plan were good, of the Second fair, but it looks as if the final outcome of the Third will be disappointing. This has been mainly due to a series of events in the last two years of the Plan which have largely neutralized an outlay substantially bigger than the original estimate. Some of these have been mentioned earlier but it may be well to recall them in view of their bearing on the design of the Fourth Plan. Apart from external crises, a bad harvest in 1964–5 and a consequent rise in the cost of living with a decline in foreign aid led to the devaluation of the rupee in June 1966.

The planners are quite definite that until actual achievements match up to projected developments, the creation of the "economic" man must take precedence over that of the "whole" man envisaged by the framers of the Constitution. Of their eight main objectives, only the last two relate directly to education and the social services.

These are worth quoting in full :

> (vii) for limiting the growth of population and ensuring better standards of living for the people, all necessary resources will be provided to enable the family planning programme to be implemented on a massive and countrywide scale;
> (viii) for the development of human resources, substantial additional facilities will be provided in the social services sector, especially in the rural areas and these will be suitably oriented in the direction of increasing productivity.

These objectives are elaborated later on. Self-reliance, we are told, requires that the policy of linking education more directly with economic development and manpower requirements should be faithfully implemented or, in other words, priority must be given to schemes of technical and vocational education which are designed to cater for the expanding demands of industry.

The anticipated outlay on the social services during the Third Plan amounted to Rs. 1422 crores, of which Rs. 484 crores were to come from the Centre and Rs. 938 crores from the States and Union Territories. The corresponding outlay proposed in the Fourth Plan is Rs. 3210 crores, Rs. 1259 from the Centre and Rs. 1951 from the State and Union Territories. The proportionate increase in the central contribution is worth noting. The main allocations in the Fourth Plan are Rs. 1350 crores for education and scientific research and Rs. 587 crores for health and family planning. The balance of Rs. 1273 crores is spread over water supply, housing and construction, welfare of backward classes, social welfare, craftsmen training and labour welfare, public co-operation, rural works, hill and special areas and rehabilitation. The percentage of the total outlay to be devoted to the social services is just over $3\frac{1}{2}$ per cent higher than in the Third Plan.

The specific proposals in the Fourth Plan for development at the various stages follow generally the lines suggested in the preliminary memoranda referred to in a previous chapter and, as might be expected, do not differ materially from those contained in the EC Report. Nor do its criticisms of the existing system. It shares the ECs opinion that the increase in enrolments during the first Three Plans has been accompanied by some deterioration in quality. It deplores the wastage at the primary stage and the high proportion of failures and poor degrees at the higher levels and makes the particular complaint that the whole system is not sufficiently geared to meet the demands of economic growth.

Pre-primary education, owing to dearth of resources, must continue to be left largely to private effort. At the elementary stage it is hoped to raise the proportion of the 6–11 age-group at school from 78·5 per cent in 1966 to 92·2 per cent in 1971, and that of the 11–14 age-group from 32·2 to 47·4 per cent in the same period. The Plan considers that the directive in the Constitution about free and compulsory education for all up to 14 is not likely to be fulfilled before 1981, which is five years sooner than the EC expects. With regard to the type of instruction to be given at this stage the Plan says "Basic education will be strengthened by developing carefully selected schools and introducing in other schools work-oriented curricula and citizenship training".

With regard to the secondary stage, by which the Plan means classes IX–XI or XII, it hoped to increase the percentage of the age-group at school from 17·8 per cent in 1966 to 22·1 per cent in 1971, but it is not satisfied that the large number of pupils who start work at the end of this course are being properly equipped. To this, it ascribes the high rate (50 per cent) of failures at the leaving examination and the increase in the number of educated unemployed. A more diversified system is clearly called for but what form or forms it should take is left to the EC.

At the university stage, the enrolment, which was just over a million in 1966, should rise to 1,600,000 by 1971, of which at least half should be in science departments. Admissions to arts and commerce courses should be restricted during the Fourth Plan and no new universities should be established, the existing ones being enlarged to accommodate the increased enrolment.

So much importance is attached throughout the Plan to the contribution to be expected from technical education to industrial and agricultural progress that it is rather surprising to find that the developments in contemplation are more modest than might have been expected. In 1966 facilities were available for the admission, annually, of 24,700 students to degree courses and 49,900 to diploma courses. The target for 1971 is 30,000 for degrees and 68,000 for diplomas. Whether new institutions will be required to cope with the increased numbers is left for consideration, presumably by the EC. An interesting proposal is that courses in management and business administration should be provided at two special institutes at Calcutta and Ahmedabad and at certain universities. The exchange of personnel between industry and teaching is recommended. Concern is expressed at the incidence of shortages in teaching cadres and of wastages at the diploma level as well as in polytechnics.

The Plan's proposals in regard to adult or social education follow accepted lines apart from the very special emphasis laid on family planning. This is ranked along with technical education as a "kingpin" in future national planning. It is recognized that, in some ways, this is the most difficult problem of all, since it is not one which can be solved by any direct form of state compulsion. There has been a cynical suggestion that the Government of India might reverse the income-tax procedure of some other countries and, instead of granting allowances for children over two in number, might authorize district boards to levy a graduated cess or tax on offspring beyond that figure. Unfortunately, most of the parents of large families in India come well below the minimum income bracket for taxation purposes. The only solution, therefore, must be to educate public opinion at local levels with the help of voluntary agencies, reinforced by a strong lead from the politicians. In this connection it is worth noting that at the third meeting of the Central Family Planning Council, held in Delhi on 3 January 1967, among the proposals discussed was one for raising the marriage age for women to 21. Dr. Sushila Nayar, the Central Minister of Health, the second woman to hold that office since 1947, said at the same meeting that the main objective was to reduce the annual birthrate from 41 to 25 per 1000 over the next ten years. She expressed some concern at the slow expansion in the number of Family Planning Centres—there are only 27,000 at the moment in the whole country—and in the supply of trained workers required to make further expansion possible. The production and distribution of various forms of contraceptives had also fallen short of expectations but it was encouraging that the Central Government had increased the allocation for family planning in the Fourth Plan from £45 million to £110 million.

A satisfactory feature of the Plan, even if it still falls short of what is needed to open the doors of higher education to poor children of ability, is the substantial increase in the provision of scholarships. The estimated expenditure under this head in 1966 was Rs. 35 crores, distributed over 2·8 per cent of the pupils at the middle stage, 8 per cent of those at the secondary stage and 18 per cent of post-matriculation students. The provision in the Fourth Plan is Rs. 54 crores for secondary, university and technical education, and Rs. 15 crores for agricultural and medical education. Most of these scholarships will take the form of loans, repayable on easy terms but still liable to prove a serious burden in the case of poorer families.

In view of the long-term proposals for improving the supply and training of teachers over the next ten to twenty years which are set out in the EC Report, it is interesting to see what the Plan has to say about progress in this all-important service during the next five years. At the school stage in 1966 there were roughly 2 million teachers, of whom 1,400,000 were trained. Although the percentage of trained teachers rose from 57 per cent in 1951 to 70 per cent in 1966, the actual number of untrained teachers increased from 320,000 to 600,000 in the same period. It has already been pointed out that acute shortages exist today in science, mathematics, technical and vocational courses and concern is expressed both in the EC Report and in the Plan about the average quality of present teachers, particularly in the subjects just mentioned. This is ascribed mainly to deficiencies in the staffing and equipment of the training colleges.

The Plan provides for an increase of 800,000 teachers at the elementary level, 520,000 for growth and 280,000 for replacement, and at the secondary level an increase of 215,000, 157,000 for growth and 58,000 for replacement. It is significant that the allowance for replacements in the case of the elementary cadre is 3 per cent while above that it is 4 per cent owing to the larger number who leave teaching for other employment. In view of their adverse comments on the quality of present teachers it is rather surprising that both the EC and the Plan propose that a substantial proportion of the new teachers should be trained through short-term or correspondence courses. It is more encouraging to find both bodies in agreement that much more should be done by universities to help solve the teacher problem by establishing strong departments of education as well as large pedagogic institutes to cater for teachers of different disciplines both in elementary and higher schools, the object being to remove existing barriers between teachers at different stages.

It is, however, rather disappointing that much wise counsel is not supplemented by the one thing really needed to solve the vital problem of attracting enough of the right kind of people into the teaching profession and that is raising their salaries and conditions of service nearer to those of most other professional workers. As already stated, the Plan is quite definite that the modest sum which it contains under this head is to be confined to offering incentives to teachers to improve their qualifications and that any question of a general rise in salaries must be taken up in connection with the normal government budget.

The Plan has a good deal to say about developments and changes in administration, based partly on the experience of previous plans and partly on the requirements of the new proposals which it contains. Apart from Centre–State relations, it raises the question of how best to ensure closer integration between programmes assigned to panchayati institutions and those administered directly under the instructions of the departments concerned at the State level. It provides Rs. 1 crore for the exploration of these and allied problems. With special reference to education and the social services, it lays emphasis on the need for both qualitative and quantitative improvement in the staffs responsible for their administration. To help the proposed reorientation of courses at the post-primary stage, subject supervisors should be appointed.

While full praise must be given to a concise and courageous appraisal of the needs, resources and problems of a new nation, it is to be regretted that the Plan, like the EC Report, seems to overlook, or at any rate to underestimate, the vital role of the

11–14 age-group in a new democracy, which, for the time being, cannot afford secondary education for all. Whether priority is to be given to the creation of the "economic" or the "whole" man, adolescence is the stage at which to discover and develop latent talent on the one hand and, on the other, to inspire all, whether talented or not, with the obligation to do their best to serve the community of which they are members. No one who has taught in a primary school, in India or elsewhere, will be satisfied that five years' schooling—still less four years, which the EC appears ready to accept in some places—can possibly train the kind of future citizen that is urgently needed by an emergent nation in this complicated and transient age.

The Plan accepts the necessity of progress from area to area in agriculture and other major sectors of national development, so why not in education, since the EC sees no prospect of the Constitution objective of free and compulsory education for all up to 14 being achieved before 1986, and it may well take longer than that? The alternative of a not-too-clearly defined one-year, part-time course for the 11–14s not at school, which, the EC suggests, is no adequate substitute for a full-time course for adolescents at a crucial stage in their development. Unless the EC takes a much more optimistic view of what can be achieved at the lower primary stage than its criticisms suggest, what is the argument for concentrating on this stage so much of the money available for general education? Is it a question of throwing sops to the proletarian Cerberus in a society where the growing gulf between the "haves" and the "have-nots" is already causing serious concern? One can only hope that the lessons of earlier industrial revolutions will not go unheeded by those now in authority and that the exhortations to prompt action in the social field of which the EC Report is full, will not fall on deaf ears.

A few years ago a foreign critic described the Third Plan as an "intricate exercise in wishful thinking". Recently, another critic has called the Fourth Plan "no more than an exercise in statistics" in which, as a practicable programme of development in existing circumstances, even its drafters can have little confidence. Readers who take the trouble to examine the forecasts in regard to finance and enrolments, both by the planners and by the EC, which are set out in the Appendixes, will be able to form their own opinion as to whether such pessimistic comments are or are not likely to be justified by what may happen during the next twenty years. That the course of events since Nehru's death has not eased matters for those in authority and the possibility that the result of the forthcoming elections may still further embarrass them are facts that even those most confident in India's ability to survive temporary setbacks cannot afford to ignore.

Conclusion

THE aim of this book has been to give some account of the
historical events and the inherent elements in the complex society
of India which have determined the progress or lack of progress
in education over the ages, or, more precisely, over the last 200
years. Although in the last few chapters there may have been
criticisms of certain phases in educational development since
1947, it is to be hoped that these have not obscured the fact that
there has been real progress in many directions, since the new
India came into being. Few people will question the importance
of a good system of education in any society, whatever its
political colour. Those who wish India well will hope that in
spite of the many internal and external difficulties which it is
now facing, it will move steadily, albeit more slowly than some
enthusiasts may wish, towards the realization of the democratic
and socialist state envisaged in its Constitution.

It would, however, be unwise to shut one's eyes or ears to the
fact that, recently, some close observers of the Indian scene who
can hardly be accused of political, still less of anti-Indian bias,
have begun to wonder whether imminent trends and pressures
may deflect India from the path which the framers of the
Constitution had in mind. The signs upon which their doubts
are founded are many and various; they include the increasing
drain of authority from the Centre to the State capitals; the
tendency of political parties, even Congress, at times of crisis to
disintegrate into factions or splinter groups; the demand of the
small educated minority, particularly among the new industrial
aristocracy, for strong government, which is not being satisfied
under the present system; the resurgence of traditional Hinduism,
as instanced by the recent reaction against the slaughter of cows

and the growth of right-wing parties like the Jan Sangh and the National Volunteer Organization. The fact that these new parties are gaining strength, mainly in the North, may tend to equate Hinduism with Hindiism and so add fuel to the language controversy, which is the outward and visible sign of regional patriotisms and fissiparous tendencies. Some of these observers are pessimistic enough to see the future political pattern in the form, not unlike Pakistan's, of a president maintained in power by the army.

One can only hope, for India's sake and the world's, that these fears are unfounded, but the fact that they exist reinforces the argument for using education to mobilize and train the rising generation not merely to serve industry but also to preserve freedom. Many years ago Rabindranath Tagore compared India to a house with the upper floor occupied by the affluent and educated and the lower by the indigent and illiterate, with no stairway in between. This, of course, was in the British period, but an Indian writer has recently expressed the same idea in a different way. "The danger", he says, "is that while the 'have-nots' move progressively to the left, the 'haves' are moving more to the right, leaving a chasm, in which Congress may easily founder." Is it not perhaps too much to expect that children under 11, upon whom at present mass education is concentrated, can be taught to appreciate the vital necessity of building this stairway or bridging this chasm?

Appendixes

IT HAS been the object of this book to give the general reader some idea of education and the social services in the new India, together with a compressed account of the historical and cultural influences which have, to varying extents, helped to influence its present polity. The foregoing chapters have necessarily contained a number of statistics but it is hoped that these have not been so voluminous as to obscure, for those not mathematically minded, the general pattern of development since 1947.

Readers who are interested in educational statistics of all kinds relating to the decade preceding Independence may be referred to the *Decennial Review of the Progress of Education in India, 1937–47.* Owing to the difficulties arising from Partition and other reasons its publication was held up for several years, and when it did appear, it attracted little attention. It does, however, make it clear that in addition to the proposals for future action put forward by the Wardha Committee, the CABE and other bodies during the period in question, there was actual progress in many branches in spite of the Second World War.

It may be well to repeat here the warning given earlier in this book that the figures contained in the *Decennial Review* relate to an unpartitioned India. Although it is estimated that by 1966 the population lost to Pakistan has been replaced by the increase in the birth rate and the fall in the death rate, there may still be considerable variations in the numbers in the respective age-groups.

The Appendixes that follow relate to (A) enrolments, (B) teachers' salaries and (C) finance.

Enrolments

In the body of this book a good many figures have been given about enrolments in the different branches of education at dates since 1944. It is not proposed to reassemble these here but it may interest readers to see in tabular form (Table 1) the ECs estimate of how these will increase between now and 1985–6, if its proposals are implemented.

Teachers' Salaries

THERE have been numerous references in this book to the imperative need for improving the salaries and conditions of service of teachers to the extent necessary to attract into the profession the number of men and women with the requisite qualifications and aptitudes to satisfy the requirements of a really national system of education. It would, however, be outside its scope to attempt to record all the steps taken in this direction at different times and places during the last thirty years. The most one can do is to summarize the main recommendations of the official bodies, which have considered this matter during the period in question and see how they compare, on the one hand with the scales at the different grades in operation today and on the other with what the EC has to propose.

The year 1937 may be taken as the beginning of this investigation, because it was then that the Wardha Committee set the pace, so far as the basic stage was concerned, by prescribing, for teachers with the necessary background and training, a minimum salary of Rs. 25 per month. Although this does not seem very liberal today, it was well above the average salary then payable in government schools, and, still further above those payable in private institutions. Between 1937 and 1944 the CABE devoted much attention to the salary problem and, when preparing its report, had available the conclusions of a special committee which it had set up to deal with salaries below the university stage. It also appointed a committee to consider the pay of university teachers, but its recommendations were not ready when the CABE was called upon to submit its Report on Post-war

Reconstruction. This is why no definite proposals for the remuneration of university teachers are to be found in the Report. With regard, however, to the pay and conditions of service of those engaged in branches other than the university sphere, the CABE made specific recommendations.

Before dealing with actual figures it laid down certain general principles applicable at all stages. In the first place men and women should be treated alike. Secondly, teachers should proceed from the minimum to the maximum of the appropriate scales by regular increments at regular intervals. Thirdly, to meet higher living costs and other factors in certain areas, it should be permissible to increase the normal scales by anything up to 50 per cent. In rural areas and other places, where suitable accommodation was not available, free houses should be provided for teachers. Where this cannot be done, 10 per cent should be added to the scale salary. In regard to what would be accepted as an essential feature of any national scale today, viz. an adequate pension scheme, the CABE only went so far as to suggest, as a beginning, a contributory provident fund, $6\frac{1}{4}$ per cent from the teacher and the same amount from the employer.

The following minimum national scales were proposed:

PRE-PRIMARY AND PRIMARY OR JUNIOR BASIC SCHOOLS

Assistants

For men and women with a matriculation certificate or equivalent and two years training, an annual rate of Rs. 360 rising by annual increments of Rs. 12 to Rs. 420 and then by biennial increments of Rs. 36 to Rs. 600.

Heads

According to the size of the school, viz.:
1 or 2   class sections   Rs. 120 above the assistants' scale
3 to 5   class sections   Rs. 600 by 48 to 840
6 to 10 class sections   Rs. 720 by 48 to 960
over 10 class sections   Rs. 960 by 48 to 1200

The CABE expressed its doubts as to whether the proposed scales, though considerably in advance of current rates, would be attractive enough.

MIDDLE OR SENIOR BASIC SCHOOLS

Assistants

Rs. 480 by annual increments of Rs. 48 to Rs. 960.

Heads

According to the size of the school, viz.:
up to 4   class sections Rs. 960   by 48 to 1200
5 to 8   class sections Rs. 1080 by 48 to 1320
over 8   class sections Rs. 1320 by 48 to 1560

HIGH SCHOOLS (LOWER AND HIGHER SECONDARY)

Assistants

(a) Non-graduates with two years training: Rs. 480 by 48 to 960.
(b) Graduates with one year training: Rs. 840 by 60 to 1800.

Heads

According to the size of the school, viz.:
up to 250 pupils on the roll Rs. 2100 by 120 to 3060
up to 500 pupils on the roll Rs. 3000 by 120 to 4200
over 500   pupils on the roll Rs. 4200 by 180 to 6000

In 1953 the Secondary Education (Mudaliar) Commission pointed out that although improved scales of pay for secondary teachers had been recommended not only by the CABE but also by the Central Pay Commission, the Kher Committee and other bodies, no steps had been taken to implement them and that such increases as had been granted had been largely nullified by the rise in the cost of living. The Commission felt that this was a matter for urgent attention and although it put forward no new proposals of its own in regard to salaries, it made some valuable suggestions about pensions and other amenities which would raise the status of the secondary teacher and make the profession generally more attractive.

UNIVERSITIES

No definite suggestions about new scales for university staffs will be found in the CABE Report for the reason already given. Five years later the University Education (Radhakrishnan) Commission made the following recommendations:

Lecturers

Rs. 3600 by 300 to 7200 per annum.

Readers

Rs. 7200 by 360 to 10,800 per annum.

Professors

Rs. 10,800 by 600 to 16,200 per annum.

A number of special allowances above the normal scales were to be available to recognize work or qualifications of outstanding merit. The influence of the new economic policy is to be seen in the proposal that professors in technical subjects may be given a personal allowance not exceeding Rs. 6000 per annum.

TECHNICAL INSTITUTIONS

The CABE adopted the following scales proposed by its Technical Education Committee:

Workshop or Laboratory Assistants

Rs. 600 by 12 to 900 per annum.

Teachers, class III

Rs. 900 by 60 to 1800 per annum.

Teachers, class II

Rs. 2100 by 120 to 3900 per annum.

Teachers, class I (including Heads of Departments).

Rs. 4800 by 300 to 12,000

Principals

Salary according to nature and size of institution.

Teachers in classes II and III above were to be entitled, like those in other branches, to allowances up to 50 per cent of their salaries to meet higher costs of living or other special factors.

ADULT OR SOCIAL EDUCATION

Owing to the great diversity in the types and standards of work covered by this branch, salary scales are impracticable but it is worth noting that the CABE proposed a minimum fee of Rs. 1 per hour.

So far this appendix has confined itself to what the Wardha Committee and subsequent official bodies have recommended in this connection. Though full effect has not been given at any time to these recommendations, there have been a number of increases since 1947, especially in the higher grades. It may, therefore, be useful to conclude this appendix with two interesting tables from the EC Report: Table 1 shows what has actually happened since 1950 and Table 2 sets out what the EC has in mind for the future.

TABLE 2

Teachers	Remuneration per mensem	
		Rs.
(1) Teachers who have completed the secondary course and have received two years of professional training.	Minimum for trained teachers .	150
	Maximum salary (to be reached in a period of about 20 years) .	250
	Selection grade (for about 15 p.c. of the cadre) .	250–300

N.B. The minimum salary of a primary teacher who has completed the secondary course should be immediately raised to Rs. 100; and in a period of five years, it should be raised to Rs. 125. Similarly, the minimum pay of a teacher, who has received two years of training, should be raised immediately to Rs. 125; and it should be raised to Rs. 150 in a period of five years. Untrained persons with the requisite academic qualifications should work on the starting salary until they are trained and become eligible for the scale.

Teachers	Remuneration per mensem	
		Rs.
(2) Graduates who have received one year's professional training.	Minimum for trained graduates .	220
	Maximum salary (to be reached in a period of 20 years) .	400
	Selection grade (for about 15 p.c. of the cadre) .	300–500

N.B. Untrained graduates should remain on their starting salary of Rs. 220 p.m. until they are trained and become eligible for the scale.

	Rs.
(3) Teachers working in secondary schools and having postgraduate qualifications .	300–600

N.B. On being trained, they should get one additional increment.

(*continued*)

TABLE 2 (*continued*)

Teachers	Remuneration per mensem	
(4) Heads of secondary schools	Depending upon the size and quality of the school and also on their qualifications, the headmasters should have one or other of the scales of pay for affiliated colleges recommended below.	
(5) Teachers in affiliated colleges	Lecturer Junior scale .	Rs. 300–25–600
	Junior scale .	400–30–640 –40–800
	Senior lecturer/reader .	700–40–1100
	Principal I II III	700–40–1100 800–50–1500 1000–50–1500

N.B. The proportion of lecturers in the senior scale to those in the junior scale should be progressively improved. By the end of the Fifth Plan, this proportion should be raised to about 75 per cent on an average.

		Rs.
(6) Teachers in university departments	Lecturer .	500–40–800 –50–950
	Reader . Professor .	700–50–1250 100–50– 1300–60– 1600

N.B. (1) One-third of the professors to be in the senior scale of Rs. 1500–1800. Scales comparable to the supertime scales in IAS to be introduced for exceptionally meritorious persons and in selected Centres of Advanced Studies. (2) The proportion of junior (lecturers) staff to senior (readers/professors) staff in the universities which is now about 3 : 1 should be gradually changed to 2 : 1.

Notes. (a) The above scales of pay for school teachers are at the current price level and include the existing dearness allowances. Suitable increases will, however, have to be made for rises in prices from time to time.

(b) Compensatory cost of living allowance given in cities, house-rent allowance or other allowances are *not* included. These will be in addition to the salary recommended above and should be given on a basis of parity.

(*continued*)

Appendix B

TABLE 2 (*continued*)

(c) The scales of pay are to be integrally related to the programmes of qualitative improvement of teachers through improved methods of selection, and improvement in general and professional education.

(d) The scales are to be given to all teachers—government, local authority or private—on the basis of parity.

Finance

THE availability of funds and the potential supply of teachers are the two main factors which must determine the practicability of all schemes for educational development. It may be of interest to those concerned with the financial aspect to set out in tabular form:

1. Expenditure on the main branches of education between 1937 and 1947 (Table 1).
2. What the CABE estimated that its Plan would cost at the end of the forty years needed to give full effect to it, i.e. by 1984 (Table 2).
3. What has actually been spent on education during the first Three Five-year Plans, i.e. between 1950–1 and 1965–6 (Table 3).
4. What the EC estimates that its proposals will cost between 1965–6 and 1985–6 (Table 4).

TABLE 1. EXPENDITURE ON EDUCATION BETWEEN 1937 AND 1947

Branch	Rs. in crores 1937–8	Rs. in crores 1946–7
Pre-primary	n.a.	n.a.
Primary (classes I–V)	8·32	18·49
Middle (classes VI–VIII)	2·57	4·80
High schools	5·63	12·23
Universities	2·76	4·57
Adult	0·02	0·11
Technical and vocational	2·46	5·16

n.a. = not available

TABLE 2. ESTIMATED COST OF CABE PLAN BY 1984

Branch or service	Estimated gross annual expenditure Rs. in crores	Estimated income from fees and private sources Rs. in crores	Estimated net expend- iture to be met from public funds Rs. in crores
Pre-primary education	3·20	—	3·20
Basic (primary and middle) education	200·00	—	200·00
High school education	79·00	29·00	50·00
University education	9·60	2·90	6·70
Technical, commercial and art education	10·00	2·00	8·00
Adult education	3·00	—	3·00
Training of teachers	6·20	1·70	4·50
School medical service*	—	—	—
Education of the handicapped*	—	—	—
Recreative and social activities	1·00	—	1·00
Employment bureaux	0·60	—	0·60
Administration†	—	—	—
TOTAL	312·60	35·60	277·00

*An amount equal to 10 per cent of the gross expenditure at the appropriate stages has been provided to meet the cost of these services.

† Provision to cover the cost of this service has been included at all stages; it is assumed that it will amount to 5 per cent of the gross expenditure.

It should be noted that the total expenditure on education in 1940–1, Rs. 30 crores, of which Rs. 17½ crores came from public funds, is not included in the above estimate but is kept as a reserve towards meeting the cost of providing for the prospective increase in population.

TABLE 4. TOTAL EDUCATIONAL EXPENDITURE, 1965–85

	1965–6	1970–1	1975–6	1980–1	1985–6
National income at 1965–6 prices—increase assumed at 6 per cent per annum (Rs. in millions)	210,000	281,000	376,000	503 000	673,000
Index of growth	100	134	179	240	320
Population estimates (medium projection in millions)	495	560	630	695	748
Index of growth	100	113	127	140	151
National income per head of population (Rs)	424	502	597	724	900
Index of growth	100	118	141	171	212
Total educational expenditure (Rs. in millions) (increase assumed at 10 per cent per annum)	6000	9663	15,562	25,063	40,364
Index of growth	100	161	259	418	673
Percentage of total educational expenditure to national income	2·9	3·4	4·1	5·0	6·0
Index of growth	100	117	141	172	207
Educational expenditure *per capita* (Rs.)	12·1	17·3	24·7	36·1	40
Index of growth	100	143	204	298	446

Index